WORLD OF CULTURE

OPERA

by Herbert Kupferberg

Newsweek Books, New York

NEWSWEEK BOOKS

Joseph L. Gardner, Editor

Janet Czarnetzki, Art Director
Jonathan Bartlett, Associate Editor
Frances J. Owles, Copy Editor
Ellen Kavier, Writer-Researcher
Susan Storer Gombocz, Picture Researcher
Mary Ann Joulwan, Designer

S. Arthur Dembner, President

ARNOLDO MONDADORI EDITORE

Giuliana Nannicini, Editor

Mariella De Battisti, Picture Researcher
Marisa Melis, Editorial Secretary
Enrico Segré, Designer
Giovanni Adamoli, Production Coordinator

Frontispiece: The Witches' Sabbath scene in a 1969 New York City Opera production of Arrigo Boito's *Mefistofele*

The Author and Editors make grateful acknowledgment for the use of quotations in the text from the following works:
The prologue to *L'Amfiparnaso* by Orazio Vecchi. Translation copyright © 1973 by Nonesuch Records, H-71286. Reprinted by permission of Nonesuch Records.
Source Readings in Music History by Oliver Strunk. Copyrght © 1950 by W.W. Norton & Company, Inc. Reprinted by permission of W.W. Norton & Company.
The Letters of Mozart and His Family. Edited and translated by Emily Anderson. Vol. III. Copyright © 1966 by St. Martin's Press. Reprinted by permission of St. Martin's Press.
London Music in 1888–1889 by Bernard Shaw. Copyright © 1937 by Bernard Shaw. Reprinted by permission of the Society of Authors.
The Case of Wagner: We Philologists by Friedrich Nietzsche. Translated by A.M. Ludovici and J.M. Kennedy. Vol. VIII of *The Complete Works of Friedrich Nietzsche*, Oscar Levy, General Editor [1909–1911]. Copyright © 1964 by Russell & Russell. Reprinted by permission of Russell & Russell.

Grateful acknowledgment is made for the use of excerpted material on pages 154–179 from the following works:
Memories of the Opera by Giulio Gatti-Casazza. Copyright © 1941 by Leon Schaefler, Ancillary Executor. Reprinted by permission of Charles Scribner's Sons.
Run-through by John Houseman. Copyright © 1972 by John Houseman. Reprinted by permission of Simon and Schuster, Inc.
Themes and Episodes by Igor Stravinsky and Robert Craft. Copyright © 1966 by Igor Stravinsky and Robert Craft. Reprinted by permission of Alfred A. Knopf, Inc.
Don't Put Your Daughter on the Stage by Margaret Webster. Copyright © 1962, 1972 by Margaret Webster. Reprinted by permission of Alfred A. Knopf, Inc.
5,000 Nights at the Opera by Rudolf Bing. Copyright © 1972 by Rudolf Bing. Reprinted by permission of Doubleday & Co., Inc.
"Infinite Pains" by Winthrop Sargeant. Copyright © 1973 by The New Yorker Magazine, Inc. Reprinted by permission of The New Yorker Magazine, Inc.
A Star in the Family by James McCracken and Sandra Warfield. Edited by Robert Daley. Copyright © 1971 by James McCracken, Sandra Warfield, and Robert Daley. Reprinted by permission of Coward, McCann & Geoghegan.
"Miss Sills Electrifies the Crowd without Benefit of Rehearsal" by Stephen R. Weisman. Copyright © 1974 by *The New York Times*. Reprinted by permission of *The New York Times*.
"Maria Callas as Pedagog" by Robert Jacobson, Copyright © 1972 by the *Los Angeles Times*. Reprinted by permission of Robert Jacobson.

ISBN: Regular edition 0-88225-117-1; ISBN; Deluxe edition 0-88225-118-x
Library of Congress Catalog Card No. 74–83891
© 1975 Europa Verlag. All rights reserved.
Printed and bound by Mondadori, Verona, Italy.

Contents

OPERA by Herbert Kupferberg

1	The Italian Connection	7
2	Opera Goes Public	21
3	Reform Movement	35
4	The Operatic Mozart	47
5	Opera Becomes Grand	61
6	Verdi: The Voice of Italy	77
7	Wagner and the Wagnerians	91
8	Realists and Romantics	105
9	A Particular Accent	119
10	Opera in the New World	133
	Epilogue: The Lively Corpse	147
BACKSTAGE AT THE OPERA		153
A CHRONOLOGY OF OPERA		180
SELECTED BIBLIOGRAPHY		185
PICTURE CREDITS		186
INDEX		188

1

The Italian Connection

AT THE METROPOLITAN OPERA HOUSE in New York City, a capacity audience is waiting expectantly for the gold curtain to rise on Mozart's *Don Giovanni*. Some have come because it is their regular subscription night. Others have been attracted by the presence of the celebrated prima donna who will sing the role of Donna Anna. Still others are there because they know that attending the opera represents a great social occasion and that no trip to New York is complete without a visit to the "Met." Somewhere in the house, perhaps among the standees or in the least expensive family circle seats, are students and young people drawn by the opportunity to hear Mozart's incomparable music sung by a fine cast. And deep within their offices sit the general manager and his assistants, pleased by the large turnout but troubled; they know that even full houses do not meet their operating costs, and they wonder where they will find the money for the next season.

This scene is not very different from that which has taken place for nearly four hundred years in virtually every opera house in the world. Almost since its inception, opera has reigned unchallenged as the most elaborate, spectacular, complex, and extravagant of all musical forms. To its adherents, it is an ártistic experience like none other, combining musical, dramatic, and visual art into such transcendent creative achievements as Mozart's *Figaro*, Verdi's *Otello*, Wagner's *Meistersinger*, and Bizet's *Carmen*. To its detractors it is a contrived and unnatural form of stage life in which people sing when they should be speaking, repeat themselves incessantly as they make their farewells, and perform feats of incredible vocal agility on their deathbeds. Wrote Joseph Addison in *The Spectator* on March 21, 1711: "There is no Question but our great Grand-children will be very curious to know the Reason why their Forefathers used to sit together like an Audience of Foreigners in their own Country . . . to hear whole Plays acted before them in a Tongue which they did not understand."

Yet not only Addison's grandchildren, but their grandchildren as well continue to attend and enjoy opera, whether in their own language or another. Modern audiences have brought a new awareness and understanding to operagoing, minimizing its social and sartorial aspects and concentrating upon what happens not only onstage, but offstage as well. After dominating opera for centuries, singers today find themselves suddenly sharing the spotlight with conductors, stage directors, and scenic designers.

Audiences have also undergone a substantial widening of tastes, aided by the extraordinary outpouring of complete opera recordings, many of which are devoted to obscure, seldom-performed works. As a consequence, traditional compartmentalization of operatic "schools" and styles is breaking down. "Wagnerians" and "Verdians" seldom feud with each other nowadays, and *bel canto* and *verismo* share the house with *sprechstimme* and *singspiel*. The old notion of "grand opera" —that nineteenth-century spectacle of vocal and visual display—has given way to the concept of opera as an art form in which music transforms stage characters into human beings with recognizable passions, tragedies, and, occasionally, triumphs. This is the spirit in which composers have created masterpieces, from Monteverdi's *Orfeo* to Berg's *Wozzeck*, and this is also the spirit in which one may seek to approach the writing of a useful history of opera.

The word *opera* itself is Italian for "work," and represents a shortened form of *opera in musica*, a "work in music." The derivation is no accident, for opera is Italian in birth, ancestry, and general outlook upon life. To be sure, there have been many fine French operas, some notable works in English, and at least one towering set of masterpieces in German. But although an opera house could manage to exist, however uncomfortably, and perform none of these, it would quickly go out of business without an Italian repertory.

So the story of opera begins in Italy, where, toward the end of the 1500s, a group of young Florentines came together and decided to do something about the state of music in their time. There is an old joke that defines a camel as a horse designed by a committee. Opera, too, with all its complexities and excesses, was designed by a committee; it is perhaps the only major art form that can claim this distinction. The committee was known as the *Camerata fiorentina*, or the "Florence Coterie," and its members numbered some of the leading young intellectuals of the city, imbued with the spirit of the Renaissance and, in the manner of young men everywhere, eager to improve on the practices of their elders.

A plaque in Florence, on the wall of a house at No. 5, Via dei Benci, still marks the site where the *Camerata* held its meetings. The group's patron was Count Giovanni de' Bardi, a mathematician, musician, and poet, and its membership included Vincenzo Galilei, a lute player and musical theoretician, perhaps more famous as the father of the astronomer Galileo Galilei; Giulio Caccini and Jacopo Peri, both singers and composers; Emilio de' Cavalieri, nobleman and composer; and Ottavio Rinuccini, a well-known poet of the day who holds the distinction of being opera's first librettist.

The *Camerata*'s announced intention was to replace the vocal musical style of its own day with the kind of music that its members believed had been sung by the ancient Greeks. Italy during the sixteenth century had attained the summit of the polyphonic style, with the great Giovanni Pierluigi da Palestrina writing works of intricate and many-textured counterpoint, in which individual voices were submerged in a great tapestry of sound. The *Camerata* longed for music that was more direct, more human. "Why cause words to be sung by four or five

So elaborate were the intermedi *both visually and musically that they sometimes overshadowed the play itself. Buontalenti's scenery for the Medici wedding* intermedi *included a backdrop (below) graphically depicting hell. As the detail (opposite) from an illustration on a Renaissance wedding chest shows, wedding parties—such as those given by the Medicis—summoned forth the finest in dress and deportment that the young Florentine noblemen could offer.*

voices so that they cannot be distinguished," wrote Vincenzo Galilei, "when the Ancients aroused the strongest passions by means of a single voice supported by a lyre? We must renounce counterpoint and different kinds of instruments and return to primitive simplicity."

Actually, the members of the *Camerata* knew very little about the kind of music the Greeks had used in their tragedies—in fact, very little is known about it to this day. But perhaps because they preferred such a style themselves, they concluded that the Greeks had employed a system of singing in which the music followed the contours of natural speech, the words were always clear and intelligible, and the melodic line mirrored the emotion of the text. This style of declamation, which became known as *recitativo*, or "recitative," has remained the spinal cord of Italian opera from that day to this.

But far more than ancient Greece, it was Renaissance Italy that had prepared the ground for the development of opera. For all their originality and inventiveness, the men of the *Camerata* built on the work of their forerunners. Music had long been used in Italy as an adjunct of both religious and secular drama. Liturgical musical plays, called *sacre rappresentazioni*, were regularly enacted either in churches or on the piazzas in front of them; given in Italian, they included stage settings, costumes, scenic illusions (Lucifer used to ride a fire-breathing dragon), and even comic interludes.

The *sacre rappresentazioni* were essentially popular works performed for the religious edification of the public at large. Musical works presented for the aristocracy were likely to be mythological rather than mystical in origin. Interludes called *intermedi*, or "intermezzi," were interspersed between the acts of spoken dramas performed at princely marriages and other noble functions. These consisted of solo songs or choral numbers with orchestral accompaniment, which in time became staged so elaborately that they overshadowed the plays they were supposed to accompany. When Ferdinando de' Medici married Cristina of Lorraine in Florence in 1589, no fewer than six *intermedi* were performed, along with a play, in the course of the evening. Forty-one musicians participated, three composers wrote the music, and the entire production was supervised by an architect with the propitious name of Bernardo Buontalenti.

Another form that contributed to opera was the pastorale, an extended poem about sylvan scenes and characters, designed for stage presentation and liberally sprinkled with songs and choruses. But it was in still another type of work, the madrigal, that musicians, rather than

The mystery plays that fascinated the general public in Renaissance Italy were another precursor of opera. Although originally a combination of spoken drama and music, the sacre rappresentazioni evolved into entirely sung presentations at the height of their development. Warnings against the devil and his evil works dominated these dramas, as can be seen in the woodcut at left, where a suitably frightening incarnation of the devil drags a young boy away from his parents. The pastorale was yet another form of popular entertainment in Italy and France. As the engraving on the opposite page shows, the pastorales featured brightly costumed singers, dancers, and actors.

Overleaf: At the Medici wedding, Buontalenti not only supervised the intermedi but was responsible for the visual aspects of Gerolamo Bargagli's play La Pellegrina. The sketches of its costumes and characters reflect the period's opulence.

DAMON ALCANDER CELADON ASTREA LISETTE DAPHNE

SILVAS ERASTO ALCIDON DELIA CORENA

poets, played the dominant role. In these songs, for two or more voices in an elaborate counterpoint, composers in Italy and elsewhere found an opportunity for a free interplay of their most fanciful and beautiful ideas. Madrigals covered a tremendous range of subject matter, from the lascivious to the spiritual; the poet Torquato Tasso wrote madrigal texts expressly for his composer friends to set to music; singers, musicians, and audiences alike took pleasure in these charming and intricate songs.

In time, composers began to string madrigals together into extended musical cycles that became known as madrigal comedies. These dramatic stories apparently were not designed to be staged; they were regarded as a delight for the ear rather than the eye. Nevertheless, the madrigal comedy represented another step in the development of the musical theater; in some cycles, singers remained behind the scenes while actors presented the story in pantomime. One madrigal comedy, which has been preserved intact and even recorded, is Orazio Vecchi's *L'Amfiparnaso*, or "At the Foot of Parnassus." Composed in 1592 and published five years later, it consists of fourteen "scenes" involving two pairs of lovers, a group of rascally servants, and several *commedia dell' arte* stock characters. A prologue, in song, provides an intriguing introduction:

Accustomed though you may be, O Illustrious Spectators,
To beholding only tragical scenes
Or comical plots
Decked out in various guises,
Do not, on that account, disdain
This comedy of ours;
Though unadorned with rich and lavish scenery,
It does, at least, contain two novelties:

11

La diessa maiestha isso furnato bianco uerde e pabonazo
d'quale abito ne attrefatte n° 9

pecta un diessa uestita pabonazo
infurnato keruelino

pecta un uestien d rotto bianchi e mag.

F   G 2726   H 1527   I 1728

2 Dioscur e Roma
fivo di 6 colori

il roggo dere

gio d'oro, d'auori e giaci   roggo tenlino panoli

13

ysetta pinza na nerbea tutta di Rosso co fondo doro. sotto esassa
Alione, N 16— Iacopo Pori Zazzerino   La nesta di questa figura incora, e grande.

Demonstrating his gifts as a singer as well as a composer, Jacopo Peri appeared in the lead role of Orpheus (drawing at left) in the premiere performance of his opera Euridice *in 1600. The surviving published version of the libretto and score (opposite, above) is the earliest operatic text available. Orazio Vecchi's madrigal comedy* L'Amfiparnaso *predated* Euridice *by six years. Thanks to the preservation of a later text of the work (opposite, below), it, too, remains an active part of our musical heritage.* L'Amfiparnaso *has received several modern productions, including a 1954 presentation at the Berkshire Music Festival at Tanglewood, in Lenox, Massachusetts.*

First, the City where this work takes place
Is the great Theater
Of the world; that's why everyone wants to hear it.
Second—but you've meanwhile guessed
That the spectacle I speak of
Is seen with the mind,
Which it enters through the ears, not through the eyes.
Wherefore keep silent,
And instead of watching, now listen.

As *L'Amfiparnaso* progresses we are given musical glimpses of everyday Italian life, both elegant and bawdy. One episode depicts Pantalone's servant Francatrippe ("French Tripe") attempting to pawn a sword at a Hebrew pawnshop on the Sabbath; although the Hebrews are described as speaking "a Babel of voices and dreadful gibberish," the composer provides them with music that is quite dignified and lovely, whereas Francatrippe more or less croaks out his words.

L'Amfiparnaso is operatic in its general structure and dramatic thrust, but its music clearly belongs to the polyphonic past. Each character is depicted not by one voice but by a group, with no fewer than five heard simultaneously in the prologue and the finale. Words overlie each other and are almost impossible to distinguish, so it is only by paying close attention to the printed text that a listener can follow the action. It was no wonder that the members of the *Camerata* sought to make their own musical dramas not only enjoyable but understandable.

Of the young scholars and dilettantes who made up the *Camerata*, at least two, Jacopo Peri and Giulio Caccini, were practicing musicians, so it was natural that they should be the first to try the new style on the stage. In 1597, Peri wrote the music for *Dafne*, a *favola per musica*, or "musical fable," telling in declamatory style the story of the nymph Daphne, who, pursued by Apollo, was turned into a laurel bush by Zeus to save her from capture. *Dafne*, which was presented in the palace of a nobleman named Jacopo Corsi, is sometimes regarded as the first opera. Its music, unfortunately, has been lost, although Ottavio Rinuccini's text is extant. Three years later Peri wrote a *dramma per musica* ("musical drama") called *Euridice*, again with a libretto written by Rinuccini. Its score has been preserved, making it the earliest opera whose music is still known to us, and its date of performance—October 6, 1600—certainly provides a convenient point from which to date the birth of opera.

Euridice was given before an admiring throng in a chamber of the Pitti Palace in Florence, with Peri himself singing the role of Orpheus. The performance was part of the festivities celebrating the wedding of Henry IV of France and Maria de' Medici. Thus, right from the outset, opera was associated with royalty and with gala social occasions. From the outset, too, opera found a source of inspiration in Greek mythology; with Peri's work, Orpheus and Eurydice began an operatic pilgrimage that has not yet ended. However, unlike most subsequent versions, Peri and Rinuccini refitted the ancient legend with a happy ending in which the lovers return safely from Hades amid choruses and dances of general rejoicing.

Peri's claim to being the first operatic composer is not entirely uncontested, because his fellow *Camerata* member, Giulio Caccini, wrote his own version of *Euridice* at about the same time. In fact, several portions of his work were incorporated into Peri's at the nuptial performance. Peri and Caccini were rivals who kept a sharp watch on each other's doings—thus beginning another long-standing tradition in opera. Both observed the new musical style of the *Camerata*, following in their music the rhythms, accents, and inflections of the words. But there was a difference in their approaches. Peri stuck largely to declamation, finding in *recitativo* all the leeway he needed to express the sentiments and emotions of his characters. Caccini, on the other hand, was inclined to broaden his melodies into the more lyrical episodes that would eventually become known as *arias* ("airs," or "songs"). The alternation of *recitativo* and *aria*, with the former setting forth the dramatic action and the latter permitting melodious reflection upon the situation, was to become the basic structural pattern for Italian opera.

Peri stayed in Florence until his death in 1633; he was affectionately known as *Il Zazzerino* ("the Long-Haired") because of his blond tresses.

But although he was appointed director of music at the court of Grand Duke Cosimo II, he never wrote another opera, and his renown remained largely local. Caccini, on the other hand, was invited to Paris for a time by Maria de' Medici, who had admired his singing. He was important in the development of the *basso continuo*, or "figured bass," a musical shorthand used by keyboard musicians in the orchestra to fill out the harmonies that supported the singers' melodies. Caccini also published a treatise entitled *Le Nuove Musiche*, or "The New Music," in which he set forth his ideas on the vocal art and urged singers always to bear in mind "the effect, the variety, and the melodic elegance of the vocal line."

Caccini was probably the first true opera singer. Although he was interested in vocal technique for its own sake, he placed prime emphasis on melody and sprinkled his performances with trills and other ornamentations. Married twice, he trained both of his wives musically and also taught his two daughters, Francesca and Settimia, to sing.

Francesca Caccini led a distinguished career of her own, not only as a singer in Italy and France, but also as a composer of numerous works, including an opera entitled *La liberazione di Ruggiero dall' isola d'Alcina* ("The Liberation of Ruggiero from the Island of Alcina"). Performed on February 2, 1625, in honor of a visit by the Polish Prince Wladislaw Sigismund to the Medici court in Florence, it was a gala spectacle that wound up in a *ballo à cavallo*—a mounted ballet performed on horses trimmed with gold and silver. The plot of *La liberazione di Ruggiero* was based on several cantos of Ariosto's *Orlando furioso*, describing how the hero Ruggiero escapes from the thrall of the sorceress Alcina—the same story set a century later by George Frideric Handel in his opera *Alcina*. As a composer, Francesca Caccini was no innovator, but she knew her craft and wrote skillfully for the voice. One contemporary describes her temperament as "fiera ed irrequieta" (fiery and restless); another praises her as "that celestial siren." In any event, she merits more than passing mention as the first woman ever to compose an opera—and one of the few to have made the attempt at all.

From the start, opera struck a responsive chord in the Italian soul. Within twenty-five years it had become the preferred elegant entertainment in such cities as Mantua, Venice, and Rome. In fact, Florence itself quickly yielded its primary position; having created the new musical form, it turned it over to others and has never subsequently been a major operatic center. Rome was receptive almost immediately, with several church dignitaries taking the lead in sponsoring performances. In 1600 Emilio de' Cavalieri's *La Rappresentazione di anima e di corpo* ("The Drama of the Body and Soul"), a sacred drama that is sometimes regarded as the first oratorio, was written in the new declamatory style. Another Roman work, Stefano Landi's *Sant' Alessio*, based on the story of a fifth-century saint, expanded the size and importance of the orchestra, which in Peri's and Caccini's works was limited to a harpsichord, several lutes, a lyre, and perhaps one or two other instruments, all hidden behind the scenes. Domenico Mazzocchi's *Catena d'Adone* ("The Chain of Adonis") gave new emphasis to the aria. Its preface notes that many such songs have been "scattered throughout the

Inheriting a predilection for opera from her father, Giulio Caccini, the talented Francesca Caccini (above) achieved great acclaim as a singer. But she also earned recognition for an even more singular milestone—being the first woman operatic composer. The birth of another new musical form, the oratorio, closely followed the rise of opera. As it developed in Italy, the oratorio was not entirely a liturgical affair but featured costumes and stage action very similar to that seen in opera. Emilio de' Cavalieri's La Rappresentazione di anima e di corpo, generally acknowledged to be the first example of this new genre, still proved to be a stageworthy vehicle when it was revived at the Salzburg Festival in 1969 (photograph at right), more than three hundred years after its first performance in Italy.

work, which breaks the tedium of the recitative." Domenico's brother Vergilio Mazzocchi teamed up with a composer named Marco Marazzoli to compose *Chi soffre, speri* ("Who Suffers May Hope"), which contains substantial episodes of romance and comedy. All through the first half of the seventeenth century, the elements that were to make up Italian opera as we know it today were falling into place.

But the form might never have prospered had it not directly turned up its first authentic genius, Claudio Monteverdi. Born in Cremona, Italy, in 1567, Monteverdi was about thirty when the Florentine *Camerata* was conducting its first operatic ventures. He would have been a great composer in any epoch, but he was particularly well suited to overcome the artificialities and expand the musical and dramatic capacities of the new style. Monteverdi's father was an accomplished composer, so Claudio was thoroughly immersed in the old polyphonic forms and, in fact, has left several books of madrigals and other secular vocal works, as well as a great body of religious choral music. He played the organ and the viol, was an accomplished singer, and, traveling in the service of Vincenzo Gonzaga, Duke of Mantua, visited both Flanders and Hungary. Most of his life he spent in Venice, where he died in 1643.

Apparently it was the Duke of Mantua who, in 1607, induced Monteverdi to try his hand at opera. Alessandro Striggio, the Mantuan state secretary, provided a libretto of *Orfeo*, and Monteverdi's music quickly demonstrated that the new form could infuse a feeling of deep human anguish into the realm of pastoral mythology. His drama proceeded from a joyous bucolic opening idyll into a scene in which Orpheus sings a tragic lament ("Tu se' morta, mia vita") on learning of Eurydice's death. There is no happy ending in this version of the old legend, although Orpheus ultimately rises to heaven while a chorus of shepherds sings below.

Orfeo was hailed by a distinguished audience, and the following year Monteverdi was commissioned to write another opera, *Arianna*, to celebrate the wedding of Francesco Gonzaga to Margherita of Savoy. The score of this work has been lost, except for the separately published "Lamento d'Arianna," a beautifully expressive aria that became one of the most famous songs of its time, and that still retains its power to move the listener.

Monteverdi perceived that musical drama could not survive merely by adhering to a set of rules or precepts, but only by shaping itself to living characters and credible situations. When Striggio, his librettist, wrote to him proposing an opera filled with sea monsters, tritons, sirens, winds, and zephyrs, Monteverdi answered: "How, my dear sir, can I imitate the speech of the Winds, if they do not talk? And how can I induce emotion through them? Arianna moved us because she was a woman, Orfeo because he was a man. . . . *Arianna* stirred me to a real lament; *Orfeo* to a true prayer; but this tale inspires me to nothing. So what, illustrious sir, do you expect music to be able to do in this?"

In 1613 Monteverdi moved to Venice, where he became *maestro di cappella* at the church of San Marco at a comfortable salary. He turned largely to church music and to madrigals but in his seventies produced

Claudio Monteverdi, opera's first genius (portrait opposite, above), wrote L'Orfeo on commission from the Duke of Mantua, who wanted a musical work to mark the marriage of his son. The original title page of the intense, dramatic score appears opposite, below. American singers Carol Neblett and Alan Titus recently helped the New York City Opera revive another Monteverdi masterpiece, the sensual L'incoronazione di Poppea (right).

two more operatic masterpieces, *Il ritorno d'Ulisse in patria* ("The Return of Ulysses to His Country") and *L'incoronazione di Poppea* ("The Coronation of Poppea"). Both works have received stagings and recordings in recent years; indeed *Poppea* is no longer an exotic item to many operagoers, thanks to revivals by the Glyndebourne Opera Festival in England, the Opera Society of Washington, D.C., the New York City Opera, and other organizations.

In his operatic setting of the story of Poppea and Nero, Monteverdi shows no sign of having attained the ripe age of seventy-four. The characters of the dissolute Roman court are vivid and vigorous, the music sensual and stirring. Love, crime, confrontations, and orgies all have their place in the story, and the music reflects and focuses on the alternating passion and pathos of the stage action. Few scenes in all opera equal the tragic dignity of that in which the philosopher Seneca serenely prepares for his death at Nero's command while a chorus of his disciples cries out to him, "Non morir, Seneca, no!" The final tableau depicts the actual coronation of Poppea at Nero's side, with strings and brasses punctuating the resounding praises of a chorus of consuls and tribunes. A less subtle composer would have ended the opera right there, but Monteverdi has the courtiers ceremoniously bow their way off the stage, leaving Poppea and Nero alone to sing a sinuous love duet that retains its voluptuous impact after nearly three-and-a-half centuries. With Monteverdi, Italian opera was no longer a tentative idea; it had become a full-fledged art.

2

Opera Goes Public

IN 1645 THE ENGLISH DIARIST JOHN EVELYN, visiting Venice at the age of twenty-five, wrote:

> This night, having with my Lord Bruce taken our places before, we went to the Opera, where comedies and other plays are represented in recitative music, by the most excellent musicians, vocal and instrumental, with a variety of scenes painted and contrived with no less art of perspective, and machines for flying in the air, and other wonderful notions: taken together, it is one of the most magnificent and expensive diversions the wit of man can invent.

Evelyn's diary is substantiated by the reports of dozens of observers of the time, all of whom agree that opera had become the most brilliant and exciting entertainment of the day. Although Rome and Mantua produced important composers and singers, it was Venice that emerged as the major operatic center of Italy and the point from which the new art radiated to other European countries. Seeking a cause for this preeminence, the English musical traveler and historian Dr. Charles Burney sourly suggested some years later that it was because the Venetians, trapped as they were on their small islands, had to create and frequent their own entertainment.

Whatever the reasons, Venice was where the term "opera" came into regular usage and, even more important, where the first public opera houses were built. Prior to the construction of the San Cassiano Theater in 1637, operatic performances were given exclusively in the palaces of the nobility. One such Roman family, the Barberini, constructed a private theater with a capacity of three thousand in which they regularly assembled audiences of their friends and retainers. When the San Cassiano Theater for the first time made the new musical spectacle available to the general public, such was the response that three more opera houses opened in Venice within the next four years, and another dozen by the end of the century.

The *modus operandi* of these theaters bears a striking resemblance to the organizational setup of the "grand opera" houses that has persisted into our own era. They were built and managed by noblemen who hoped to profit from them. The San Cassiano Theater had five tiers of boxes ringing the auditorium in the now-familiar horseshoe shape. Boxes were subscribed to annually by noble families, while admission to the pit was sold nightly to the public, who had to stand

Advanced techniques in stage-craft and scenic design made opera in seventeenth-century Italy an opulent and richly satisfying pageant. Sometimes audiences were entertained by the sight of singers and musicians descending from the heavens on clouds, while painted backdrops hid the technical equipment needed to perform such "miracles." In other instances they were dazzled by finely appointed stage designs, such as that seen in the painting at left.

21

throughout the performance—like the "groundlings" in Shakespeare's Globe Theater, which also flourished in the early seventeenth century. In Venice it became a custom to distribute unsold tickets to gondoliers, who were known for their enthusiasm. One French visitor wrote disdainfully of the applause and shouted approbation of the *gondolieri*, particularly for female performers: "Nothing is so remarkable as the pleasant benedictions and the ridiculous wishes of the gondoliers in the pit to the women singers." The inhabitants of the boxes had their own peccadilloes as well—they entertained, dined, played chess, and slept during the performances, bestirring themselves only at the approach of a familiar aria or a favorite singer.

The craze for opera in Venice, and the rewards to be found there, led composers to produce their most notable works in that city; for example, Monteverdi's *Ulysses* and *Poppea* both had their premieres there in 1641 and 1642 respectively. But as enchanted as the Venetians were with opera's musical attributes, they were equally carried away by its spectacular aspects. The scenic art reached unprecedented refinement, with much of its inspiration coming from architecture—great rows of columns receding in perspective, huge vaulting arches and domes soaring over the stage. Ingenious machinery moved clouds and various apparitions into place; singers impersonating gods were often called upon to declaim their music from lofty perches or even suspended from wires. In Francesco Manelli's *Andromeda*, the first opera given at the new San Cassiano Theater, the audience was entranced to hear Jupiter and Juno singing a duet as they literally ascended to the heavens.

But just as it took actors to bring drama to life, so were singers necessary to provide flesh and blood for even the most elaborately staged operas. The Florentine *Camerata* invented opera, but with its emphasis on declamation by individual voices it also brought into being that extraordinary creature, the opera singer. Within a few years vocalists who could negotiate the new musical styles with greater finesse and flair than their competitors were in demand throughout Italy. People came to hear Francesca Caccini, whom they called "La Cecchina"—a nickname for Francesca—or Vittoria Archieli, who sang the title role in Peri's *Euridice* in 1600, with the same eagerness that modern audiences flock to a performance by Joan Sutherland or Beverly Sills.

For reasons difficult to explain either musically or psychologically, the higher singing voice has always had a more powerful impact on listeners than the lower. From Peri's day on, the fattest parts—and payments—have gone to sopranos and tenors rather than to altos and basses. Between 1650 and 1750, the voice that dominated Italian opera was that of the *castrato*—the male soprano. The *castrati*, men who in boyhood had had their testicles surgically removed, sang both male and female roles with equal ease and aplomb. Their prevalence was due in part to the Church's edict against women appearing on the stage, although this ban was frequently ignored in Italian cities other than Rome. But, aside from this, the *castrati* became the rage because they provided uniquely stirring, powerful singing. The Church, though officially disapproving of the operation that produced them, took the prag-

Opera's first "star" was the castrato Carlo Broschi, known as Farinelli. Opposite, Farinelli is seen in one of the multitude of idealized portraits that celebrated his fame, while the caricature below shows him during a performance as a female character.

matic attitude that it would be sinful to waste a fine *castrato* voice if one came along, with the result that eunuchs continued to sing in the Sistine Chapel Choir well into the nineteenth century.

Many of the *castrati* claimed that their condition had resulted from a childhood fall, or an attack by a dog, pig, or other animal. However, parents of boys with good voices are known to have had them emasculated in the hope of lucrative professional careers. An English visitor to Rome in 1705 gave a graphic description of the operation: first the boy was put into a warm bath "to soften and supple the parts, and make them more tractable," then his jugular vein was pressed until he fell into a semicoma, "and then the action could be performed with scarce any pain to the patient."

Musically, the result of the castration procedure was the production of a singer who had the pure, high-ranging voice of a woman, combined with the lung capacity and muscular power of a man. Actually, the *castrato* voice possessed a certain clear sexless quality of its own, and many of its owners developed a prodigious technique and a staying power that few female singers could match. Whatever it was, audiences in Italy (and later in England) went into a frenzy of adulation over the *castrati*. Often clumsy and stolid on the stage (and off as well) these vocal capons earned huge sums, developed fanatical followings, and regularly packed the house. "Evviva il coltello!" (long live the little knife), audiences would shout ecstatically as the *castrato* triumphantly concluded a particularly florid or brilliant passage.

While scenic splendors were certainly a much-enjoyed feature of opera, the settings themselves inevitably fell into some conventional patterns. Sebastiano Serlio's handbook on operatic architecture illustrates the basic formulas followed in designing the background for opera seria *(top) and* opera buffa *(above). The chief aspect of Serlio's design was his focusing of the action in the open center of the stage. Another designer, Tommaso Borgonio, applied Serlio's principle in the setting shown opposite for the opera* Lisimaco, *premiered in Venice in 1673.*

The most famous of all *castrati* was the great Farinelli, whose real name was Carlo Broschi, and who lived from 1705 to 1782 (for some reason, longevity was fairly commonplace among the *castrati*). According to a famous musical tale, Farinelli studied as a young boy with the great pedagogue Niccolò Porpora, who kept him for six years incessantly repeating elementary vocal exercises. Finally Farinelli went to him and asked despairingly, "When may I sing?" and Porpora answered, "Go, my son. You are now the first singer in Italy."

Whether or not the story is true (it is also told sometimes of another *castrato*, Caffarelli, born Gaetano Majorano, for whom Handel wrote the "Largo" in *Serse*), there is no doubt that Farinelli was capable of almost incredible vocal feats. In one opera in Rome he was called upon to sing a long and difficult run simultaneously with a trumpet player in the orchestra; finally the trumpeter, exhausted and out of wind, had to give up, leaving Farinelli to complete the passage unchallenged. His brother wrote an aria for him that was so difficult it became known as the "Concerto for Larynx"; no one else could sing it. Portraits of him, which were painted by the dozens, found eager buyers. When he appeared in London, it was to such adulation that the artist William Hogarth depicted in his *Rake's Progress* series a lady at the opera crying out: "One God and one Farinelli!"

Farinelli's career reached its climax when he was engaged by the Queen of Spain, Elizabeth Farnese, to become singer-in-residence, at a fabulous salary, to the half-mad King Philip V. Farinelli claimed afterward that he sang the same four songs to Philip every night for ten years, thereby preserving a modicum of sanity in the monarch. In any event, he finally retired to a castle located near Bologna and spent his last years in ease and affluence, a well-padded symbol of opera's first Golden Age of singers.

Thanks largely to the *castrati*, star singers quickly became the most visible (and also the most audible) symbol of opera. Theater operators moved to build shows around them. As a result, less money was spent on the purchase of expensive scenery, and the chorus was reduced in size or even eliminated, the savings permitting the impresarios to bid higher for the most popular singers. Composers, needless to say, were paid miserably in comparison. Their remuneration for a completed operatic score usually averaged between the equivalents of $100 and $150, and copyright was nonexistent.

Nevertheless, the financial emphasis upon solo singers was not necessarily injurious to opera. With less lavish scenic designs, and the size of casts and choruses reduced, composers and librettists were forced to concentrate on the protagonists and develop musical-dramatic situations that could hold an audience's interest. Opera was not yet ready to deal with the conditions of everyday life, but at least the gods and goddesses began to give way to historical or semihistorical figures. A stately and rather solemn style called *opera seria* developed, with *castrati* generally playing the parts of the magnanimous and high-minded rulers who were its usual heroes. A bit later *opera buffa*, a corresponding comic form stemming from the old *commedia dell' arte*, began to attract audiences; one such work, Giovanni Battista Pergolesi's *La serva padrona*

("The Maid Turned Mistress," 1733), continues to find appreciative listeners today.

The most significant Italian opera composer of the first part of the eighteenth century was Alessandro Scarlatti, founder of a Neapolitan school of composers, and father of the famous harpsichordist Domenico Scarlatti. Alessandro Scarlatti allegedly wrote 115 operas, but posterity has managed to lose most of them. Those scores that do remain are admired by scholars but rarely performed. Scarlatti is credited with developing the Italian opera overture, and with establishing solidly the *da capo* ("from the beginning") aria—that is, an aria with a principal section, a contrasting middle section, and a repetition of the principal section. This "A-B-A" form has been carried over into modern times, remaining a standard device ever since.

For all of Scarlatti's contributions, the prime progenitors of *opera seria* were not composers but two poets and librettists, Pietro Trapassi, better known under the nom de plume of Metastasio, and Apostolo Zeno. Between them these two men succeeded in formalizing the patterns of Italian opera and practically monopolizing all the available subjects relating to the heroes of antiquity or the nobility. Metastasio's plots in particular were set and reset to music by one composer after another. Some of his librettos were adapted into as many as seventy different musical versions; even Mozart used one in his next-to-last opera, *La clemenza di Tito*.

Both Zeno and Metastasio were Italian in birth, language, and outlook, but they did most of their work and lived much of their lives at the imperial court of the Habsburgs in Vienna. For by now opera had spread far beyond Italy and had begun to take roots in the German-speaking lands of central Europe as well as in England and France.

In the German language regions, opera naturally found its most receptive soil in the south, which was both geographically and artistically closest to Italy. In 1666 the Venetian composer Marc' Antonio Cesti was invited to Vienna to perform *Il pomo d'oro* ("The Golden Apple") to celebrate the nuptials of the Emperor Leopold I and the Infanta Margherita of Spain. It was a magnificent event, and the proportions of the work were appropriately enormous: five acts, sixty-six scenes, twenty-four stage settings, and forty-eight individual roles in addition to the chorus. Few other courts in what are now Austria and Germany could match this kind of opulence, but some of them tried. In the South German states Italian operas were performed under princely or ducal patronage in Salzburg, Prague, Innsbruck, Ratisbon, and Munich. The North's first public opera house was opened in the free Hanseatic city of Hamburg in 1678. However, the first indigenous German opera is considered to be Heinrich Schütz's *Dafne*, composed in 1627 to nothing less than Ottavio Rinuccini's text, originally designed for Jacopo Peri in Florence.

German opera as such was slow in developing, although Reinhard Keiser struggled valiantly, writing more than a hundred scores, most of them given at the Hamburg Opera House. The famous Georg Philipp Telemann wrote at least twenty operas for the same institution. However, with the closing of that theater in 1738, German opera went into an eclipse that would end only with Mozart. The German taste ran more to instrumental music than to vocal music, and the language was too heavy and opaque to fit comfortably the typical patterns of the recitative. Yet the operatic influence was steadily growing. Germany's greatest composer, Johann Sebastian Bach, never wrote an opera; yet the style is present in several of his "secular cantatas," including *Phoebus and Pan* and the *Coffee Cantata*. That legendary old lady who attended the premiere of Bach's supremely dramatic *Passion According to St. Matthew*, which took place in Leipzig in 1729, was not so far wrong when she cried out: "God, save us, my children! It is just as if one were at an opera-comedy!"

The British also failed to nurture their own operatic school, even though its beginnings seemed promising. The Elizabethan age produced not only a wealth of great plays and poetry, but also a species of musical stage works called the "masque," a kind of semiopera built largely around solo singers. In 1656 a five-act work in music entitled *The Siege of Rhodes* was staged, with a text by William D'Avenant (or Davenant) and music by several composers, among them Henry Lawes, Matthew Locke, and Captain Henry Cooke, a military man who was an excellent bass singer and a favorite of Samuel Pepys. Lawes, Locke, and John Blow all wrote vocal stage music of distinction; in fact, John Milton, who presumably was sensitive to the treatment of the English language, praised Lawes's declamatory musical style in 1646 with a sonnet that began:

> Harry, whose tuneful and well-measured song
> First taught our English music how to span
> Words with just note and accent . . . .

Milton notwithstanding, the composer who "first taught . . . English music how to span words" was not Lawes but Henry Purcell, who was born around 1659 and died at the age of thirty-five. As a composer, Purcell was active in many styles, both vocal and instrumental. He wrote considerable church music, about two hundred songs, and much vocal incidental music to such plays as Shakespeare's *A Midsummer Night's Dream* (under the title of *The Fairy Queen*) and Dryden's *The Indian Queen*. He also wrote a miniature masterpiece called *Dido and Aeneas*, which has stood for nearly three hundred years as the first and possibly the greatest English opera.

Dido and Aeneas was composed in 1689 for a performance by the pupils of a fashionable girls' school run by one Josias Priest in Chelsea. Without elaborate scenery or ostentatious singers as distractions, Purcell was able to write an opera that was simple, direct, and concentrated in its dramatic lyricism. His story was taken from Virgil, and told of the Trojan hero Aeneas's escape from the fallen city of Troy to Carthage, his love affair there with Queen Dido, and finally his departure from her side to found the city of Rome. Purcell's work lasts only an hour, but it is so compact in structure and so sturdy in melody that it produces the effect of a much longer opera. It has arias, duets, a witches' chorus, a sailors' chorus, an echo chorus, and a climactic confrontation between the two lovers, with the bereft Dido singing a final lament, "When I am laid in earth," that is one of opera's most moving expressions of grief. Purcell showed in *Dido and Aeneas* that it is perfectly possible to adapt the recitative style to the sound of the English language, but few subsequent composers have been able to emulate him.

Purcell's early death destroyed any possibility of an indigenous English opera developing in the eighteenth century, but it is doubtful that this would have occurred in any case, for the Italian *opera seria* suddenly conquered London almost as thoroughly as it had swept over Naples, Rome, and Venice. It was implanted in England by itinerant Italian singers and musicians, as well as by Englishmen who had been exposed to the craze on visits to the Continent. Its principal exponent in

In his tragically brief musical career, English composer Henry Purcell (portrait opposite) wrote much music for the stage, but only one work that can truly be called an opera, Dido and Aeneas. *Despite the moving and dramatic nature of Purcell's score,* Dido and Aeneas *received only two public productions following its premiere in 1689. It remained a lost work until the Royal College of Music staged a revival of the opera in 1895 to celebrate the bicentennial of Purcell's death. Today,* Dido and Aeneas *is frequently seen in opera houses throughout the world, including a recent production at London's Covent Garden (right).*

Overleaf: In a perfect wedding of artist and subject matter, William Hogarth, England's finest pictorial satirist, produced a series of paintings showing high points of John Gay's parody of baroque opera, The Beggar's Opera. *In this canvas Hogarth captures the action in Act III.*

England, and certainly its supreme master, was George Frideric Handel, who was born in Halle, Germany, in 1685 (the same year as Johann Sebastian Bach), and died in London in 1759.

Handel is one of the most remarkable personages in music history. As a young man in Germany, he excelled as an organist and a harpsichordist as well as a composer. He might have succeeded the legendary Dietrich Buxtehude as organist at Lübeck, an important post, but the conditions of employment required him to marry the incumbent's daughter, and after looking the lady over, Handel declined the job. Fräulein Buxtehude must have been singularly ill-favored, for the position was similarly rejected by J. S. Bach and by Johann Mattheson, one of Germany's earliest operatic composers.

In 1706 Handel journeyed to Italy, where he soon began composing such successful operas as *Rodrigo* and *Agrippina*. In 1711 he went to London and scored another triumph with *Rinaldo*, an opera concocted from arias and other material that had been written for earlier works. Handel felt so much at home in England that when one of his old German patrons, the Elector of Hanover, was summoned to the throne as George I, he decided to remain there permanently. He became a British subject in 1727.

During his operatic career in London, Handel became not only a composer and a conductor, but an impresario as well. In 1720, along

with two Italians, Giovanni Bononcini and Attilio Aristi, he became a director of the Royal Academy of Music, whose function was largely to present Italian opera. Handel was sent to the Continent to round up the best Italian singers he could find, including *castrati* and female sopranos; among the latter he engaged the famous Francesca Cuzzoni, who was squat and homely, but whose agile, bewitching voice won her a contract for two thousand pounds per annum.

The Royal Academy's operatic productions made handsome profits for a time, but Handel and Bononcini had a falling-out, and their rivalry somehow became enmeshed in the politics of the day, with King George and the Tories supporting the German-born composer, and the duke of Marlborough and the Whigs backing the Italian. Literary as well as musical London was bemused by the conflict, with John Byrom writing the famous rhyme:

> Some say, compar'd to Bononcini,
> That Mynheer Handel's but a ninny;
> Others aver that he to Handel
> Is scarcely fit to hold a candle;
> Strange all this difference should be
> 'Twixt Tweedledum and Tweedledee.

George Frideric Handel was a master of the opera seria, which went out of style in the nineteenth century because of its vocal artificialities and stylized stage action. The New York City Opera scored a great success in 1966 with a production of Handel's Julius Caesar, which showcased two of the company's leading performers, Beverly Sills and Norman Treigle (right). Three of Handel's operas, Atalanta, Alcina, and Berenice, received their first performance in the original Covent Garden Theatre (watercolor below), which was opened in 1732.

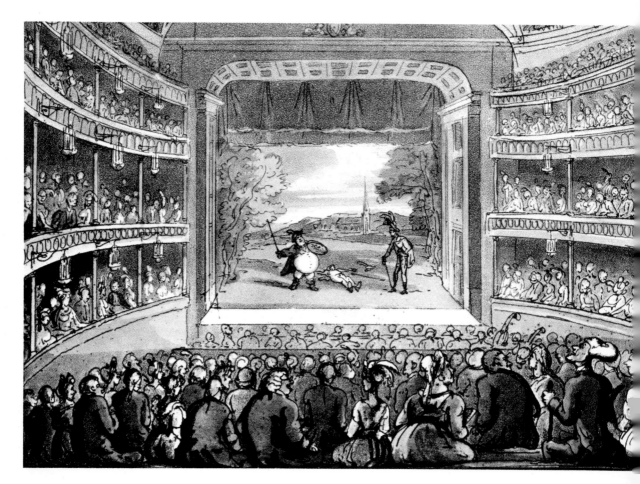

The rivalry was even reflected on the stage of the King's Theater, where Cuzzoni and her principal competitor, Faustina Bordoni, engaged in a hair-pulling match during a performance of Bononcini's *Astianatte*. Eventually Bononcini retired from the fray and left London, but other impresarios arose to challenge Handel. One of them was the famous singing teacher Porpora, who induced his old pupil, the *castrato* Farinelli, to come to London. Handel always managed to retain his primacy as an *opera seria* composer, but he went bankrupt doing it, and after giving London some thirty-five operas he turned to oratorio, producing such masterpieces as *Saul*, *Israel in Egypt*, and *Messiah*.

What was Handelian opera like? We are in a better position to answer that question today than at any time since the composer's death simply because such works as *Alcina*, *Ariodante*, *Julius Caesar* (or *Giulio Cesare*, to use the Italian form that Handel employed), *Rodelinda*, and others have been revived in recent years either on the stage or in recordings. These operas are not particularly theatrical, with little in the way of suspenseful situations or character confrontations. But while dramatic action is minimal, the music is wonderfully alive in delineating character and expressing emotional states. *Julius Caesar*, which has been revived successfully by the New York City Opera, is a case in point; basically proceeding through a succession of recitatives, arias, choruses, and two duets, it manages to emerge as much a work of human warmth as one of musical stateliness. And it also affords the opportunity for some magnificent singing, with the *castrato* part of Caesar allotted to a bass-baritone, and that of Cleopatra—as in the original version—taken by a coloratura soprano capable of altitudinous vocal ornamentations.

One of the blows that contributed to the demise of Handel's Italian operas in London was the production in 1728 of *The Beggar's Opera*, a ballad opera with music drawn largely from popular airs arranged by Johann Christoph Pepusch, a German settled in England, and a satiric text by John Gay, depicting the seamy side of London life. Presented at a theater run by John Rich, it was an instant success, so much so that, as one wag put it, it "made Gay rich and Rich gay." *Opera seria*, with its lofty pretensions and its foreign accents, suddenly seemed remote and artificial compared to this irreverent and lusty work, performed in a language everyone could understand. For the time being, at least, Italian opera was finished in England. *The Beggar's Opera* and its successors enjoyed a vogue for some years, and then performances of these, too, began to taper off. Two centuries later, in 1928, John Gay's saga about Polly Peachum and the bold Macheath was modernized by Kurt Weill and Bertolt Brecht into *Die Dreigroschenoper*, and in 1952 Marc Blitzstein produced an American version called *The Threepenny Opera*, which had a tremendous success and made "Mack the Knife" the most popular song of the day. Curiously, it has taken the twentieth century to give new life both to Handel's operas and to the acidulous little work that helped sweep them into obscurity.

3

Reform Movement

OF THE COUNTRIES OUTSIDE ITALY, the only one that was able to establish early its own operatic school and style was France. The French, like the Italians, had produced medieval musical plays that might be considered forerunners of opera—including the liturgical drama *The Play of Daniel*, performed at Beauvais in the twelfth century, and Adam de la Halle's *Le Jeu de Robin et de Marion* ("The Game of Robin and Marion"), a charming pastoral playlet that stems from late in the thirteenth century.

It was the Italian-born Cardinal Mazarin who first introduced Italian opera to France in the first half of the seventeenth century. In 1643 he ordered that musicians be sent from Rome to Paris, and the following year he specifically requested Leonora Baroni, a singer with glowing eyes, whom one French musician extolled as "the wonder of the world, who made me forget my mortal state, so that I thought I was already among the angels, sharing the joys of the blessed." The logical French much preferred beautiful sopranos to *castrati*, who were regarded as slightly ridiculous and who never won acceptance in France. Mazarin kept on bringing Italian performers to Paris and succeeded in interesting the young King Louis XIV in their art. In 1647 the Roman composer Luigi Rossi spent several months there, supervising a production of his version of *Orfeo* at the Palais-Royal.

Although the modern French writer Romain Rolland regarded Rossi as the founder of French opera, that honor is generally accorded to Jean-Baptiste Lully, a transplanted Italian who arrived in Paris at the age of fourteen and spent the rest of his life there. Lully became the principal musical luminary at the court of the Sun King, and was given letters patent to establish an "Académie Royale de Musique," which eventually became the Grand Opéra. He also provided ballet music for several of Molière's plays, including *Le Bourgeois Gentilhomme*, and he composed about fifteen operas, mostly on classical subjects, turning them out at the rate of one a year.

Lully's operas were invariably serious and stately, beginning with a dignified two-part overture (whose form he devised) and an apostrophe to the monarch. He wrote to the king's taste rather than the public's, and was careful about the subjects he chose, working closely with a librettist named Philippe Quinault. Among his operas were

The burgeoning popularity of opera in Italy soon strained the capacity of available performing space, and a spate of new theaters were built over the next two centuries. Almost every city of importance had at least one. Among the loveliest was the Teatro Regio in Turin, which continued in operation until it was gutted by fire in 1936. The painting at left shows performers and spectators during the theater's opening production, Francesco Feo's L'Arsace, in 1741.

works such as *Alceste*, *Thésée*, *Amadis de Gaule*, *Roland*, and *Acis et Galatée*. Ballet was an integral part of these, for the French taste demanded elaborate dance sequences in all stage productions. One of Lully's greatest accomplishments was the creation of a French style of recitative, patterned on dramatic declamation and shaped to the formal measures of the French tongue rather than the songful Italian.

Lully's successor, Jean-Philippe Rameau, was French-born, though he spent a year as a young man traveling in Italy. An organist and musical theoretician, Rameau wrote a treatise that helped establish harmony as a science. He was fifty years old when he began writing operas, and he put greater emphasis on the role of the orchestra than had any previous composer. Many of his contemporaries regarded his music as too complex and learned. But unlike Lully, whose operas lie dormant, several of Rameau's works have achieved modern revivals, notably *Les Indes galantes*, which received a spectacular pro-

duction at the Paris Opéra in 1952, and *Castor et Pollux* and *Hippolyte et Aricie*, both of which have been recorded.

With its emphasis on ballet and orchestra, its elegant recitative, and its general ceremonial atmosphere, French opera was distinctive from Italian. But not all Frenchmen approved. Some were so enchanted when a visiting Italian troupe performed Pergolesi's *La serva padrona* in 1752 that they began to agitate for more Italian and less French opera. The ensuing battle between the factions, which became known as La Guerre des Bouffons ("The War of the Buffoons"), was symptomatic of a general demand for musical stage works that were more natural and popular in spirit than those of the old *opera seria* type. Opera nearly everywhere, as a matter of fact, was in drastic need of reform. In its first century and a half it had developed certain artificialities, quirks, and conventions, even absurdities, that had begun to adulterate its original concept as a *dramma per musica*.

As far back as 1720 an accomplished Italian composer named Benedetto Marcello launched a satiric attack on current operatic customs in a pamphlet that was entitled *Il teatro alla moda*, or "The Theater à la Mode." The pamphlet was addressed to "Poets, Composers . . . Singers of either sex, Impresarios, Musicians, Designers . . . Costumers, Pages, Supernumeraries, Prompters, Copyists, Protectors and Mothers of Lady Singers, and other Persons connected with the Theater." And in it Marcello gave advice to each of the principals concerned with opera. The composer, he wrote ironically, should speed up or slow down the pace of an aria to suit the fancies of the singers. The librettist should never bother to read the ancient Greek and Latin authors, since they had never bothered to read him. The director should see that the best arias are given to the prima donna, and that if cuts are necessary "he will not permit the removal of arias or ritornelli, but rather of entire scenes." Marcello's sharpest thrusts were reserved for the singers, male and female, who, he said, "will ignore the other singers on the stage and will, instead, bow to the spectators and smile at the orchestra, so that the audience may understand that he or she is not the Prince Zoroaster but Signor Forconi; not the Empress Filastroca but Signora Giandussa Pelatutti."

Another reform-minded pamphleteer was Francesco Algarotti, who in *Saggio sopra l'opera in musica*, an essay on opera published in 1755, urged that musical drama be so constructed as "to delight the eyes and the ears, to rouse up and affect the hearts of an audience, without the risk of sinning against reason or common sense."

Several Italian composers, among them Nicola Jommelli and Tommaso Traetta, made efforts at curbing the old abuses, but when reform was finally achieved, it took place not in Italy but in Vienna. Its instigator was Christoph Willibald von Gluck, one of the first truly international opera composers, who was born in Bavaria in 1714 and educated in Prague and Milan. Gluck traveled widely in Italy, visited London and Paris, toured in Germany with an itinerant opera company, and finally settled, married, and died in Vienna.

Gluck's earliest operas gave little indication of the revolutionary changes he was to bring about, although they were produced in Italy

with reasonable success. He traveled to Paris, where he met Rameau, and then to London, where he wrote two unsuccessful operas for the Haymarket Theater, which was running in competition with Handel's company. Handel himself was unimpressed, telling friends that Gluck knew no more about counterpoint than his cook. It so happened that Handel's cook was a professional musician; still, the remark could hardly have been intended as complimentary.

Gluck's reforms were ushered in not by himself alone but through his association with Ranieri de' Calzabigi, a poet with strong ideas about what opera ought to be, and who, like Gluck, lived in Vienna, which was still devoted to operas composed to librettos by Metastasio. Gluck openly acknowledged his indebtedness to Calzabigi in his preface to *Alceste*, in which he wrote that his intentions were

> to divest [the music of *Alceste*] entirely of all those abuses introduced into it either by the mistaken vanity of singers or by the too great complaisance of composers, which have so long disfigured Italian opera. . . . I have tried to restrict music to its true office of serving poetry . . . by following the situations of the story, without interrupting the action or stifling it with a useless superfluity of ornaments. . . . I believed that my greatest labor should be devoted to seeking a noble simplicity.

This was the sort of manifesto that might have won the approval of the *Camerata* a century and a half earlier, and curiously, the first opera to embody Gluck's ideals was a setting by Calzabigi of the Orpheus story, which had served the Florentines so well.

The Calzabigi-Gluck *Orfeo ed Euridice* was performed at Vienna

on October 5, 1762, and holds the distinction of being the oldest opera still in the repertoire of most major opera houses. By any standard it is a remarkable work, for the poet and the composer made good their pledge to dispense with all superfluity and excess. The story is direct, moving, and strongly personalized, from the opening lament of Orpheus at Euridice's tomb, through his dramatic descent to Hell with the Furies seeking to bar his entrance, and the contrasting serenity of a scene in the Elysian fields, to his climactic, sorrowful outcry when he looks back and again loses his beloved. Ironically, Gluck's *Orfeo* lives on not because it was a "reform" opera, but because it contains such beautiful and deeply felt music as the arias "Che puro ciel" (What pure light) and "Che farò senza Euridice" (What shall I do without my Euridice). Gluck wrote the part of Orfeo for a *castrato* named Gae-

When rigid stylistic formulations threatened to ossify the art of opera, its course was changed by the reforms of Christoph Willibald von Gluck (left, above). Beginning with Orfeo ed Euridice, *seen at left, below, in a 1968 production at Milan's La Scala Theater, Gluck and his librettist Calzabigi stripped away the artificialities born of mere vocal display to allow a direct development of story and character. The qualities of simplicity and clarity so essential to Gluck's style were exemplified in his masterful opera* Alceste. *The sketch at right shows the main setting chosen by La Scala designer Piero Zuffi for a recent production of Gluck's work.*

tano Guadagni, but when he composed a French version for performance in Paris in 1774, he rewrote the part for a tenor. Today it is usually sung by a contralto or mezzo-soprano.

Gluck followed *Orfeo* with *Alceste*, a much larger work, which also adhered to the new principles and is known today at least through the celebrated heroic aria "Divinités du Styx." Not altogether satisfied with the effect his operas were producing in Vienna, Gluck decided to try his fortunes in Paris, where he remained for six years, writing such works as *Iphigénie en Aulide, Armide,* and *Iphigénie en Tauride,* the last of which some critics regard as his masterpiece.

Gluck's stay in Paris led to a renewal of the "War of the Buffoons" of twenty-five years earlier, with a group of pro-Italian operagoers proclaiming the superiority of Nicola Piccinni, a composer from Naples who arrived in France in 1776. Benjamin Franklin happened to be in Paris at the time as United States commissioner and commented

Appointed by Louis XIV as a virtual musical dictator, Jean-Baptiste Lully created a French operatic style. Among his many stage works was Phaëton (score at left), which premiered in 1683. Lully insisted that his performers, such as the Mlles. Christhophe and Aubry (shown in the drawings right, above), be accomplished actresses as well as singers. Giovanni Pergolesi's La serva padrona (far right) is a comic masterpiece that introduced many of the conventions upon which the opera buffa style developed and flourished.

tartly that the French must be a happy people indeed if they had no grievances or subjects of contention "but the perfections and imperfections of foreign music." In any event, Gluck was generally regarded as the winner of the competition with Piccinni. The two men continued to remain on fairly good terms, and when Gluck, who had left Paris in failing health, died in 1787, Piccinni tried to organize a series of annual concerts in his memory.

Gluck's influence on succeeding generations was indirect rather than direct; he had no disciples and established no school. But his insis-

tence that musical drama must make sense as well as sounds was not forgotten. He humanized *opera seria* and carried it as far as it could go as a musical form. Important as his influence was, however, the real reform of opera—which moved it far closer than it had ever been before to the everyday world of reality—came not in *opera seria* but in the realm of comedy, *opera buffa*.

Comic opera had been more or less a musical stepchild for years, represented by such sporadic efforts as *Chi soffre*, *speri* by Mazzocchi and Marazolli in 1637. Early in the eighteenth century, the form seems suddenly to have flowered almost simultaneously under various names in different countries—the *opera buffa* of Italy, the *opéra comique* of France, the ballad opera of England, the *zarzuela* of Spain, and the *singspiel* of Germany. Reference has already been made to Pergolesi's *La serva padrona*, a sparkling little work about a maidservant who artfully tricks her half-willing bachelor master into marrying her. Pergolesi was a brilliant but lame and sickly composer who died of consumption at the age of twenty-six. *La serva padrona* was written as an intermezzo, a snippet of an opera to be played for comic relief between the acts of an *opera seria*. In fact, during its Parisian performance of 1752, which launched the "War of the Buffoons," it was put on during the intervals of Lully's *Acis et Galatée*.

La serva padrona displays the elements that gave *opera buffa* its extraordinary range, flexibility, and popular appeal. There are piquant and melodic arias for the maid Serpina and her master Uberto; a swift moving recitative over a crisp, dry keyboard accompaniment (*recitativo secco*) that permits rapid-fire musical conversation; and a general brightness and cheeriness to the tunes. Also, the leading male character in *La serva padrona* is a bass, a virile type of voice woefully neglected by *opera seria*.

It was not long before composers began to add greater substance and complexity to the *opera buffa* form. Among those who were most successful at it were Baldassare Galuppi, who was celebrated for other reasons in a poem by Robert Browning; Giovanni Paisiello, who composed opera's first, but not last, *Barber of Seville*; and Domenico Cimarosa, whose *Il matrimonio segreto* ("The Secret Marriage") survives, although his seventy-five other operas have been forgotten. Librettos for such works were provided by writers, some quite distinguished, with a flair for comedy and a knowledge of the theater. The playwright Carlo Goldoni became, in effect, the Metastasio of *opera buffa*, producing farcical plots that served generations of musicians. As late as 1906, the composer Ermanno Wolf-Ferrari used a Goldoni story for his opera *I quattro rusteghi* ("The Four Rustics"). Even the leading symphonist of the era, Joseph Haydn, composed a dozen *opere buffe*. One of Haydn's operas, *Il mondo della luna* (1777), enjoys an occasional revival in English under the title "The Man in the Moon."

Producing nearly eighty operas in twenty-nine years, Domenico Cimarosa was one of the most prolific and engaging composers in the opera buffa *style. However, only one of his operas is still alive today—*Il matrimonio segreto *(scene at left). This work so delighted the emperor at its premiere in Vienna that he ordered supper for the cast and insisted they repeat the entire performance that same night. Parisian audiences first saw Pergolesi's* La serva padrona *in 1746, but its impact was slight in comparison to the tumult it caused in French opera circles after a second production given in 1752. The playbill seen at right, above, commemorates that occasion.*

La serva padrona had no less an impact on France than on Italy, for its Paris production impelled French composers to turn to their own brand of comic opera. *Opéra comique* might be said to go back to Adam de la Halle's *Robin et Marion*, but it began to find wide audiences at such festive events as the famous Foire Saint-Germain, the great medieval Parisian trade and agriculture fair. There, the actors would perform light plays and invite the audience to join in singing the refrains of the songs. The Foire productions eventually led to the establishment of a Théâtre de l'Opéra-Comique, which performed musical plays made up of lively tunes linked by stretches of comic dialogue. Among the early composers of such works was Charles Simon Favart, whose name is still honored on the square in front of the Opéra-Comique building in Paris. Alluding to the *opéra comique's* rather questionable beginnings

in the rough-and-tumble Parisian fairs, Voltaire wrote to Favart: "You are the first to have made a decent and ingenious amusement out of a form of production that before you did not concern polite society."

The concept of *opéra comique* was also aided, however unintentionally, by no less a personage than Jean Jacques Rousseau, the back-to-nature philosopher who composed in 1752 a little work called *Le Devin du village* ("The Village Soothsayer"). Rousseau intended to write in an Italianate style, for he disliked French music intensely, proclaiming that "the French have no music and never will, or if they ever should, so much the worse for them." For his remarks, Jean Jacques was burned in effigy by the singers and musicians of the Opéra, but ironically *Le Devin du village* came out sounding considerably more French than Italian.

Opéra comique experienced the same rapid acceptance and growth as *opera buffa*. Even Gluck tried it out in such works as *L'Ivrogne corrigé* ("The Reformed Drunkard," 1760), but the most popular *opéra comique* composers in France were such men as Egidio Duni, who was Italian by birth; François André Philidor, who also became a famous chess master; Pierre Alexandre Monsigny, who wrote a dozen operas within fifteen years and then none at all during the next forty; and Belgian-born André Grétry, the most accomplished of them all. The song of Blondel the minstrel, "O Richard, o mon roi," from Grétry's romantic *Richard Coeur de Lion*, became a kind of anthem for the *ancien régime* in France. Foolishly sung by Marie-Antoinette at a Guards' dinner at Versailles on October 1, 1789, it helped inflame the mobs of the French Revolution.

In Germany, as in England, serious opera remained largely an Italian import, with native composers producing not even an isolated masterpiece like *Dido and Aeneas*. But a popular musical theater began to flourish, with little operas based on either the French *opéra comique* or the English ballad opera. One such work was *Der Teufel ist Los* (1752) with music by Johann Christian Standfuss, which was adapted from Charles Coffey's English comedy *The Devil to Pay*. Another popular piece was Johann Adam Hiller's *Die Jagd* ("The Hunt"), patterned on a work by Monsigny.

The Germans called their brand of comic opera *singspiel*, or "singspeech," in which, like the French popular opera, spoken dialogue carried the burden of the action, with musical numbers permitting the characters to comment melodiously on the situation. *Singspiel* became so popular in German-speaking lands that in 1778 Emperor Joseph II established a special company in Vienna to present such works. Only four years later it was performing an opera entitled *Die Entführung aus dem Serail* written by a young Austrian composer who had visited England, France, Italy, and Germany, and who transcended the musical style of all nations.

4

The Operatic Mozart

Wolfgang Amadeus Mozart comes closest of all musicians to being the universal composer. He wrote operas and symphonies, chamber music and church music, solo and concerted works for virtually every instrument, not excluding mechanical clocks and musical glasses. Probably more of his compositions are still in active use today than any other composer in history—his only possible challenger being Johann Sebastian Bach. Yet he lived for less than thirty-six years, from January 27, 1756, to December 5, 1791. His middle name means "beloved of God," but his life exemplifies Menander's ancient saying: "Whom the gods love dies young."

Mozart was a child prodigy; in fact, he and Felix Mendelssohn, who lived half a century later, were the most precocious young musicians that music has ever known. He was born in Salzburg, a German town with an Italian atmosphere and close to Vienna, central Europe's artistic metropolis. But many of his early years were spent in travel with his father, Leopold Mozart, a distinguished violin teacher who was eager to show off the youthful musical marvel of the age. When Wolfgang was seven, he set off with his father and his eleven-year-old sister Nannerl for a three-year-tour of Europe, nearly half of which was spent in London. As a boy, Mozart hobnobbed with King George III, Maria Theresa, and Marie Antoinette, and was lavishly praised by such celebrated musical figures as old Metastasio the librettist, and by Johann Hasse, the most prolific and successful of German opera composers. His father, a shrewd musician no less than a doting parent, wrote home: "Our high and mighty Wolfgang knows everything in this, his eighth year, that one can require of a man of forty."

None of this attention and adulation appears to have spoiled him in the least, however. He was a perfectly natural and cheerful child, who took it as quite a normal thing that he should discuss musical problems seriously with composers, singers, and instrumentalists far older than he, and give keyboard concerts before audiences who were clearly astounded by his technique and musicianship. By the age of ten he was one of the most famous individuals in Europe, and he remained so to the end of his life. But even though his talents as a performer and creator grew with the years, the novelty of his accomplishments inevitably diminished. At the age of twenty-five he decided to leave the secure but confining post of court musician to the archbishop of Salzburg in the hope of supporting himself as a pianist and composer in

Mozart's Don Giovanni *is one of the supreme baritone roles. At left is Francesco d'Andrade, a late-nineteenth-century interpreter. Critic George Bernard Shaw wrote of him: "D'Andrade made a passable libertine; but all libertines are not Don Giovannis, though all Don Giovannis are libertines"—thus succinctly stating the challenge of the role.*

47

Vienna—perhaps the first major musician ever to attempt a career as a freelance. From then to the end of his life his story was one of financial struggle with only intermittent success. Whether through a misunderstanding or lack of ready cash, he wound up in a pauper's grave somewhere in Vienna, so that no real monument to him remains except his music.

Throughout his life, Mozart produced music at a rapid, almost feverish pace, almost as if he knew he would have only a brief span in which to complete his work. In opera, the branch of his activity that concerns us here, he began by writing childish entertainments, one of which, a Latin comedy with music entitled *Apollo et Hyacinthus*, was actually performed by students at the University of Salzburg in 1767. The following year he came up with *Bastien und Bastienne*, a little *singspiel* with a libretto based on Rousseau's *Le Devin du village*. It was given an outdoor performance in the Vienna garden of Dr. Franz Anton Mesmer, the discoverer of "animal magnetism." *Bastien und Bastienne* holds an immortality of sorts because its overture begins with a tune that bears a startling resemblance to the famous opening theme of Beethoven's *Eroica* Symphony, written thirty-five years later.

It may seem slightly ridiculous to consider seriously operas written by a teenage boy, but the fact remains that most of the works composed by Mozart in this period were staged in his own time, and some are available today in complete recordings. In 1768, when he was twelve, he composed an opera called *La finta semplice* ("The Pretended Simpleton"), which became a center of intrigue at the Imperial Court of Vienna. Leopold Mozart had the impression that Emperor Joseph II wished to have the opera performed; but when Wolfgang completed the work, the director of the Imperial Opera, Giuseppe Affligio, kept on postponing its production. Leopold suspected certain elements at the court, Gluck among them, of refusing to permit a child to present an opera in such august surroundings. Eventually the Mozarts had to take the opera back to Salzburg with them.

Over the next few years, Wolfgang produced other operas: *Mitridate, rè di Ponto* ("Mithridates, King of Pontus," 1770) and *Lucio Silla* (1772), both of which were *opere serie*; and *Ascanio in Alba* (1771) and *Il sogno di Scipione* ("The Dream of Scipio," 1772), occasional pieces for a wedding and for the enthronement of an archbishop. Greater charm is evident in *Il rè pastore* ("The Shepherd King," 1775), whose lovely aria "L'amerò, sarò constante" (I will love her, I will be constant) is still sung in the concert hall.

Most significant of all Mozart's early operas is *La finta giardiniera* ("The Pretended Gardener"), which scored a genuine public success at the Munich Carnival in 1775. Despite its absurd plot about a noblewoman disguised as a garden girl, the audience was carried away by the music, which is in turn lively and tender and which climaxes in two splendidly dramatic ensembles. Mozart himself wrote to his mother, Anna Maria Mozart, that it was "impossible to describe the applause . . . after each aria there was a terrific din and cries of 'Viva Maestro.'" Characteristically, he concludes the letter with "one thousand kisses to Bimberl"—the family dog.

Envisaged by Emperor Francis Joseph I as the crowning achievement in the redesigned center of Vienna, the Vienna Royal Opera opened on May 25, 1869, with a gala performance of Don Giovanni. (drawing below). The selection of a work by Mozart (portrait at right) to celebrate this auspicious occasion was a fitting tribute to the genius of a composer whose operas had met with relative indifference in the Vienna of his lifetime.

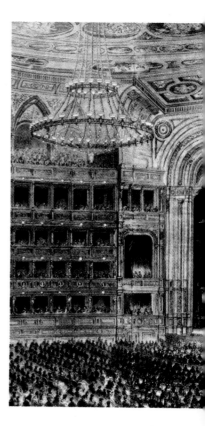

Five years later, Mozart was again invited to compose an opera for the Munich Carnival, this time an *opera seria*. The resulting work, *Idomeneo, rè di Creta* ("Idomeneus, King of Crete"), still receives occasional performances and is highly prized by connoisseurs. Although *opera seria* was already a fossilized form of music, the twenty-five-year-old composer managed to breathe life into it for one last time. The story is a typically stilted narrative about a monarch forced by a rash vow to sacrifice his only son, but Mozart humanizes the characters through his vocal and orchestral writing. Professor Edward J. Dent, the British authority on Mozart's operas, calls the quartet "Andro ramingo e solo" (Alone, I go to wander) "perhaps the most beautiful ensemble ever composed for the stage."

Idomeneo brought Mozart into close contact for the first time with singers and their vagaries. The role of Idomeneo was sung by Anton Raaff, a sixty-five-year-old tenor whose voice was all but worn out, while that of Idamante, the king's son, was entrusted to an inexperienced and clumsy young *castrato*, Vincenzo dal Prato. Mozart managed to give old Raaff music that he could sing effectively without too much strain, and he jollied the younger man, whom he referred to privately as "mio molto amato castrato Dal Prato" (my much beloved castrato Dal Prato), into giving the performance of his life.

With *Idomeneo*, Mozart entered his maturity as an opera composer. Two signal events in his personal life also occurred at about this time —he made his final break with the mean-spirited Salzburg archbishop, Hieronymus von Colloredo, and he became betrothed to Constanze Weber, the youngest of a family of three singing daughters. Constanze was a second choice, Mozart having unsuccessfully courted the middle daughter, Aloysia, who was among other things a finer singer.

In the midst of these personal crises came an invitation to write an opera for the national theater, which had been established by Emperor Joseph II to perform popular German operas in Vienna. Gottlieb Stephanie, the director of the theater, wrote the libretto himself, a pleasantly exotic farrago about a Spanish lady who falls into the hands of a Turkish pasha and is finally rescued by her suitor, who manages to gain entry into the palace disguised as an architect. The opera, at first called *Belmont und Constanze* (Mozart must have been pleased at the coincidence of names between the heroine and his own bride-to-be), finally ended up with the title *Die Entführung aus dem Serail* ("The Abduction from the Seraglio," 1782).

In *Die Entführung* Mozart once again tailored his music to the singers at hand with brilliant results—rumbling comic arias for Ludwig Fischer, the basso who sang the part of the drunken gardener Osmin, and spectacular vocal displays for Caterina Cavalieri, the accomplished soprano who played Constanze. The famous "Martern aller Arten" (Tortures past enduring) aria has been a showpiece for sopranos ever since its first performance. Mozart even worked on the text with the librettist, laying down the dictum: "In opera the poetry must be the obedient daughter of the music."

As beautiful and exhilarating as much of the music is, *Die Entführung* is a hodgepodge of an entertainment rather than a cohesive work

of art. The part of the pasha is spoken throughout, for instance, so that this crucial role is never established musically. A few years later Mozart and Stephanie collaborated on a brief one-act work entitled *Der Schauspieldirektor* ("The Impresario"), which had some imposing music but a witless plot about two feuding sopranos. The most memorable number in *Der Schauspieldirektor* is its lively overture.

Until now, Mozart had not had very good fortune with his librettists. But in 1783 he met Lorenzo da Ponte, who had just been appointed official poet to the imperial theaters in Vienna, and with him created the three masterful Italian operas, *Le nozze di Figaro* ("The Marriage of Figaro," 1786), *Don Giovanni* (1787), and *Così fan tutte* ("Thus Do They All," 1790).

Da Ponte was a highly skilled manipulator of words—and of other things as well. Born Emanuele Conegliano to poor Jewish parents in the ghetto of Ceneda, Italy, he underwent baptism at the age of fourteen, studied at a seminary, and became a Catholic priest. But this in no way prevented him from leading a generally dissolute life as well as becoming a literary lion in Vienna. Eventually he emigrated to the United States, where he became, in turn, a grocer in New Jersey and a professor of Italian literature at Columbia College before dying in New York at the age of eighty-nine.

So far as Mozart was concerned, da Ponte was a poet who could provide librettos that were abundant in incident and rich in characterization, with well-knit plots that built steadily toward dramatic climaxes. This was *opera buffa* raised to undreamed-of heights musically and peopled with real human beings caught up in conflicts stemming from their own ambitions, intrigues, and personalities. Mozart himself suggested Beaumarchais' *Le Mariage de Figaro* to da Ponte as a subject for an opera. He was not interested in the original French play's political aspects or its revolutionary implications; for him it was basically a drama, filled with people whose concerns and emotions he could make his own—Figaro, the shrewd valet who could outthink and outmaneu-

Along with Mozart's achievements in the Italian style, he helped lay the foundation of German opera with his singspiel Die Entführung aus dem Serail, *premiered in Vienna in 1782 (playbill above). The* singspiel *form, originally comic in design, was later turned to serious use by Mozart himself in* The Magic Flute *and by Beethoven in* Fidelio. *Today,* Die Entführung *is a popular favorite, especially enjoyed by youthful audiences. The photograph at right shows Anneliese Rothenberger and Kurt Böhme portraying the roles of Constanze and Osmin in a recent production in Munich. —*

ver his master; Susanna, the bright and tenderhearted maid; Cherubino, the lovesick young page; the Count, choleric and lecherous but not a bad fellow beneath it all; the Countess, striving desperately to retain her husband's waning affections; and various minor denizens of the "Castle of Count Almaviva, about three leagues from Seville."

To comprehend fully Mozart's transformation of *opera buffa*, it is necessary to remember that by the time he wrote *Figaro* he had also achieved mastery in other musical forms—symphonies, concertos, and string quartets. Thus he was able to bring to opera an instrumental depth and subtlety no other composer before him had possessed. In his hands vocal music took on a complexity and life of its own, with the melodies moving in unexpected directions and modulations, somewhat in the manner of symphonic themes.

As expressive as the arias themselves are, it is the ensembles in *Figaro* that make it such an inexhaustible and unfailing delight. The finale of Act II, especially, is a perfect fusion of musical development and dramatic action. The Count believes he has discovered his wife deceiving him with the page boy Cherubino but is persuaded otherwise by the Countess and Susanna; Figaro enters and inadvertently almost gives the plot away, requiring some more nimble talking by the women; a gardener bursts in to announce that he has seen a man (actually the page) jump from the window; Figaro convinces everyone (almost including himself) that *he* was the man who jumped; finally the stage is filled with nearly all the principal characters arguing, expostulating, and jostling as they present their points of view simultaneously. In twenty minutes of marvelous music Mozart presents a microcosm of the human comedy with all its passion and intrigue, pathos and irony.

The Marriage of Figaro was an immediate success in Vienna in 1786. Irish tenor Michael Kelly, who sang the minor roles of Don Basi-

lio and Don Curzio, has left in his *Reminiscences* an endearing picture of Mozart being moved by the sound of his own music:

> I remember at the first rehearsal of the full band, Mozart was on the stage with his crimson pelisse and gold-laced cocked hat, giving the time of the music to the orchestra. Figaro's song, "Non più andrai, farfallone amoroso," [baritone Francesco] Bennuci gave with the greatest animation and power of voice.
>
> I was standing close to Mozart, who, *sotto voce*, was repeating, Bravo! Bravo! Bennuci! and when Bennuci came to the fine passage, "Cherubino, alla vittoria, alla gloria militar" . . . the effect was electricity itself, for the whole of the performers on the stage, and those in the orchestra, as if actuated by one feeling of delight, vociferated "Bravo! Bravo! *Maestro! Viva, viva, grande* Mozart!"

Unfortunately *Figaro*'s acclaim in Vienna was transitory; after nine performances it was dropped in favor of *Una cosa rara*, a work by the Spaniard Vicente Martin y Soler. However, when *Figaro* was staged by the Italian opera company in Prague, 150 miles from Vienna, it filled the theater night after night. The delighted management immediately invited Mozart to the Bohemian capital, and there, he wrote home, he heard "nothing but *Figaro*" talked about, played, and sung. Because of its success the company's director, Pasquale Bondini, commissioned Mozart to write another opera, a decision to which the world owes *Don Giovanni*.

This time it was da Ponte who suggested as the subject the legendary Spanish lover Don Juan, particularly as represented in a tale called "The Stone Guest," in which the statue of the Commendatore, killed by the Don, accepts an invitation to supper and drags the miscreant off to Hell. For *Don Giovanni*, Mozart and da Ponte dropped the designation *opera buffa* and called it instead a *dramma giocoso*. Technically there is little difference in the terms, but "jocose drama" somehow conveys a more ominous and portentous image. Its overture opens in D minor (unlike *Figaro*'s D major) and blends straight into a scene in which Don Juan attempts to rape Donna Anna and then slays her father when he comes to her aid; all this takes place before the eyes of his sardonic but horrified servant Leporello.

The demonic aspects of *Don Giovanni* were undoubtedly exaggerated by the Romantic era, but they are present nevertheless and dominate the climax of the opera in which the defiant Don meets his doom to ghostly winds and solemn brasses. As in *Figaro*, there are magnificent ensembles, including one in which three small onstage orchestras play simultaneously during a ball in the Don's palace. There is also some pliantly beautiful use of recitative, as in Giovanni's lightly caressing phrases just before he begins the celebrated duet "Là ci darem la mano" (There you will give me your hand) with the peasant girl Zerlina.

Don Giovanni, like *Figaro* before it, scored a tremendous success in Prague, but when it was produced in Vienna, with a few additions to please the singers there, the response was less enthusiastic. The emperor remarked, "Such music is not meat for the teeth of my Viennese," to which Mozart replied, "Give them time to chew on it."

Mozart's The Marriage of Figaro *brought to the stage a gallery of human characters unmatched previously in opera for their individuality and reality. Some of these figures were later depicted in silhouette (seen above, clockwise from top, left): Count Almaviva, Susanna, the Countess, and Cherubino. In the Act II finale, nearly all the principal players come together in a confrontation for which Mozart wrote a complex, intricate ensemble that is a marvel of musical drama. The photograph at left shows that climactic moment as it is performed in the current New York City Opera production.*

Overleaf: *Still filled with defiance and bravado, Don Giovanni, played by Metropolitan Opera bass Cesare Siepi, enjoys a lavish, though ominous, banquet as the final, tragic act of Mozart's* Don Giovanni *begins.*

Three years later, Joseph II, taking another chance on his Viennese, commissioned Mozart and da Ponte to try one more opera, *Così fan tutte*. The plot was slight and, on the face of it, absurd—a cynical old bachelor, Don Alfonso, undertakes to prove the inconstancy of women to two young officers, and he succeeds by having them disappear and return in disguise, each successfully wooing the other's sweetheart. For all the artificiality of the situation and characters, Mozart succeeded in writing music of exquisite charm, humor, and even wistful tenderness. In all his operas, nothing is more touching than the achingly beautiful farewell trio "Soave sia il vento" (Gentle be the wind), written for the unusual combination of soprano, mezzo-soprano, and baritone, the voices alternately in unison and intertwining.

Barely two years of life were left to Mozart after *Così*, and in that time he produced two more operas. The first, *La clemenza di Tito* ("The Clemency of Titus"), was an *opera seria*, commissioned for the coronation at Prague of Emperor Leopold II as king of Bohemia in September, 1791. This time, however, Mozart was unable to overcome the sterility of the *opera seria* form. With its convoluted plot about a magnanimous monarch and its inevitable *castrato* character, *La clemenza di Tito* has its moments of beauty, including a charming little love duet, "Ah, perdona," but today it remains the least performed of Mozart's mature operas.

Two later Mozart operas, Così fan tutte *and* The Magic Flute, *show an undiminished range of musical inventiveness.* Così fan tutte *(photographed at left, above, during a performance at the Salzburg Festival) is a sophisticated but touching exploration of the nature of love. By contrast, the mystical spirit that pervades* The Magic Flute *is portrayed in a drawing of the Queen of Night (above), executed for an early nineteenth-century production that was given in Munich.*

If the coronation of a king couldn't inspire Mozart to a masterpiece at this stage of his life, the idea of an opera written for the common people in their own language could. Among Mozart's acquaintances was a traveling impresario-actor-singer named Emanuel Schikaneder, who in 1791 was running a popular theater just outside the city limits of Vienna. There he presented musical entertainments that put strong emphasis on comedy, spectacle, and even live animals. Most of Mozart's previous operas had been given at the official and fashionable Burgtheater; now Schikaneder invited him to write for his considerably less-refined Theater auf der Wieden. The libretto, by Schikaneder himself, was *Die Zauberflöte* ("The Magic Flute"), a fairy-tale story about a prince who sets out to rescue a princess from an evil sorcerer, only to find that the latter is, in reality, the high priest of a noble and humane order, which the young couple eventually join.

Both Schikaneder and Mozart were Freemasons, and efforts have been made to find Masonic significance in the rituals that Tamino and Pamina undergo as they are initiated into Sarastro's order, and even in the three majestic trombone chords which begin the overture and recur at solemn moments throughout the opera. Mozart wrote *The Magic Flute* on two levels. In Sarastro's realm the music has a remarkably spiritual and ethical quality—"the only music yet written," George Bernard Shaw has said, "that would not sound out of place in the mouth of God." But in the everyday world of Papageno, a loquacious and amiable birdcatcher who is helping Tamino in his search, the music is simple, songlike, and gay.

The Magic Flute is a *singspiel* in form, with spoken dialogue and lusty jokes, most of which were written in for Schikaneder, who played the part of Papageno himself. In the opera, Papageno uses a magic glockenspiel to ward off danger just as Tamino uses a magic flute, with the actual playing of the instruments entrusted to two musicians offstage. Mozart himself, in a letter to his wife, reported a delightful incident that took place one night while he was attending a performance at the theater:

> During Papageno's aria with the glockenspiel I went behind the scenes, as I felt a sort of impulse to-day to play it myself. Well, just for fun, at

the point where Schikaneder has a pause, I played an arpeggio. He was startled, looked behind the wings and saw me. When he had his next pause, I played no arpeggio. This time he stopped and refused to go on. I guessed what he was thinking and again played a chord. He then struck the glockenspiel and said "*Shut up.*" Whereupon everyone laughed. I am inclined to think that this joke taught many of the audience for the first time that Papageno does not play the instrument himself. By the way, you have no idea how charming the music sounds when you hear it from a box close to the orchestra.

Die Zauberflöte is the first great opera written in the German language and as such may be said to mark the true starting point of German opera. A huge popular success, it packed Schikaneder's theater night after night. Over the next ten years it was given there 223 times and taken up by many other German theaters as well.

Unfortunately, all this came too late for Mozart, who by now was exhausted and ill, as well as being at low ebb financially. What Schikaneder paid him for *The Magic Flute* is not known, but he had received the equivalent of about two hundred dollars from the Prague Opera for *Don Giovanni* with a hundred dollars more for the Vienna production, and about four hundred dollars for *Così fan tutte*. In his last days he was kept afloat mainly by generous loans from a friend, Michael Puchberg. On November 20, 1791, Mozart took to his bed for the last time. Most authorities today believe he had chronic kidney disease, but whatever it was, the physicians of the time were helpless to save him. As he lay dying, he would keep his watch open on his pillow on the nights *The Magic Flute* was being performed, and follow its progress in his mind. It consoled him somewhat that vast audiences were coming to see and hear his last stage work; perhaps he also sensed that they would continue to do so in times to come.

Paradoxically, the nineteenth century tended to regard Mozart as a composer of operatic miniatures rather than masterpieces. The only one of his operas to remain consistently in the repertory was *Don Giovanni*, whose dashing hero appealed to the Romantic imagination. *Così fan tutte* was regarded as such a triviality that efforts were made to refit the music to a more "respectable" libretto. In Paris *The Magic Flute* was for a time equipped with a new plot and additional music and set before the public under the title of *The Mysteries of Isis*.

Even the early twentieth century was remiss in its appreciation of Mozart's more important operas; incredible as it seems, the Metropolitan Opera went twenty-three years, starting in 1917, without a single performance of *The Marriage of Figaro*. Fortunately a brilliant revival in 1940, with Ezio Pinza as Figaro, augmented beautiful performances (subsequently recorded) by the Glyndebourne Opera Festival of England during the 1930s, sparking a Mozart revival that has never diminished. George Bernard Shaw, while a young music critic in Victorian London, said that all his musical self-respect was based on his keen appreciation of Mozart; in like manner, the twentieth century can claim among its artistic accomplishments the restoration of Mozart to his proper place at the summit of the operatic art.

Sets and costumes designed by Marc Chagall highlighted the Metropolitan Opera's new production of The Magic Flute *in 1967. In the scene below, Tamino and Pamina stand before Sarastro, who will sanction their entry into the holy order.*

6ᵉ année. — N° 21   Un numéro 10 centimes   4 juillet 1867

LE HANNETON

ILLUSTRÉ, SATIRIQUE ET LITTÉRAIRE

ROSSINI

Monsieur D. Azam

Dantan fit jadis la Caricature du Compositeur Pesarese
Aujourd'hui devenu Pianiste de la quatrième Classe il ne
s'oppose pas a ce qu'elle soit Publiée dans votre Journal

G. Rossini

Passy 28 Juin 1867

5

Opera Becomes Grand

TALLEYRAND, the French diplomat who served both the Emperor Napoleon and the restored Bourbon kings with equal efficiency and cynicism, once remarked: "Anyone who has not lived before 1789 has not tasted the sweetness of life." He was referring, of course, to the French Revolution, which, two years before the death of Mozart, had irreparably shaken the established political and social order in Europe and opened the way to the modern era. Relatively few people had enjoyed the "sweetness" of which Talleyrand spoke, but there is no doubt that aristocratic patronage had enabled the arts, at least, to flourish with a certain degree of elegance and refinement.

The upheavals of the Revolution forced opera to seek new patrons, new subject matter, and new musical directions. These developed most strongly in Paris, which, during the first half of the nineteenth century, became the unchallenged operatic capital of Europe. But the Revolution unloosed new artistic currents elsewhere, too. In Germany, opera became suffused with a romanticism that was to culminate in the musical dramas of Richard Wagner. In Italy, the voice reaffirmed its supremacy and ushered in the era of *bel canto*. And in France, where composers of all nationalities gravitated, the prevailing taste for eye- and ear-filling splendor eventually led to the elaborate spectacle known as "grand opera."

No composer in any land was more in sympathy with the ideals of the French Revolution than the German Ludwig van Beethoven. Brusque, plainspoken, profoundly republican in instinct, he accepted the patronage of the aristocracy but not its outlook. His genius was basically symphonic, but in 1805 he composed his one opera, *Fidelio*, a dramatic work about a political captive immured in a Spanish prison from which he is freed only by the efforts of his devoted wife Leonore, who dons a male disguise to gain entry into his jail.

Beethoven himself later said of *Fidelio* that "of all my children, this was born in the greatest labor." He revised and rewrote it over a period of years, one result being that it was left with no fewer than four overtures (now known as the *Fidelio* Overture and the *Leonore* Overtures Nos. 1, 2 and 3). Various criticisms have been leveled against *Fidelio*: it is musically inconsistent, varying in style from the trivial to the heroic; it makes inordinate demands on its singers, with its wide-ranging vocal leaps; and its libretto is occasionally awkward, as when the prisoner

Florestan, after two full years in a black dungeon, greets us with the words: "Gott! welch Dunkel hier!" (God, it's dark in here!).

Nevertheless, Beethoven made of *Fidelio* a magnificent and ennobling work. The story, with its amalgam of human suffering, wifely devotion, and the eventual triumph of right and justice fired his imagination, and he utilized his full orchestral mastery to bring it to life. Beethoven was always prone to push his singers to the uttermost, and he achieved exalted results in *Fidelio*.

None of the German or Austrian symphonic masters who followed Beethoven was able to achieve a success in opera. Franz Schubert made numerous attempts without ever writing a stageworthy work; Felix Mendelssohn gave up after one youthful try, turning instead, like Handel, to oratorio; and Robert Schumann completed one opera, *Genoveva*, which has since been forgotten.

The only German composer of the era to become a major operatic figure was Carl Maria von Weber, a first cousin of the Constanze Weber who married Mozart. Weber's career nearly ended at age nineteen when he drank a cup of corrosive acid, mistaking it for wine; but he survived this mishap and went on to become an operatic conductor and impresario in Breslau, Prague, and Dresden. All the while he was writing his own operas, and he achieved a sensation with *Der Freischütz* ("The Free-shooter"), performed in Berlin in 1821.

Where the old Florentine composers had sought their inspiration in Greek myths, Weber entered the realm of Teutonic fairy tale, legend, and the supernatural. *Der Freischütz* is about a forester who sells his soul to Samiel, the Black Huntsman, in exchange for seven magic bullets. Its scene in the Wolf's Glen, in which Samiel forges the bullets, is still one of the eeriest in opera, with muttered voices over a spooky orchestral and choral background. Other scenes offer musically spacious arias for the principal characters, and vigorous and charming rustic choruses. The "deutsches Volk," beloved of Wagner, makes its bow in Weber's opera.

Der Freischütz has a reputation for historical significance, because it opened the era of German operatic romanticism and challenged the supremacy of the Italian style. But its appeal has always been principally to Germans, and it has never really entered the international repertory. Nor did Weber quite repeat his success in his two subsequent works, *Euryanthe* and *Oberon*. The latter was commissioned by London's Covent Garden, and Weber, spent with consumption, went there in 1826 to conduct the opening performances and collect his fee of one thousand pounds. He died in England the night before he was scheduled to leave for home. Today most listeners know his three most famous works chiefly through their splendidly scored, richly romantic overtures, but these are heard far more frequently in the concert hall than in the opera house.

In Italy, the advent of the nineteenth century was not a particularly propitious time for opera. Leading composers had a way of heading north for Paris, where they Frenchified both their life styles and their musical techniques. One of the most popular "Italian" composers of the era was Johann Simon Mayr, a facile Bavarian who settled in Bergamo,

Not until the regime of Arturo Toscanini, beginning in 1898, did La Scala Theater in Milan get around to staging Beethoven's Fidelio. *The poster at left, above, advertises its first performance. One generally marks the birth of German romantic opera by the premiere in 1821 of Carl Maria von Weber's* Der Freischütz. *The sketch at left shows the original costumes worn by the opera's principal characters—Samiel, the wild huntsman (left), and Caspar, a young hunter (right). Composed in the space of only twenty-seven days,* L'italiana in Algeri *is one of Rossini's most entertaining creations. It is seen in the photograph above, taken during a 1973 performance at La Scala.*

where he turned out a succession of operas more substantial in style and content than those of many of his native competitors.

But in 1792, the year after Mozart's death, Gioacchino Rossini was born in Pesaro, and it was almost as if Italian opera marked time while he grew up. The wait was not a long one, for Rossini began writing operas before he was twenty, and he turned them out at an incredible pace—twenty in the eight years from 1815 to 1823. He composed serious dramas, including a setting of Shakespeare's *Othello*, which held the stage until Verdi's far more powerful work eclipsed it. His supreme accomplishments, however, were in comedy, a field in which he was an absolute master. *L'italiana in Algeri* ("The Italian Girl in Algiers"), *La scala di seta* ("The Silken Ladder"), *La gazza ladra* ("The Thieving Magpie"), *Cenerentola* ("Cinderella")—their overtures alone would make up a joyous evening in the concert hall.

The thoroughly theatrical quality of Rossini's music is not least among the characteristics that guarantee its permanence. His father was a town trumpeter who also played in various provincial theaters; Rossini learned early the importance of direct communication with an audience. A curious echo of this appears in a work of modern fiction, James M. Cain's *Serenade*, a novel published in 1937. An operatic baritone and a merchant-ship skipper are arguing the merits of various composers, especially Beethoven and Rossini. The singer wins the argument with this tirade:

Listen, symphonies are not all of music. When you get to the overtures, Beethoven's name is not at the top, and Rossini's is. . . . Rossini loved the theater, and that's why he could write an overture. He takes you into the theater—hell, you can even feel them getting into their seats, and smell the theater smell, and see the lights go up on the curtain.

Posterity, with unerring instinct, has seized upon *Il barbiere di Siviglia* (1816) as the quintessential Rossini opera. Rossini is supposed to have composed it in thirteen days, leading to Donizetti's legendary comment: "Ah, yes, but then Rossini always *was* lazy." Since Paisiello's version of *The Barber of Seville*, written in 1782, was still a favorite in Italy, Rossini thought it politic to seek the older composer's permission for setting the same story. Paisiello gave his consent, little dreaming that the new *Barber* would efface the old.

Right from the opening chorus, in which a group of hired serenaders adjure each other noisily to be absolutely quiet, *The Barber of Seville* is the stuff of sheer musical farce. Figaro's sprightly "Largo al factotum" (Room for the factotum) is the classic example of the *opera buffa* patter song, in which the Italian language and the musical notes seem inextricable from each other. Also very much in evidence is the "Rossini Crescendo," in which the music increases dizzily in tempo and volume, and the "ensemble of perplexity," in which the various charac-

ters, individually and in overlapping combinations, insist melodiously and repeatedly that the situation is most vexing and they really do not know what to do. Somehow, they always manage to do something.

The Barber and his other successes made Rossini the most sought after opera composer of the day and virtually assured his departure for cities where the rewards were more lucrative. He tried Vienna and London, but after marrying Isabella Colbran, a Spanish soprano, and composing *Semiramide*, a tragic opera about a Babylonian queen, he settled in Paris, where we will meet him again shortly.

Rossini's departure in 1823 left the development of Italian opera largely in the hands of two young men, twenty-two-year-old Vincenzo Bellini and twenty-six-year-old Gaetano Donizetti. Between them they helped evolve *bel canto*—literally "beautiful song," but more comprehensively an operatic style characterized by smooth and expressive vocalism, often with a minimum of dramatic impact or logic.

Bellini, like his friend Frédéric Chopin, led a short and not particularly merry life. He was continually falling in love with his prima donnas, his health was bad, and he never really found a sense of either personal or artistic fulfillment. Thus it is no wonder that his operas so often sound like one long sigh. His most durable creation has proved to be *Norma* (1831), a beautiful and stately work about a Druid priestess in Britain who is secretly in love with a Roman proconsul. Norma's great aria "Casta diva" (Chaste goddess) exemplifies the Bellini style of elegant and flowing vocalism.

Not unexpectedly, opera like this, where dramatic suspense counted for little and vocal expertise for everything, depended then (as it does now) on the prowess of the singers involved. Giuditta Pasta, who was said to be able to sing contralto as easily as she sang soprano, created the role of Norma. Giulia Grisi appeared in the first *I Puritani* ("The Puritans," 1835), in one of the first authentically all-star casts in history, its other members being the tenor Giovanni Battista Rubini, the baritone Antonio Tamburini, and the bass Luigi Lablache. Another famous *bel canto* interpreter, especially in *La sonnambula* ("The Sleepwalker," 1831), was Maria Malibran, whose extraordinary voice, and figure described as "rounded to a becoming degree of embonpoint," made her as intriguing a personality to Bellini as to everyone else in the musical world. Later on, Jenny Lind joined the ranks of notable Bellini protagonists.

Most of these singers were equally at home in the operas of Donizetti, which had somewhat more dramatic cohesiveness than those of Bellini. Donizetti turned out some seventy operas, and several of his comic works, such as *L'élisir d'amore* ("The Elixir of Love," 1832), *La fille du regiment* ("The Daughter of the Regiment," 1840), and *Don Pasquale* (1843), have stood up very well. More than a hundred years later, the appearance of a twentieth-century crop of *bel canto* sopranos, among them the Americans Maria Callas and Beverly Sills and the Australian Joan Sutherland, led to renewed interest in Donizetti's "historical" operas, including three sagas involving British royalty—*Anna Bolena*, *Roberto Devereux*, and *Maria Stuarda*—all revived by the New York City Opera in the 1970s.

GIUDITTA PASTA

Inspired by the first of three plays Beaumarchais wrote about the comic adventures of Figaro (portrayed by Hermann Prey left, above), Rossini's Il barbiere di Siviglia *is as beloved a part of operatic repertory as is Mozart's opera based on the same character. The engraving at left shows a scene in Rossini's work in which Figaro shaves Bartolo while Rosina supposedly takes a singing lesson. Giuditta Pasta, one of the most celebrated performers of the early nineteenth century, is shown in the engraving above singing the title role in* Norma, *which Bellini wrote especially for her.*

Joan Sutherland's 1959 Covent Garden appearance in Donizetti's Lucia di Lammermoor *established her as one of the leading sopranos of this era. Two years later she repeated her triumph as Lucia in her Metropolitan Opera debut (left). Luigi Cherubini and his pupil Daniel Auber were leading figures in French opera during the first half of the nineteenth century. Cherubini's* Médée *(published libretto above) has been revived in modern times to display the talents of dramatic sopranos such as Maria Callas. Auber's* La Muette de Portici *(playbill below), an enormously influential precursor of French grand opera, is rarely performed today.*

But his masterpiece, which seems likely to remain in the repertory as long as sopranos exist, is *Lucia di Lammermoor* (1835), based on Sir Walter Scott's novel *The Bride of Lammermoor*. Donizetti, like Bellini, was enamored of "mad scenes," episodes in which a character (invariably a soprano) loses her senses in a series of florid vocal runs and roulades. *Lucia* boasts the most dazzling mad scene of all, and, in its famous sextet, a superb dramatic ensemble that never fails to stir the listener. Novelists from Gustave Flaubert in *Madame Bovary* to E. M. Forster in *Where Angels Fear to Tread* have depicted *Lucia di Lammermoor* as the ideal romantic opera and have put it to use memorably for background purposes.

Donizetti lived longer than Bellini and wrote far more, but his end was equally sad, for he suffered increasingly from mental breakdowns and melancholia, and he eventually died in his native town, Bergamo, as mad as any of his heroines. But he had preserved and enhanced the Italian operatic tradition before passing it to its supreme master, Giuseppi Verdi.

At various epochs in their careers, both Bellini and Donizetti spent considerable time in Paris; in fact, works like *I Puritani* and *Don Pasquale* had their premieres there. The French capital had been a magnet to foreign musicians since the days of Louis XIV, and with the Revolution and the rise of Napoleon it became a center of artistic ferment, producing a new middle-class audience for what had been essentially an aristocratic entertainment.

The Revolution itself created little of note operatically; typical of the French product was a popular work by Henri Montan Berton entitled *Les rigueurs du cloître* ("The Rigors of the Cloister," 1790), in which a young nun about to be imprisoned by a wicked abbess is rescued by a detachment of Revolutionary troops.

Under Napoleon, the most favored musicians in Paris were two transplanted Italians, Luigi Cherubini, best known today for his *Médée* ("Medea"), which is occasionally revived, and Gasparo Spontini, composer of *La Vestale* ("The Vestal") and *Fernand Cortez*, both written in the *tragédie lyrique* style of Gluck but with spectacular stage effects that presage the era of grand opera. Beethoven was an admirer of Cherubini, and his *Fidelio* was supposedly modeled on the "rescue operas" popular in Paris, in which a hero or heroine is snatched from death at the last moment by the arrival of a loved one. Along with their taste for spectacular and heroic opera, French audiences never lost their affection for the lighter *opéra comique*, as evidenced by such successful works as François-Adrien Boieldieu's *La Dame blanche* ("The White Lady," 1825), Ferdinand Hérold's *Zampa* (1831), and Adolphe-Charles Adam's *Le Postillon de Longjumeau* ("The Coachman of Longjumeau," 1836), although Adam is certainly even better known for his quintessentially romantic ballet *Giselle*.

Curiously, both the serious and comic French traditions combined to produce grand opera. In 1828 Daniel-François-Esprit Auber, a composer with a genius for *opéra comique* (among his subsequent works were *Fra Diavolo* and *Le Domino noir*), wrote for the Opéra a large-scale work called *Masaniello*, or *La Muette de Portici* ("The Mute Girl of Portici"). Its subject was a revolt led in Naples by a fisherman named Masaniello against Spanish occupying forces in 1647, and its climax involves nothing less than the eruption of Mount Vesuvius, an event that actually occurred in 1631. Auber's *Muette* was one of the first operas to be turned to political uses; when it was performed in Brussels in 1830 its scenes of patriotic fervor helped ignite a popular uprising against Dutch occupying troops that led to the establishment of Belgium as an independent state.

So far as the French were concerned, *La Muette de Portici* brought together all the elements of stirring musical theater—a vigorous but melodic score, plenty of spectacle and ballet, and a story filled with both action and romance. The immediate success of *La Muette* was enormous (Auber's name still designates one of Paris's most prestigious streets, alongside the Opéra), and other works in a similar style were obviously called for.

A few years before *La Muette de Portici*, Gioacchino Rossini had arrived in Paris to become an immediate musical and social lion. At first he was appointed director of the Théâtre des Italiens, an institution founded by Napoleon to produce the best Italian operas in Paris; later he was showered with such prestigious titles as "First Composer of the King" and "Inspector-General of Singing in France," each garnished with an impressive stipend. In his first years in Paris, Rossini produced three operas of his own, all with French texts: *Le Siège de Corinthe* ("The Siege of Corinth") and *Moïse en Egypte* ("Moses in Egypt"), both of which were rewrites of earlier Italian works, and *Le Comte Ory* ("Count Ory"), which was genuinely new.

With the success of Auber's *Muette*, Rossini decided to try something in the same vein. The result was *William Tell*, performed to critical acclaim at the Paris Opéra in 1829 with the renowned dramatic tenor Adolphe Nourrit in the title role. Rossini's *William Tell* has always been a work spoken of almost in awe, yet actual performances of it have tended to be minimal. Its stirring overture, however, has become a concert hall favorite, not to mention the signature of American radio's Lone Ranger. Even in Rossini's time, *Tell* underwent cutting and excerpting at the Paris Opéra. A famous story tells of that theater's director encountering Rossini on the street one day and informing him heartily, "Tonight we're giving Act II of *William Tell*," and Rossini replying in mock surprise, "What—*all* of it?"

Rossini was thirty-seven years old when *Tell* was produced, and although he lived for thirty-eight years more he never wrote another opera. Instead he took a new wife, Olympe Pélissier, described by one authority as "a prominent demimondaine with a variegated past," and settled comfortably into a house in Passy, where he earned a reputation as a wit, a gourmet, and an amiable, if somewhat cynical, elder statesman of music. Every musician passing through Paris came to call on him, from Franz Liszt to Richard Wagner. Few men have enjoyed their fame as amply or as leisurely. In his later years he composed only a handful of instrumental pieces that he gathered under the title *Les Péchés de Vieillesse* ("Sins of Old Age") and an admirable religious work, *La Petite Messe Solennelle* ("Little Solemn Mass"). To the latter

The famed American soprano Beverly Sills made her La Scala debut in a 1969 revival of Rossini's Le Siège de Corinthe *(photograph opposite, with co-star Marilyn Horne). Immensely prolific in his youth, Rossini abandoned opera at the age of thirty-seven following the presentation in Paris of* William Tell *(drawing below), whose overture is a popular concert work.*

he attached a plaintive and punning note: "Dear God: . . . Have I for once written real sacred music [*musique sacrée*] or merely damned bad music [*sacrée musique*]? I was born for *opera buffa* as Thou knowest. . . . So blessed be Thou and grant me Paradise."

Considerable though Rossini's contribution was, the true master of French grand opera turned out to be not an Italian but a German. Giacomo (really Jakob) Meyerbeer was the son of a Berlin banker and Jewish communal leader. He displayed musical talents early and was advised to sharpen them in Italy by Antonio Salieri, an old opera com-

The sketch above shows the eerie, midnight dance of the nuns, a famous scene in Giacomo Meyerbeer's first triumph at the Paris Opéra, Robert le Diable.

poser who had been a rival of Mozart. He wrote several works in Italy, and one, *Il crociato in Egitto* ("The Crusade in Egypt"), was such a success that a performance was scheduled for Paris in 1826. Meyerbeer went there to supervise it and was so smitten with the city and its musical life that he forthwith became a Parisian. While there, he began a collaboration with Eugène Scribe, author of the libretto of *La Muette de Portici*, who was a master at concocting operatic texts that blended history, spectacle, romance—and a touch of sensationalism.

The first joint effort of Meyerbeer and Scribe was *Robert le Diable* ("Robert the Devil," 1831), a grotesque tale laid in thirteenth-century Sicily. Its hero, Robert Duke of Normandy, who is the son of a mortal woman and an offspring of Satan, is barely saved from a trip to the infernal regions by the love of a good woman, Princess Isabella. In one of the scenes that titillated Parisian audiences of the 1830s, an orgy of faithless nuns dance about Robert in a convent cemetery in an effort to make him break off a magical cypress branch that will seal his doom. After seeing *Robert le Diable* the sensitive Frédéric Chopin wrote: "I don't know whether there has ever been such magnificence in a theater. . . . It is a masterpiece of the new school, in which devils (huge choirs) sing through speaking-trumpets, and souls rise from graves. . . . There is a diorama in the theater against which, at the end, you see the interior of a church, a whole church, at Christmas or Easter, lighted up . . . nothing of the sort could be put on anywhere else. Meyerbeer has immortalized himself."

Even more spectacular, if possible, was *Les Huguenots* (1836), based on the French religious wars of the sixteenth century and culminating in a depiction of the St. Bartholomew's Day massacre, which demanded seven absolutely first-rate lead singers, a huge chorus, and massive panoply. Similarly scaled were *Le Prophète* (1849), about the Anabaptist theocrat John of Leyden, and *L'Africaine* (1865), whose hero is the explorer Vasco da Gama. Meyerbeer's success naturally led to emulation of his style by other composers. Also surviving from the period, at least by reputation, is Fromental Halévy's *La Juive* ("The Jewess," 1835), whose heroine is executed by being dropped, on stage, into a vat of boiling oil.

Perhaps the most remarkable aspect of Meyerbeer's operas is not the tremendous vogue they enjoyed in their own time but their total disappearance today. Their inordinate length, their wearying spectacle, their remote and often absurd plots have proved too great a burden for the occasional passages of vigorous and even brilliant music. Meyerbeer exercised considerable influence on composers who came after him, including both Verdi and Wagner, but save for isolated numbers like "O Paradis!" from *L'Africaine* and the Coronation March from *Le Prophète*, his operas, which once towered over the musical scene, today are as dead as the dinosaur.

The epoch of grand opera brought not only changes on the operatic stage, but significant alterations in the audience. With aristocratic support a thing of the past, theaters depended for their survival upon ticket sales to the public. Not the least of the accomplishments of *Robert le Diable* was that it put the Paris Opéra on its feet financially.

Overleaf: Covent Garden's 1969 production of Les Troyens *represented the first time the work had been performed exactly as Berlioz wrote it—without cuts or revisions—more than one hundred years earlier.*

The great Parisian working class lacked both the money and the leisure to attend the opera, but the new bourgeois and mercantile class had both.

From 1830 to 1848 France was ruled by Louis Philippe, the "citizen-king," who walked around Paris carrying an umbrella like any middle-class stroller and whose advice to his subjects was: "Get rich!" For the bourgeoisie, the opera was a place not only for musical enjoyment and stage spectacle, but also for social display and even business transactions. When Madame Bovary's husband wants to relieve the tedium of their small-town life with a touch of glamour and excitement, he takes her to the opera in Rouen. Flaubert neatly depicts the operatic audience of the time:

> The theater began to fill; opera glasses came out of cases; and subscribers exchanged greetings as they glimpsed one another across the house. The arts, for them, were a relaxation from the worries of buying and selling; that was why they had come; but it was quite impossible for them to forget business even here, and their conversation was about cotton, spirits, and indigo.

The Meyerbeer era was also a golden age for the "claque," the hired applauders whose task was to stimulate ovations for a particular singer or opera. No one can date with certainty the first appearance of the claqueur on the operatic scene; his art goes back at least to the *gondolieri* of Monteverdi's Venice, and persists to the present. But it reached its pinnacle in the Paris of the 1830s, when a certain Auguste Levasseur, "a veritable Hercules in size, and gifted with extraordinary hands," according to one contemporary, was said to have earned as much annually as *chef de claque* as any of the leading singers.

Strangely, while French grand opera was being all but monopolized by foreign musicians like Rossini and Meyerbeer, the native-born Hector Berlioz was struggling to win recognition as a symphonic and operatic composer alike. The fate of Berlioz's operas, especially his epic *Les Troyens* ("The Trojans," 1856–58), is exactly the reverse of Meyerbeer's—ignored and unplayed in their own time, they are being staged to admiration and acclaim today.

Berlioz, whose father was a doctor in a town in southeast France, was sent to Paris in 1822 to study medicine. He said afterward that he "might have added another name to the long list of bad doctors" but for a visit he paid to the Opéra on a night when Salieri's *Les Danaïdes* was being given. The opera was in the style of Gluck, who was Berlioz's hero. The next day he irritated his laboratory partner by singing the arias while they sawed through the skull of the cadaver they were dissecting. Eventually, after a fearful quarrel with his father, he gave up medicine and enrolled at the Paris Conservatory. From then on he became a habitué of the Opéra, especially when Gluck's works were being performed; one night when cymbals were inserted into a ballet sequence that the composer had scored only for strings, Berlioz shouted out in midperformance to the startled audience: "There are no cymbals there! Who has dared to correct Gluck?"

Romantic, original, and impatient with all established rules and

Now recognized as one of the unique talents in musical history, Hector Berlioz (engraving above) died a lonely and bitter man who suffered the fate of virtually never seeing his works performed exactly as he composed them. A far more successful contemporary of Berlioz's was Charles Gounod (photograph at right, below). Much of his continuing fame rests upon the opera Faust, *which achieved worldwide acclaim following its first performance in Paris in 1859. Jean-Baptiste Faure, a baritone with the Opéra, was a leading interpreter of the character Méphistophélès (right, above).*

practices, Berlioz wrote highly charged music for vast assemblages of performers. At twenty-six he completed his *Symphonie fantastique*; seven years later he married the Irish Shakespearean actress Harriet Smithson, to whom it was dedicated. His opera *Benvenuto Cellini* aroused little interest when it was performed at the Opéra in 1838, and his *Béatrice et Bénédict* had to be premiered outside France, in Baden-Baden, in 1862.

Berlioz's operatic fame rests on two works, *La Damnation de Faust* (1846) and *Les Troyens*. The former was written as a "dramatic legend" and is often given in concert version, but it is quite viable in an operatic adaptation made by Raoul Gunsbourg in 1893, in which form it was presented for years at the Paris Opéra.

Les Troyens is a magnificent five-hour-long musical panorama encompassing the fall of Troy to the Greeks, the arrival of the escaped Trojan hero Aeneas in Carthage, his love affair with Queen Dido, and ultimately his departure to found the city of Rome. Purcell had set the same story to music two centuries earlier in *Dido and Aeneas*, but it is extremely doubtful that Berlioz knew this version; he drew his inspiration straight from Virgil and added a dash of Shakespeare to a text that he wrote himself. *Les Troyens* is the operatic style of Gluck carried to its logical and majestic extreme—classical in form and grandeur but with an amplitude of orchestral richness and emotional intensity previously unknown in French opera. Berlioz himself never saw a complete performance of *Les Troyens*. In fact, only in modern times has it been given uncut with any degree of frequency, and it did not reach New York's Metropolitan Opera until 1973.

The one mid-nineteenth-century French opera that has never dropped out of circulation is Charles Gounod's *Faust*. Gounod was an able and sensitive musician who added touches of Italian lyricism and German mysticism to an inherently French style. He composed a ponderous *Roméo et Juliette* (1867), which is performed today somewhat more often than it should be, and *Mireille* (1864), a charming Provençal opera, which is played somewhat less.

Although Gounod's *Faust* (1859) reduces Goethe's philosophical drama to a sentimental tale of boy-meets-girl, boy-loses-girl, all under the auspices of a debonair Devil, it contains nevertheless a good deal of stirring and touching music, including a lengthy love scene of genuine ardor. Filled with melodies and adorned by an appealing heroine, *Faust* became possibly the most popular opera of its time, and was translated and performed in a dozen languages. With an Italian text, it opened the new Metropolitan Opera House in New York City on the evening of October 22, 1883.

To many modern ears *Faust* has begun to fade, but this writer confesses a special weakness for it, for it was the first opera he ever attended. To be young and to hear for the first time the final trio from *Faust* soaring ever higher can be an indelible experience. Charles Gounod did not attain the ultimate in the French operatic art—that distinction was reserved for Georges Bizet a quarter of a century later—but in *Faust* he consummates, and perhaps even vindicates, the era of French grand opera.

6

Verdi: The Voice of Italy

In 1906 the British poet Alfred Noyes published "The Barrel-Organ," which, in the course of a description of the color and variety of London life, reflected the prevalent critical view about the music of Giuseppe Verdi:

> And there *La Traviata* sighs
>   Another sadder song;
> And there *Il Trovatore* cries
>   A tale of deeper wrong....
> Though the music's only Verdi there's a world
>   to make it sweet....

For many years, especially during the ascendancy of the Wagnerian concept of *Gesamtkunstwerke* ("total work of art"), some academicians and critics tended to dismiss Verdi's operas as "barrel-organ music," his orchestra as a "big guitar," and his arias as undeniably effective but just a bit crude. The public, the ultimate arbiter of the longevity of art, never accepted this view, with the result that Verdi has remained the most popular operatic composer for nearly a hundred years. Today his music is held in higher scholarly regard than ever, and if another Alfred Noyes were to write a poem about him, it would be unlikely to contain the disdainful phrase "*only* Verdi."

Verdi and Wagner, who were to embody the two great antitheses of operatic style—Italian versus German, vocal versus orchestral—were born in the same year, 1813. Perhaps more than any of the other great composers, Verdi was a true son of the soil and of the people; his father was an innkeeper in the dusty village of Le Roncole in northern Italy. Even after attaining wealth and fame, and being feted throughout Europe, Verdi persisted in regarding himself in spirit as "a peasant of Le Roncole," and purchased a villa nearby, where he spent much of his time in agricultural production and research.

Verdi's boyhood was one of hard labor, but he loved the music he heard in the local church and from strolling players. His father, though totally ignorant of the art himself, managed to procure for his son a patched-up old spinet piano and eventually let him go to the nearest town, Busseto, for music lessons and general schooling. At Busseto, the young man was soon doing orchestrations and composing pieces for the local Philharmonic Society, an organization of amateur enthusiasts, and for the town brass band. He became a protégé of Antonio Barezzi, the

Known popularly as La Scala, the full name of Milan's world-famous opera house is the Teatro alla Scala. During the nineteenth century it played a central role in shaping Italian operatic history by presenting the masterpieces of such composers as Rossini, Donizetti, Bellini, and Verdi. The painting at left shows the entrance to La Scala as it appeared in the 1850s.

leading merchant of Busseto, and eventually married his daughter Margherita, by whom he had a son and a daughter. Barezzi sent him to Milan to register at its famous Conservatory, but that institution rejected him as unqualified, to its everlasting embarrassment. Undaunted, Verdi pursued his studies with private teachers.

At the age of twenty-five, while living in Milan and being supported mainly by his benefactor and father-in-law Barezzi, Verdi had his first opera produced at La Scala Theater. Entitled *Oberto, Conte di San Boni facio* and written largely in the style of Bellini, it achieved only a mild success, but the impresario of La Scala, Bartolomeo Merelli, was sufficiently impressed to sign a contract with Verdi to compose three more operas.

At this point the young composer was struck by overwhelming tragedy. Within a short period of time his wife and two children died of illnesses. In the midst of these disasters he had to produce the first opera of his new contract, which ironically was to be a comedy entitled *Un giorno di regno* ("King for a Day"). Not surprisingly, it was a total failure, and Verdi, exhausted and embittered, prevailed upon Merelli to tear up his contract. But the impresario was a persistent man; three months later he ran into Verdi in the street on a snowy evening in Milan, and on the pretext of seeking advice about what to do with a new libretto submitted to him, persuaded the young man to take it home to read. It was an opera that had been written by Temistocle Solera about the biblical king Nebuchadnezzar. Verdi, by his own account, carried the manuscript home and threw it on a table, where it fell open at a chorus beginning with the words "Va, pensiero, sull'ali dorate" (Go, thought, on golden wings). His imagination fired by this song of the captive Jews in Babylon, Verdi read the entire libretto three times and spent a sleepless night, yet nevertheless persisted in his resolve to compose no more. The next day, he recounts, he went to return the manuscript to Merelli:

"Eh," [the impresario] said, "it's beautiful!"

"Very beautiful!"

"Well then, set it to music!"

"Positively no! I don't want to have anything to do with it!"

"Set it to music, I tell you, set it to music!"

With these words, he stuffed the pamphlet into my overcoat pocket, seized me by the shoulders, and not only threw me out of his office but slammed the door in my face and locked himself in.

Now what?

I went home with *Nabucco* in my pocket. This verse today, tomorrow that ... and little by little the opera was written.

Nabucco had an electrifying impact upon its first audience in 1842, and still undergoes revival as the opera that really launched Verdi's artistic career. To understand the extraordinary impression it and many of his other early operas had upon their first listeners, it is necessary to remember that Italy in Verdi's time, far from being an independent country, was a collection of various regions for the most part under Austrian domination. Verdi himself was regarded politically not as an

Rigoletto Atto III.

Rigoletto. Gilda! mia Gilda! È mor-ta!... A la mala - di - zio - - - - - - - ne!!

Though Parisian audiences rioted to show their displeasure with Victor Hugo's drama Hernani *(drawing at left, above), Italian audiences responded warmly to its romantic and melodramatic themes when Verdi produced an opera based on the Hugo text in 1844. Through the years the dashing and noble Ernani has been portrayed by many outstanding tenors, including Enrico Caruso (left, below). Following* Ernani, *Verdi found the seeds of another, even more successful opera,* Rigoletto, *in the plot of a second Hugo play. This story of a frustrated and abused court jester became such a favorite in its own day that photographs of its action were used to illustrate postal cards such as the one depicting Gilda's death scene at right, above.*

"Italian" but as a citizen of the duchy of Parma, a designation that rankled him as it did most of his countrymen in like circumstances. Verdi's life coincided with the development of the Risorgimento, the movement for unification and liberation of Italy, which ended in triumph in 1870. The letters of the name "Verdi" happened to coincide with the initials of the patriotic rallying cry "Vittorio Emmanuele Re D'Italia," so that by shouting "Viva Verdi!" it was possible for a crowd to demonstrate on behalf of Victor Emmanuel II, who was then king of Sardinia and who later became the first king of a united Italy.

Similarly Verdi's music itself seemed to express patriotic yearnings. Thus, the "Va, pensiero" chorus in Nabucco became the outcry not of the exiles in Biblical Babylon but of the Italians oppressed in their own land. The symbolism was carried on in such works as *I Lombardi* ("The Lombards," 1843), *Ernani* ("Hernani," 1844), *Giovanna d'Arco* ("Joan of Arc," 1845) and *La battaglia di Legnano* ("The Battle of Legnano," 1849), all of which celebrated feats of arms, acts of heroism, or love of country. *Attila* (1846) was cheered for the lines sung by the resolute Roman general Ezio to the all-conquering Hun: "Avrai tu l'universo, resti l'Italia a me" (You may have the universe, but let Italy remain mine).

The appeal, however, of Verdi's operas was due not only to their patriotic implications but also to their vigorous rhythms, direct melodies, lusty choruses, and forthright dramatic situations. The orchestrations could be crude and the vocal style unsubtle, but music of such furious vitality was something new on the operatic stage; it was as though fresh blood had been pumped into an ancient art. And with this pulsating feeling of life there went a growing sense of characterization, so that the period costumes and historical trappings seemed to fade, revealing beneath them individuals with passions, desires, and emotions very much like those of the people in the audience.

For all their rough power, Verdi's early operas were by no means cohesive works of art; it was only with *Rigoletto* (1851), his sixteenth opera, that he began the almost unbroken sequence of masterly works by which he is known today.

Rigoletto itself has a highly unusual hero, a hunchbacked cripple, a man of sensibility forced to earn his living by playing the part of a callous court jester. Both physically and psychologically Rigoletto is a pathetic figure, and Verdi explores in his music his differing relations with his libertine master the duke, his beloved daughter Gilda, and the corrupt Mantuan court of which he is a part.

In the second scene of Act I the composer exhibits a subtlety of musical characterization such as he (or few other composers) had seldom displayed before. Rigoletto encounters on the street a professional assassin named Sparafucile who offers—for a price—to dispatch any enemy for him; over a sinuous and sinister accompaniment figure in the cellos the two men, baritone and bass, converse, discussing the possible time, place, and circumstances of such an eventuality. The music, hovering somewhere between melody and speech, could hardly be more chilling or foreboding; it is one of the most memorable duets in all opera.

Equally memorable is the aria "La donna è mobile" (Woman is fickle), which characterizes Rigoletto's frivolous master, the duke of Mantua, perfectly. It was such a catchy tune that Verdi did all he could to prevent it from leaking out in advance of the first performance, even to the extent of warning the tenor not to practice it outside the theater. Finally, the celebrated quartet delineates its four participants individually, even as it blends their voices into a remarkable ensemble. Small wonder that Rossini, nearing sixty, said of *Rigoletto*, "In this music I at last recognize Verdi's genius," and used to have the quartet performed at his Saturday night soirées in Passy.

Il Trovatore ("The Troubadour," 1853), if anything, exceeded

Despite a convoluted and unconvincing story, the power and beauty of Verdi's score has made Il Trovatore *(below) an unquestioned audience favorite. By contrast,* Les Vêpres siciliennes *is one of Verdi's more obscure operas. In 1974, the Metropolitan Opera mounted its first production of this work— originally seen at the Paris Opéra in 1855—with the Spanish diva Montserrat Caballé singing the lead role of Elena (photograph at right). Verdi was fortunate after the death of his first wife to meet Giuseppina Strepponi (right, below), an Italian soprano whose sympathetic personality made her a perfect companion for the composer.*

Rigoletto in its impact on audiences; from the unison Anvil Chorus to the dramatic "Miserere" ensemble, it offered a powerful blend of romance and emotionalism. *La Traviata* ("The Erring One," 1853), represented a still greater refinement; this story of a Parisian courtesan (taken from the younger Dumas' *La Dame aux Camelias*) was told in music with more intimacy and orchestral delicacy than Verdi had previously shown. *Traviata*'s opening night was a fiasco, however, partly because the leading lady was played by a soprano whose ample physical endowments belied her supposed suffering from the last stages of consumption, and partly because the work was played in the costumes of its own time—the first modern-dress opera in history—which audiences refused to accept. Verdi, with characteristic stoicism, wrote to a friend, "Il tempo deciderà" (Time will decide)—and so it has.

For a number of years Verdi had been living with Giuseppina Strepponi, a soprano who had performed in *Nabucco* and who had been an early admirer of his music. Verdi was as indifferent to public opinion about his personal life as about his artistic achievements; and although he never abjured the Roman Catholic Church he never paid much attention to it either. However, the couple was finally married formally in April, 1859, in a small village in Savoy; in all, Verdi and "Peppina" spent nearly half a century together in a warm and mutually fulfilling relationship.

A year after his marriage Verdi began a five-year career as a deputy in the Italian parliament; he had no wish to enter politics, but his friend Count Cavour urged him to stand for election as a symbol of Italian achievement and unity. He was never comfortable in the legislature, however, and in 1865 he resigned, telling a friend: "The 450 deputies are in reality only 449, because, as a deputy, Verdi does not exist."

For fifteen years following *La Traviata* Verdi, by now acknowledged as the unchallenged master of Italian opera, continued to produce new works at regular intervals. *Les Vêpres siciliennes* ("The Sicilian Vespers"), written for the Paris Opéra in 1855, was the weakest of

81

Between the composition of the brilliant Rigoletto-Trovatore-Traviata *trilogy and the masterful* Aïda, *Verdi (portrait at right) wrote several operas of mixed styles and successes. The composer traveled to St. Petersburg for the premiere of* La forza del destino, *a sprawling but poignant opera whose melodic score keeps it in the repertory of many opera houses. The photograph at left shows a 1964 Metropolitan Opera production of Forza. Censorship problems forced Verdi to shift the locale of* A Masked Ball *from eighteenth-century Stockholm to seventeenth-century Boston before the opera could be performed in Italy. However, as the drawings at far right show, the costumes for this opera do not necessarily have a strongly American flavor.*

this group. Verdi detested the Opéra, referring to it derisively as "La Grande Boutique" (The Big Shop), and he disliked the *Vêpres* libretto, which Scribe had been commissioned to write for him. *Don Carlos,* also composed for the Paris Opéra, in 1867, came off considerably better, but it is notable more for its fine individual scenes than for its general dramatic cohesiveness. Both *The Sicilian Vespers* and *Don Carlos* are generally performed today in Italian translations.

Three of Verdi's operas from this period, *Simon Boccanegra* (1857), *Un ballo in maschera* ("A Masked Ball," 1859), and *La forza del destino* ("The Force of Destiny," 1862) are near-masterpieces, even though—perhaps because of a pervasive quality of dramatic darkness and gloom—they have not won the popularity of the *Rigoletto-Trovatore-Traviata* triumvirate. *A Masked Ball* suffered also from the interference of Roman censorship officials, who objected to the depiction of a king (even a king of Sweden) on the stage. Accordingly, the story of courtly intrigue and illicit amours was shifted to colonial America, with its hero becoming "Count Riccardo, Governor of Boston." G.B. Shaw,

that inveterate and astute observer of musical matters in Victorian England, gives this description of how Verdi met his musical challenges in one of the great scenes of *A Masked Ball:*

> The hero has made an assignation with the heroine in one of those romantically lonely spots which are always to be found in operas. A band of conspirators resolves to seize the opportunity to murder him. His friend Renato, getting wind of their design, arrives before them, and persuades him to fly, taking upon himself the charge of the lady, who is veiled, and whose identity and place of residence he swears as a good knight to refrain from discovering. When the conspirators capture him and find that they have the wrong man they propose to amuse themselves

Overleaf: The score of Aïda *is certainly one of Verdi's most magnificent achievements. It combines passages of intimate character delineations with ensembles that capture the essence of grand opera. One of Verdi's most frequently presented works,* Aïda *is shown here during an outdoor performance at the Verona amphitheater.*

by taking a look at the lady. Renato defends her; but she, to save him from being killed, unveils herself and turns out to be Renato's own wife. This is no doubt a very thrilling stage climax: it is easy for a dramatist to work up to it. But it is not quite so easy to get away from it; for when the veil is off the bolt is shot; and the difficulty is what is to be said next. The librettist solves the problem by falling back on the chaffing of Renato by the conspirators. Verdi seizes on this with genuine humorous power in his most boldly popular style, giving just the right vein of blackguardly irony and mischievous mirth to the passage, and getting the necessary respite before the final storm, in which the woman's shame, the man's agony of jealousy and wounded friendship, and the malicious chuckling of the conspirators provide material for one of those concerted pieces in which Italian opera is at its best.

Aïda, the final great opera of Verdi's "middle period," was composed in 1871 on commission from the Khedive of Egypt for a new theater in Cairo as part of the celebration of the opening of the Suez Canal. Never had ceremonial panoply and individual tragedy been combined so skillfully and richly into one musical fabric; *Aïda* has remained ever since the grandest of grand operas, and also the most touching.

Verdi was fifty-eight when he wrote *Aïda*, and for the next few years he retired to his estate, composing a charmingly melodic string quartet for his own diversion, and a boldly operatic *Requiem Mass* in honor of the novelist Alessandro Manzoni, whose death had moved him deeply. *Aïda* captured one world capital after another; about the only dissenter was a young man who wrote complaining that he hadn't liked it and asking that Verdi refund him the price of his admission, train fare, and dinner. Verdi sent him the money for the ticket and the fare, but declined to pay for the meal on the grounds that he could just as well have eaten at home.

In 1887, when Verdi was seventy-four, the world was suddenly informed that it could expect another opera from his hand, this time on the subject of Othello. Verdi had long been an admirer of Shakespeare, whom he read in Italian translations; he had composed a *Macbeth* opera in 1847, and for years had projected a *King Lear*, which unfortunately never came to fruition. During his seventies he began an association with Arrigo Boito, a young composer and poet who had himself written a notable opera on the Faust theme, *Mefistofele*. Boito wrote for Verdi a dramatically taut Othello libretto, which admirably follows the spirit and often even the words of Shakespeare's play.

Verdi's music for *Otello* is similarly Shakespearean in its grandeur, poetry, and probing of character. Although the protagonists still sing arias, they are arias that are no longer regular in form or expansive in melody. The first act demonstrates at once the dramatic and musical cohesiveness that marks Verdi's new style. It starts with a tremendous dissonant thunderclap that greets Otello's ship as it nears the shore of Cyprus during a storm, and moves through Iago's betrayal of Cassio and the latter's subsequent disgrace to an ecstatic, soaring love duet between Otello and Desdemona. *Otello* represents the highest achievement of

Italian operatic art; Verdi said afterward that he almost hated to finish it: "Oh, glory, glory! I so loved my solitude in the company of Otello and Desdemona! Now the crowd, always greedy for something new, has taken them from me, leaving me only the memory of our secret conversations, our dear, past intimacy."

Amazingly, Verdi had one opera left to write. At the age of eighty, with Boito once more as his literary collaborator, he produced another Shakespearean work, *Falstaff*. This was the first comedy he had under-taken since the ill-omened *Un giorno di regno* of over fifty years before, and here once again he composed a work of truly Shakespear-ean proportions. The comic music of *Falstaff* is a perfect counterpart

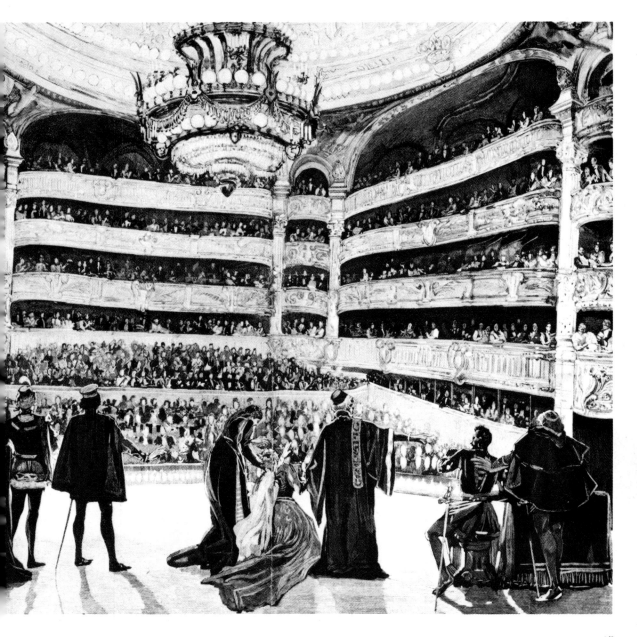

to the tragic music of *Otello*—its orchestration irresistibly brilliant and subtle, its swift melodies as dry and sparkling as champagne. As an octogenarian, Verdi was able to compose wistful love music for Nannetta and Fenton, as well as amply pontifical passages for Falstaff himself. Verdi had always been able to characterize an individual musically in an aria; in *Falstaff* he does it in a single word, as in the obsequious yet ironic "Reverenza" (Your Grace) with which Dame Quickly repeatedly salutes the Fat Knight. For the finale, and for his farewell to the world of opera, Verdi has his whole cast sing the words "All the world's a jest"—to that most learned of musical forms, the fugue!

Perhaps it was inevitable that in his old age Verdi should be charged with imitating Wagner. His great German rival had died in 1883, evoking from Verdi a sincere expression of regret, for he respected the German's accomplishments even though he knew that their concepts of opera were diametrically opposed. Such similarities as exist between Wagner and late Verdi are superficial, representing the common musical store of the time. "Do you think that under this sun and under this sky I could have composed *Tristan* or the *Ring*?" the Italian composer wrote to a friend. Both Verdi and Wagner would have written the same operas in the same manner had the other never existed.

During the winter of 1901, Verdi, now eighty-eight, was spending some time in Milan in a suite he kept at the Hotel di Milano, being cared for by a cousin. Peppina was dead; many of his friends were also gone; as honored and revered as he was, he was a weary, lonely old man. In his hotel room on the morning of January 21, a shirt stud fell to the floor as he was dressing. His cousin had left the room and would be back in a moment, but Verdi, as independent as ever, got down on his hands and knees and groped for the stud under the bed. He suffered a stroke and was found unconscious. It took him a week to die.

Italy, stricken by the news, planned a great funeral, but when his will was opened it read: "I wish my funeral to be very simple, and to take place at daybreak or in the evening at the time of the Ave Maria, without music or singing."

His wish was respected. But a few months later it became necessary to rebury him in the final resting place he had specified, the chapel of a home for aged musicians he had built in Milan. This time, will or no will, a multitude of Italians, great and small, filled the streets. And as the coffin passed, they raised their voices spontaneously in the hymn through which he had first spoken to their hearts sixty years before: "Va, pensiero, sull'ali dorate."

Intrigued by the challenge of composing music for Shakespeare's Othello *(engraving at left), Verdi ended a period of retirement that followed the staging of* Aïda *and set to work in collaboration with librettist Arrigo Boito. Otello premiered at La Scala in 1887, where it was immediately recognized as one of Verdi's most powerful accomplishments. In his final opera Verdi again turned to a Shakespearean character, Sir John Falstaff (drawing, below, left), for his motivation. In the photograph below, at right, Rolando Panerai plays the corpulent knight, with Luisa Maragliano as co-star, in a production of* Falstaff *mounted for the 1970 May Music Festival in Florence.*

Stadttheater Zürich

Parsifal

Ein Bühnenweihfestspiel
von Richard Wagner

Sechs Aufführungen 1913

| Sonntag 31. August | Freitag 5. September | Dienstag 9. September |
| Mittwoch 3. September | Sonntag 7. September | Donnerstag 11. September |

Billettbestellungen können an die Kasse des Stadttheaters und an das

7

Wagner and the Wagnerians

VERDI'S LONG AND FRUITFUL CAREER did more than leave opera with a new store of stageworthy works; it also left it with a new audience. His music had a wide popular appeal such as opera had not previously known. Now, not only the aristocrats and the *nouveaux riches* became familiar with the arias from *Rigoletto* and *Traviata*; shoemakers, barbers, and fishermen as well could be heard singing and whistling the melodies. The monied classes continued to occupy the boxes, but the rest of the house began to represent a genuine cross section of the population.

With the change in the character of the audience came a growing seriousness in the general atmosphere of the opera house itself. Partially this was due to such nonmusical developments as improved lighting systems. Originally theaters were illuminated by candles, many of which burned throughout the performance. But during the latter part of the nineteenth century, when gas chandeliers, and then electric lights, were introduced, it became possible to darken the auditorium. These innovations helped reduce socializing during performances and concentrate attention upon the stage.

Nevertheless, some musicians and music lovers persisted in regarding Italian opera as a somewhat frivolous entertainment unworthy of the same attention one brought to a Beethoven symphony or string quartet. No one subscribed more heartily to this view than Richard Wagner, who, born in the same year as Giuseppe Verdi and certainly aware of his work, sedulously avoided ever mentioning his contemporary by name in all his extensive writings and correspondence.

Wagner is one of the most remarkable, contradictory, and influential composers in the annals of music. His career is a total negation of any theory that holds that only a noble artist can produce noble works. In his personal life, Wagner was one of the most ambitious, unscrupulous, faithless, vain, bigoted, and intolerant individuals known to history. He was a womanizer and a squanderer, and the sort of virulent anti-Semite who would have been perfectly at home in Adolf Hitler's cultural hierarchy. Even his warmest and most human opera, *Die Meistersinger von Nürnberg* ("The Mastersingers of Nuremberg"), cannot conclude without an apotheosis of "holy German art"—presumably holier than any other. Yet his "music dramas," as he called his compositions, brought about some of the most revolutionary changes opera had ever known, added at least ten works to the standard oper-

atic repertory, led to reforms in production and staging practices, and affected the course of music for years.

Wagner was born in Leipzig, the son of a minor police official who died when the infant was six months old. A short time thereafter, his mother married an actor named Ludwig Geyer, and there is some suspicion that the latter was actually Wagner's father—an intriguing possibility, since Geyer was Jewish-born. Wagner received a substantial education in both nonmusical and musical subjects; his earliest inspirations were Beethoven's symphonies and Weber's operas. In his youth he composed two operas, *Die Feen* ("The Fairies") and *Das Liebesverbot* ("The Ban on Love"), both highly unoriginal, and followed these with the Meyerbeerian *Rienzi*, which he began composing in 1837 at Riga, where he was director of the opera, and whose stirring overture still survives. Hopeful of finding fame and fortune in Meyerbeer's Paris he set sail for France, but the most productive aspect of the trip was a stormy sea passage that gave him the idea for *Der fliegende Holländer* ("The Flying Dutchman").

In Paris, Wagner not only failed to get his works produced but went deeply into debt and spent three weeks in a debtors' prison. However, his fortunes took a turn for the better in 1842, when the Dresden Opera produced *Rienzi*, and then *The Flying Dutchman*, and invited him to settle there as musical director, which he did for six years.

In 1836 Wagner had married Minna Planer, an actress; but although the two were not formally separated until 1861, their relationship was marked by disputes, quarrels, and infidelities on a Wagnerian scale. In 1850 he almost eloped with Jessie Laussot, a young Englishwoman married to a French wine merchant, and a few years later he fell in love with Mathilde Wesendonk, the wife of a wealthy businessman who befriended and supported him while he was writing *Tristan und Isolde*. In 1864 he began an affair with Cosima von Bülow, wife of the great conductor Hans von Bülow and daughter of Franz Liszt. Cosima bore him three children, Isolde, Eva, and Siegfried, out of wedlock, before von Bülow divorced her in 1870, enabling Wagner to marry her.

Between these major love affairs Wagner amused himself with a succession of minor amatory excursions such as Don Giovanni himself might have envied. Here is a portion of a letter written in 1863 (when he was fifty years old) to a young woman he had engaged to keep house for him while he was living in Penzing, a suburb of Vienna:

> Dear little Marie,—I shall be home again next Wednesday. . . . Now, my best sweetheart, have everything in the house very nice, so that I can get a cozy rest, which I very much need. Everything must be quite tidy and—well warmed. See that everything is very nice in the lovely study; if it is hot, open it a little, so that the study may be warm; and perfume it nicely: buy the best bottles of scent, so as to give it a nice odor. Ach Gott! How delighted I am to be able to rest again with you there. (I hope the rose-colored pants are ready?) Aye, aye! You must be very pretty and charming; I deserve to have a thoroughly good time once more.

Eager and ardent as the sentiments are, they are a world removed from the passionate yet spiritualized "love-death" music of *Tristan und Isolde*, which he had just written.

Wagner's *Tannhäuser* (1845) and *Lohengrin* (1850) were, like *The Flying Dutchman*, full-bodied German romantic operas in the tradition of Weber, though far more richly orchestrated. Wagner became involved in the Revolution of 1848 in Germany, and as a consequence was forced to flee the country. He stayed briefly with Liszt in Weimar but eventually settled in Zurich, where he met the Wesendonks and where he remained for eight years. The revolutionary ferment seemed to have given freshness and new impetus to his musical ideas, for he began to work on the poems and the music that were to fuse into his titanic epic of four music dramas *Der Ring des Nibelungen* ("The Ring of the Nibelungs").

Wagner, who fancied himself as great a poet, dramatist, and philosopher as he was a musician, set forth the concept of the *Gesamtkunstwerke*, the total art work, as opposed to the Italian or French musical stage product. "The mistake in the art form of the opera," he wrote, "consists in this, that a means of expression (music) was made the end, and the end to be expressed (the drama) was made a means." His history was a bit shaky; actually it had not been an Italian or a Frenchman but Mozart himself who had said that "in opera the poetry must be the obedient daughter of the music." In the Wagnerian scheme of things,

poetry and music were entitled to at least equal status; after all, he was writing both himself.

The greatest protagonist in all Wagnerian music drama after *Lohengrin* is the orchestra. Essentially Wagner was a symphonist rather than a vocal composer; *The Ring* is a work of orchestral eloquence, with the voices carried along on its surface as by irresistible tides and deep-flowing currents. Wagner did away with the old concept of operas divided into "numbers"—that is, separate arias, duets, choruses, and other set pieces (which were actually numbered in the printed score)—and replaced it with a continual, ceaseless ebb and flow of music. He made extensive use of the *leitmotiv*, or "leading theme," a kind of musical label that identifies a particular personage or idea, and that recurs in the orchestra at appropriate moments, often in subtly altered form.

Wagner's *Ring*, drawn from Teutonic myth, tells the story of a magic ring first stolen from three Rhine maidens by the evil dwarf Alberich and taken from him in turn by the god Wotan; recovered by the hero Siegfried, the ring exerts a curse on all who touch it and is finally returned to the depths of the Rhine, while Wotan's castle, Valhalla, itself undergoes destruction.

Wagner unfolded this epic in four works, *Das Rheingold* ("The Rhinegold," 1869), *Die Walküre* ("The Valkyrie," 1870), *Siegfried* (1876), and *Götterdämmerung* ("The Twilight of the Gods," 1876)— all but the first being of inordinate length, considerable repetitiveness, and studded with passages that seem interminable to all but devotees. Certain vocal episodes of *The Ring*, such as the ecstatic love duet between Siegmund and Sieglinde in *Walküre* and Wotan's moving farewell to his daughter Brünhilde in the same opera, are of a surpassing beauty; and the cycle abounds in orchestral passages such as the Ride of the Valkyries and Magic Fire music in *Die Walküre*, the Forest Murmurs in *Siegfried*, and Siegfried's Funeral Music and Rhine Journey in *Götterdämmerung*, that demonstrate Wagner's symphonic mastery.

To experience the full impact of *The Ring* one must listen to it *in toto* and preferably *in sequitur*, accepting its slower sections along with its climaxes. Opportunities to hear the entire *Ring* cycle performed on the stage are still fairly infrequent, but the release of complete recordings under the direction of George Solti, Wilhelm Furtwängler, and others has made the works available to all.

Amazingly, while Wagner was planning and working on this gigantic epic about gods and demigods, he was also composing two masterpieces, *Tristan und Isolde* (1865) and *Die Meistersinger* (1868), of more human dimensions. *Tristan* suffers from a mystical, elliptical libretto whose complete meaning probably was clear only to Wagner himself, but its love music engulfs a listener in a veritable tide of chromatic sound that conveys a rare sense of yearning and emotion.

Meistersinger started out in Wagner's mind as a modest comedy but evolved into a majestic nationalistic work celebrating the medieval guilds of mastersingers, and especially Hans Sachs the cobbler, who is probably the most sympathetic character Wagner ever drew. *Meistersinger* is at once the most approachable, exalted, and genuinely operatic of Wagner's later works, re-creating in music an entire gallery of

Nicola Benois of La Scala created the setting shown at right, above, for the first scene in Act III of Wagner's Götterdämmerung. *In the nineteenth-century engraving above, Wagner's tragic lovers Tristan and Isolde prepare to drink from a goblet containing a potion they expect will bring them death, but which instead liberates their love. Wagner's* Ring *cycle begins with the innocent frivolity of the three Rhine maidens (photograph at right, below), impersonated here by a trio of Paris Opéra singers around 1900.*

sixteenth-century men and women, and putting into human terms the ancient struggle between tradition and innovation in art. In his final work, *Parsifal* (1882), Wagner composed the ultimate in mystical abstraction, a work about the Holy Grail and its knights. He called it a *Bühnenfestspiel*, a "stage dedication festival play"; Friedrich Nietzsche, the philosopher who began as an ardent Wagnerite but later turned against the *Meister*, sardonically described it as "Christianity arranged for Wagnerians."

Difficult as it was to compose his enormous works, Wagner found it even more arduous to get them produced on the stage, both because of their complexity and because of the notoriety surrounding their composer. A production of *Tannhäuser* in Paris in 1861 stirred both anti- and pro-Wagner demonstrations, and was finally withdrawn. For years Wagner labored patiently over such scores as *Tristan* and *The Ring* with no assurance that anyone would ever actually stage them. But in May, 1864, King Ludwig II ascended the throne of Bavaria, and Wagner's whole life immediately changed. Ludwig, who was eighteen years old, admired Wagner's music with the passion of a romantic youth, and he forthwith invited the composer to Munich and promised to do "everything in my power to make up to you for what you have suffered in the past. . . . O, I have looked forward to the time when I could do this! I have hardly dared indulge myself in the hope so soon to be able to prove my love to you."

Ludwig, a profligate builder of castles, was in later years to be declared insane and to drown himself in the Starnberger See. But in 1864 he welcomed Wagner to Munich, paid off his debts, gave him a house and a stipend, and saw to it that his works were produced on the stage. So intense was his infatuation with Wagner and his ideas that some Bavarians, in and out of the court, were made uneasy by the composer's influence over the young king. Within two years Ludwig had to ask Wagner to leave the city for a time; once again he took up residence in Switzerland.

For years Wagner had cherished the thought of building his own theater, where his works could be performed to his specifications and under his control, and he now undertook a European concert tour to raise money for the project. The town of Bayreuth, near Nuremberg, was selected as the site, and with the help of public subscriptions and a huge loan from Ludwig, the theater was built and opened in 1876 with the first complete performance anywhere of *The Ring*. Bayreuth has ever since remained the great Wagnerian shrine and has set international styles and standards for the performance of his music dramas, especially *The Ring*. Its general air of sobriety and solemnity has also contributed to the seriousness with which opera in general has come to be treated in theaters elsewhere.

Wagner died February 13, 1883, while wintering in Venice, and his body was conveyed north to Bayreuth for burial while bands along the way played Siegfried's Funeral Music from *Götterdämmerung*. He died believing that he had written "the music of the future," but the French composer Claude Debussy may have come closer to the truth (insofar as we can judge it today) when he said that Wagner represented "a beautiful sunset that was mistaken for a dawn."

Wagner certainly represented the climax of German romantic opera, and for a time other composers—not all of them German—tried to emulate his mythological, mist-shrouded works. The Frenchman Ernest Reyer wrote an opera, *Sigurd* (1884), that at least in subject matter was thoroughly Wagnerian, and some Parisian enthusiasts even published a periodical entitled *La Revue Wagnérienne*.

But it took a Wagner to write genuinely Wagnerian works, and his influence has ebbed slowly during the twentieth century. In some ways, his true heirs were symphonists such as Anton Bruckner and Gustav Mahler rather than opera composers, although Wagner certainly gave the operatic orchestra a status and a function it had never achieved before, and he established, if he did not invent, the *leitmotiv* as a universal operatic device. Oddly, for all their orchestral magnificence and emphasis on dramaturgy, Wagner's works rely heavily for their appeal —as all operas do—upon the quality of their singers. In fact, with their demands for vocal power and endurance, they brought into being a new breed of stentorian male singer, the *Heldentenor*, or "heroic tenor," with equally heroic sopranos to match. A first-class orchestra and a strong conductor are Wagnerian essentials, but it is only when singers like Lauritz Melchior, Kirsten Flagstad, and Birgit Nilsson are on the scene that Valhalla seems truly to become the abode of the gods.

So pervasive was Wagner's presence that other nineteenth-century German opera seems hardly to exist. Light opera never died out, as attested by such works as Gustav Albert Lortzing's *Czar and Carpenter* (1837), still a favorite in Germany; Friedrich von Flotow's *Martha* (1847), with a famous tenor aria, "M'appari" (Like a dream), usually sung in Italian; Otto Nicolai's *Merry Wives of Windsor* (1849), known at least by its vivacious overture; Peter Cornelius's *Barber of Baghdad* (1858), a thoroughly appealing and unduly neglected romantic comedy; and Hermann Goetz's *The Taming of the Shrew* (1874), which George Bernard Shaw pronounced a masterpiece. But none of these had the success of Engelbert Humperdinck's *Hänsel und Gretel* (1893), which artfully combined a familiar folktale and some rich

Wagnerian orchestration into a work of enduring popularity.

Wagner's successor as the predominant figure in German opera was Richard Strauss, who lived from 1864 to 1949, long enough to become a celebrated conductor, to achieve fame as a composer of such symphonic tone poems as *Don Juan, Till Eulenspiegel*, and *Death and Transfiguration*, and to write fifteen operas, many of which are still performed. In 1935 he accepted a post from the Nazis (President of the Reich Music Chamber), although he later fell out with the Hitler regime and was officially denazified in 1948.

Strauss's first great operatic success—sensation might be a more accurate word—was *Salome* (1905), written in the Wagnerian style and based on Oscar Wilde's play about John the Baptist and the licentious princess of Judea. The climax of the opera occurs when Salome performs the Dance of the Seven Veils in order to win the privilege of having John's severed head presented to her on a silver platter, a scene that provoked dismay among operagoers accustomed to more staid subject matter. When the Metropolitan Opera first presented *Salome* in 1907, many subscribers fled indignantly into the night at the sight of soprano Olive Fremstad fondling the prophet's head, and one critic dismissed the work as "operatic offal." However, Strauss's sensuous score long ago established itself in the opera house, with modern audiences regarding Salome's sexual transports with equanimity and even anticipation. The major problem in producing the work nowadays is to find a soprano with the requisite vocal power and a physique suitably voluptuous for shedding the seven veils.

Strauss's *Elektra* (1909), his first collaboration with the Austrian

Richard Strauss created two remarkable roles for dramatic sopranos in Salome *and* Elektra. *In the engraving above, Salome performs the Dance of the Seven Veils; below, Birgit Nilsson sings the role of Elektra.*

librettist Hugo von Hofmannsthal, was another Wagnerian work with a high degree of shock impact and a madwoman as its heroine. But two years later in *Der Rosenkavalier* ("The Knight of the Rose"), Strauss and Hofmannsthal produced an altogether different kind of opera, a romantic comedy that, for all its orchestral luxuriance, represents a turn away from Wagner.

Rosenkavalier, easily the most popular of Strauss's operas, is a sentimental story of a young man who has been conducting an affair with an older noblewoman, but leaves her to wed a pretty young girl who herself is about to be pushed reluctantly into a marriage with a boorish but wealthy baron. Richard Strauss was no relation to Johann Strauss, but *Der Rosenkavalier* is liberally bestrewn with engaging waltz melodies—something of an anachronism, since the scene is eighteenth-century Vienna, a good half century before the waltz became popular. The opera abounds in rich character parts, such as Ochs, the bumptious baron; the Feldmarschallin, or field marshal's wife, conducting one last affair with a youthful lover; and Octavian, the young man in question, a spiritual and musical descendant of the similarly ardent Cherubino in Mozart's *Marriage of Figaro*.

Like Cherubino, Octavian represents what is sometimes called a "trouser role"—a male character played by a female singer. There are a number of these in nineteenth-century opera, such as Urbain in *Les Huguenots*, Siebel in *Faust*, and Oscar in *A Masked Ball*, and they are sometimes regarded as relics of the ancient *castrati*. However, far from representing heroic roles they invariable depict young people just coming into maturity and musically provide a welcome sense of contrast. In *Rosenkavalier* the mezzo-soprano voice of Octavian blends enchantingly with the two higher sopranos of the Marschallin and Sophie in the beautiful final trio and duet.

Strauss and Hofmannsthal followed *Rosenkavalier* with *Ariadne auf Naxos* ("Ariadne on Naxos," 1912), a play-within-a-play with charming episodes but an unusually complicated structure. Most of their succeeding operas have dropped from view, although *Die Frau ohne Schatten* ("The Woman Without a Shadow," 1919) and *Arabella* (1933) are sometimes revived. Strauss's last opera, *Capriccio* (1942), is a curious work whose subject is the art of opera itself and whose setting is Paris at the time of the Gluck-Piccinni controversy. Strauss himself described it as a "conversation piece for music" that was not for the public but "only a fine dish for connoisseurs." Most of them have yet to discover it.

Strauss was the last towering figure among German operatic composers. A few operas that have been written since have their enthusiasts, but none has had very wide acceptance—*Tiefland* ("Lowland," 1903) by Eugène d'Albert, a Scottish-born German citizen; *Palestrina* (1917) by Hans Pfitzner, highly regarded in Germany and totally ignored elsewhere; *Doktor Faust* (1925), an ambitious treatment of the Faust legend by Ferruccio Busoni, a distinguished composer of mixed German and Italian parentage; and *Die tote Stadt* ("The Dead City," 1920) by Erich Korngold, who was born in Brünn, Moravia, in 1897, became a child prodigy in Vienna, and, some years after writing this early opera, emigrated to the United States where he became a Hollywood sound-track composer.

Vienna was the birthplace of both Arnold Schoenberg and his disciple Alban Berg, whose departures from traditional tonal harmony helped shape—or misshape, depending upon the listener's point of view —modern music. Schoenberg's major operatic effort, *Moses und Aron*, was left unfinished and is rarely staged, but Berg's *Wozzeck*, which aroused a storm of protests at its premiere in Berlin in 1925, has not only survived but has also been widely recognized as a modern operatic masterpiece.

By any standard *Wozzeck* is a remarkable work. Written atonally

Abandoning the tragic themes of his early works, Strauss composed one of the most popular of all comic operas, Der Rosenkavalier, *which received its first performance at the Royal Opera House in Dresden in 1911 (playbill at left). Believing his opera* Moses und Aron *to be a virtually unproducible work, Arnold Schoenberg left it incomplete. However, critically acclaimed productions in Zurich in 1957, and at the Berlin Festival two years later, proved Schoenberg wrong in his estimate. The photograph at right, taken during a performance in Berlin, shows the opera's protagonists.*

Alban Berg wrote only two operas, Wozzeck *and the incomplete* Lulu, *but nevertheless was able to demonstrate the potent effect modern musical techniques could create on the stage.* Wozzeck, *photograph at left, is one of the few contemporary operas regularly appearing in the repertory of major companies.* Lulu *(as shown above) was presented at the 1974 Festival of Two Worlds in Spoleto, Italy, by the noted film director Roman Polanski.*

—or without a definite key center—it demonstrates convincingly the theatrical potential of the modern style. It dispenses with traditional singing, replacing it with *sprechstimme,* a kind of declamation that is midway between song and speech. As in almost all Germanic post-Wagnerian works, the orchestra is dominant, with the score organized along symphonic lines to include such sections as a passacaglia, a scherzo, and a fantasia and fugue.

None of this would be important were it not that *Wozzeck* onstage is a powerful and moving musical drama. For all its modernity it is based on a play dating from 1837 by Georg Büchner, a German revolutionary dramatist who died at the age of twenty-three. Its "hero" is an army private named Wozzeck, who identifies himself at the outset as a member of "Wir arme Leut" (we poor people). As the story unfolds he is degraded by his captain, maltreated by a regimental doctor, deceived by the sluttish woman with whom he lives, and ultimately driven to murder and suicide.

Wozzeck can be viewed as a psychological drama of the debasement of human beings by a vicious and unfeeling world. Beyond its symbolism, the opera has a phantasmagoric, nightmarish quality that makes it a memorable experience even for operagoers who prefer more traditional and comfortable music. Berg died before he could complete another stage work, *Lulu,* which musically is even more radical; but in *Wozzeck* he left a personal imprint upon modern opera that seems indelible half a century later.

8

Realists and Romantics

In 1875, one year before *The Ring of the Nibelungs* had its first complete performance in Bayreuth, a rather modest opera called *Carmen* was presented at the Opéra-Comique in Paris. Its composer, Georges Bizet, was a thirty-six-year-old musician whose accomplishments to date, including an exotic Indian opera entitled *Les Pêcheurs de perles* ("The Pearl Fishers," 1863), had not quite fulfilled the promise of his early years. *Carmen*'s subsequent success, and its universal preeminence as a "vehicle" for a star mezzo-soprano, have somewhat obscured its artistic and historical significance. It did more than give opera one of its most alluring female characters: it opened an era of realism and naturalism, not only in France, but also in Italy, where the new style became known as *verismo*, from the Italian word for "truth."

To one enthusiastic observer, the philosopher Nietzsche, who had become disenchanted both personally and artistically with Richard Wagner, *Carmen* seemed to return opera to its proper sphere, that of Mediterranean clarity. From Turin in 1888 he wrote:

> Yesterday—would you believe it?—I heard Bizet's masterpiece for the twentieth time. Once more I attended with the same gentle reverence; once again I did not run away. This triumph over my impatience surprises me. How such a work completes one! Through it one almost becomes a "masterpiece" oneself.—And, as a matter of fact, each time I heard *Carmen* it seemed to me that I was more of a philosopher, a better philosopher than at other times. . . . Bizet's music seems to me perfect. It comes forward lightly, gracefully, stylishly. It is lovable, it does not sweat. . . . This music is wicked, refined, fatalistic: and withal remains popular,—it possesses the refinement of a race, not of an individual. . . . With it one bids farewell to the damp north and to all the fog of the Wagnerian ideal.

As much as by any other single element, Bizet's Carmen *is distinguished by the psychological truth with which its main characters are portrayed. In the scene at left from Act I of the Metropolitan Opera's 1972 production, Carmen (Marilyn Horne) entices Don José (James McCracken) into releasing the ropes that bind her hands—the beginning of her tragic manipulation of José.*

Many of *Carmen*'s initial listeners were considerably less impressed. The composer was accused of "Wagnerism" because of the rich texture of his orchestration and his use of recurrent devices like a "Fate" motif. He was also denounced for having written an immoral work for the Opéra-Comique, which usually drew a family audience unaccustomed to an opera about a wild gypsy girl who seduces an upstanding young soldier and is stabbed to death by him—in the full view of the audience—after she has thrown him over for a bullfighter. Wrote one indignant critic: "What do you think, chaste mothers of families, good fathers

105

relying on the reputation of the past, hoping to entertain your daughters and your wives with a pleasant and decent evening?"

Despite several such press reactions *Carmen*, on the strength of its vivid melodies, its brilliant orchestral score, and its taut and compelling story, made its way throughout Europe, becoming as popular in Italy and Germany as in France. Bizet, unfortunately, did not live long enough to see its universal triumph; he died three months after its premiere, on the night of its thirty-first performance at the Comique.

Remarkably, although *Carmen* retains an unshakable hold on modern audiences, it is almost always seen today in an adulterated form —as a grand opera, rather than an *opéra comique*. As noted earlier, *opéra comique* originated as a light musical form in which musical episodes were linked by stretches of spoken dialogue. In Bizet's *Carmen* the musical substance was dramatic rather than diverting, but the spoken interludes remained. However, when the work was sent out after the composer's death to be performed in Vienna, London, and New York, the French spoken dialogue was scrapped and replaced with accompanied recitatives concocted by Ernest Guiraud, a friend and colleague of Bizet's. Guiraud did a conscientious job and adapted most of his musical declamation from Bizet's own melodic material, but the use of recitatives blunts the musical and dramatic thrust of *Carmen*. To hear this opera performed in its original form, as at the Opéra-Comique in Paris during the 1940s and 1950s, or in its stylish 1972 production at the Metropolitan Opera in New York, is to view a masterpiece restored.

NB *Carmen* will probably retain the affection of audiences because of such "Spanish" elements as the Habanera sung by the gypsy girl or the virile verses of Escamillo the bullfighter, but its greatness lies in its vivid individual portraiture and its abundant dramatic vitality—as in the scene in a smugglers' mountain camp, where the four principal characters, with their conflicting loves and rivalries, are brought into juxtaposition. *Carmen*'s basic qualities remained unimpaired even in the 1943 Broadway adaptation by Oscar Hammerstein II called *Carmen Jones*, in which the locale was transferred to a World War II training camp, with Don José turned into a draftee named Joe, and Escamillo into Husky Miller, a prizefighter.

Like Mozart at nearly the same age, Bizet ended his career at thirty-six with a masterpiece; but he had just found his true bearings in opera, and who can say what he might have achieved had he lived longer?

One effect of *Carmen* was to give the Opéra-Comique a certain status as a theater willing to take chances and experiment, unlike the relatively conservative Opéra, which in 1875 took occupancy of its current home, an ornately conspicuous edifice in the center of Paris. Through the latter part of the nineteenth century it was the Comique rather than the Opéra that gave the premieres of most of the new French operas that entered the permanent repertory—Ambroise Thomas's warmly melodic *Mignon* in 1866, Jacques Offenbach's bizarre and brilliant *Les Contes d'Hoffmann* ("The Tales of Hoffmann") in 1881, Léo Delibes's exotic *Lakmé* in 1883, Edouard Lalo's vigorous and color-

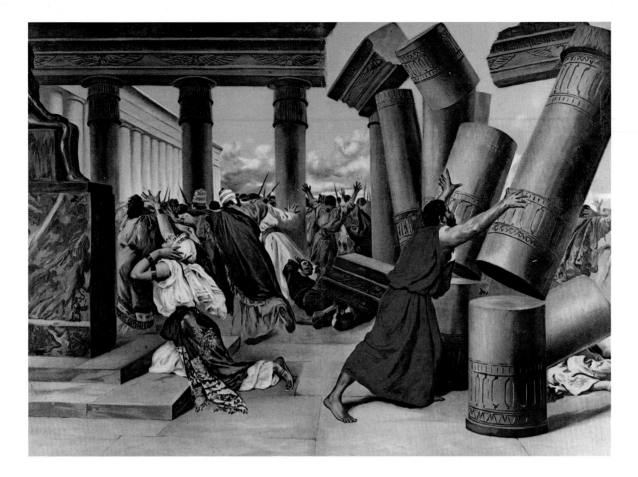

ful *Le Roi d'Ys* ("The King of Ys") in 1888. However, Camille Saint-Saëns' *Samson et Dalila*, which stood in a tradition of Old Testament operas dating back at least to Etienne Méhul's *Joseph* of 1807, had to be produced by German admirers in Weimar in 1877 before it won acceptance in its own country.

The most popular French composer during this period was Jules Massenet, who produced some twenty operas over the years. Massenet was forever combining religion and eroticism into a salable commodity. In *Manon* (1884), his most enduring work, a young nobleman falls in love with a charming but highly accessible young woman; when she eventually leaves him he decides to become a priest, but she entices him back by visiting him at the seminary of St. Sulpice, her insinuating phrases artfully contrasting with austere religious chants. *Thäis* (1894) presents the spectacle of a Greek courtesan exercising her wiles over a Cenobite monk named Athanaël. A New Orleans Opera production of *Thäis* in 1973 achieved the ultimate in verisimilitude when soprano Carol Neblett appeared in the title role naked. Among Massenet's other notable works are *Werther* (1892), based on Goethe's novel, and *Le Jongleur de Notre Dame* ("The Juggler of Our Lady," 1902), based on a medieval miracle play.

Massenet's blend of sentimentality and sensationalism sometimes seems a bit too calculating, but he was an able and even individualistic musician with a flair for melody and a strong theatrical instinct. His operas, with their distinctive gracefulness and occasional dramatic force, have become perennial favorites in France, and survive, though more fitfully, in other lands as well.

With the turn of the century the Opéra-Comique premiered two works that represented high points in modern French opera yet were poles apart in their methods and subject matter—Gustave Charpentier's realistic *Louise* (1900) and Claude Debussy's impressionistic *Pelléas et Mélisande* (1902). *Louise* is the most naturalistic of French operas; Charpentier, who was forty when he wrote it, was much interested in the welfare of the working classes, and one might almost describe *Louise* as the first socialist opera. Its central figure is a working girl who longs for the liberation of women from parental tyranny and bourgeois morality; its settings include such scenes as a tenement apartment and a factory filled with young women at sewing machines; among its characters are a ragpicker, a milkwoman, a junkman, and other poor people; and some of its most striking music consists of the cries of Paris street vendors. Both in sight and in sound, the City of Light itself seems to come alive. But for all its realism *Louise* is actually a romantic tragic opera. Nowadays it seems even more so, with the setting of a vanished epoch adding to it a patina of nostalgia.

Debussy's *Pelléas et Mélisande* is nothing like *Louise*; for that matter, it is unlike any other opera ever written. Taking its text virtually intact from a play by Maurice Maeterlinck, it is a depiction in veiled and filmy music of a mysterious romance between shadowy figures in a mythological kingdom. The orchestration is like sunlight glinting through clouds, and the vocal line is almost a chant that follows the contours of the words themselves. *Pelléas* is a unique opera, without antecedents or descendants; at times it almost seems like a musical apotheosis of the French language itself. Perhaps it falls into the classification of those specialized works that Shakespeare called "caviar to the general," yet for listeners sensitive to its musical and linguistic nuances it offers an operatic experience like no other.

Claude Debussy spent ten years on the composition of Pelléas et Mélisande, *the only purely Impressionist work in opera repertory. In the photograph at left, taken during a performance at Spoleto, Pelléas and Mélisande realize their love for one another. A far more conventional opera in style and content is Alfredo Catalani's* Loreley, *which premiered in Turin in 1890 and is still a part of the regular repertoire at La Scala (above).*

Debussy, like many other French composers, was profoundly aware of Wagner's music; though he ultimately rejected it, he made his pilgrimage to Bayreuth as a young man and was duly impressed by what he saw and heard. Italian operatic composers, on the other hand, rarely went to Bayreuth; in the 1880s and 1890s most of them paid little attention to the Wagnerian method. They really had no need of it, for they were able to take Giuseppe Verdi as their principal guide, seeking to emulate his success by adopting his style. Several moderately durable works that resulted were Amilcare Ponchielli's melodramatic *La Gioconda* ("The Ballad Singer," 1876); Umberto Giordano's *Andrea Chénier* (1896), interesting for its French Revolutionary background; and Alfredo Catalani's *La Wally* (1892), a work of refined lyricism despite a grim plot that climaxes in its heroine's death in an avalanche.

None of these created anything like the sensation stirred in May, 1890, in Rome by the first performance of a fiercely melodramatic one-act opera entitled *Cavalleria rusticana* ("Rustic Chivalry") by an unknown, twenty-six-year-old composer, Pietro Mascagni. *Cavalleria rusticana* was an outgrowth of one of the earliest manifestations of commercialism in music—a competition for the best one-act opera, organized at three-year intervals by the publishing house of Sonzogno.

Mascagni, who won over seventy-two other entries, was an obscure music teacher and a conductor of the municipal band in the small town of Cerignola; there had been weeks in his life when he existed on a plate of macaroni a day. *Cavalleria* changed his financial condition overnight, for audiences responded at once to its emotional melodies and passionate action. The opera begins with a serenade and ends with a scream; between them it presents in highly charged music a story of infidelity and vengeance in a sunbaked Sicilian town. Mascagni never produced another comparable success, although he lived to 1945 and kept trying.

Much the same effect was produced by another classic of *verismo*, Ruggiero Leoncavallo's *I Pagliacci* ("The Clowns," 1892). Leoncavallo, a somewhat more worldly and polished composer than Mascagni, wrote *Pagliacci* for Sonzogno in a frank attempt to emulate *Cavalleria*'s triumph, and he succeeded amazingly with an opera that was equally direct, realistic, and brutal. He built his story on what he said was an actual incident involving passion, jealousy, and murder within the ranks of a traveling theatrical troupe playing in a small Calabrian village. Its raw emotionalism reached a peak of intensity in the tenor aria "Vesti la giubba" (Put on the costume), whose climactic outburst of "Ridi, Pagliaccio" (Laugh, Clown) has come to serve for many people as almost a symbol of opera in general. The aria has been recorded for all time by Enrico Caruso, possessor of the most golden of all Golden Age voices.

Like Mascagni, Leoncavallo never attained anything else remotely approaching the success of *I Pagliacci*, though he wrote a dozen other

Sharing the bill in opera houses throughout the world, Leoncavallo's I Pagliacci (drawing above) and Mascagni's Cavalleria rusticana (scene at left) represent the peak achievements of the Italian verismo style. Each opera has one act overflowing with melodramatic developments and passionate confrontations; each remains as audience pleasing today as at its premiere in the 1890s. With Manon Lescaut, Giacomo Puccini emerged as the popular successor to his countryman Verdi. Among the many fine interpreters of Puccini's avaricious heroine is the American soprano Dorothy Kirsten, seen in the photograph at right.

operas. *Cavalleria* and *Pagliacci*, brief in duration and kindred in spirit, are usually presented as a double bill. Artistically, the combination represents the apex of the "veristic" movement; commercially, it constitutes a salable "ham and eggs" staple for many an opera house.

In 1884, Giuseppe Verdi wrote in a letter to a friend: "I have heard the composer Puccini well spoken of. I have seen a letter, too, reporting all kinds of good things about him. He follows the new tendencies, which is only natural, but he keeps strictly to melody, and that is neither new nor old."

Considering that Giacomo Puccini was then only twenty-six years old, and had not as yet written *La Bohème*, *Tosca*, or *Madama Butterfly*, the reports to Verdi were remarkably prescient. Puccini, who lived from 1858 to 1924, comes as close as anyone ever has, and perhaps ever will, to being Verdi's successor in Italian opera; and in many theaters he ranks immediately after his compatriot as the most frequently performed composer.

Puccini came from a long line of musicians, but he himself did not resolve on a career as an operatic composer until he heard a performance of *Aida* at the age of eighteen. His own first opera, *Le Villi* ("The Wilis"), was composed in 1883 and submitted in the Sonzogno competition for that year. It did not win even an honorable mention but was taken up by Sonzogno's rival company, Ricordi, which thus moved into the enviable position of being publishers to both Verdi and Puccini. *Le Villi*, a supernatural affair set in the Black Forest, was followed by *Edgar* (1889), a medieval romance laid against a Flemish background. In 1893 Puccini found his true style in *Manon Lescaut*, telling the same story as Massenet's earlier work in music of less elegance but rather more vigor.

La Bohème in 1896 made Puccini world famous. Within two years it was playing in opera houses from Mexico City to Zagreb. Based on

A calculated blend of music and melodrama, Tosca *requires brilliance in acting and voice from each of its leading players. The striking poster at left was designed to publicize* Tosca's *premiere at the Teatro Costanzi, Rome, in January, 1900. By contrast,* La Bohème, *often considered Puccini's finest work, combines moments of intense drama and passion with lighter interludes. The lovers Rodolfo and Mimi are flanked by Marcello and Musetta in the photograph below of an early production.*

Henry Murger's *Scenes de la vie de Bohème* ("Scenes of Bohemian Life"), with an excellent libretto by Luigi Illica and Giuseppe Giacosa, it contains the essence of Puccini's operatic style—a sentimental and touching story, impassioned melodies, and a keen sense of dramatic irony. In his operas Puccini had a habit of playing back the music of Act I during Act IV with tremendous effectiveness: thus, when Mimi, the frail and attractive young working girl, lies dying at the end of *La Bohème* with the poet Rodolfo at her side, they repeat the same melodies they sang when they first met and fell in love in his garret. Such numbers as the arias in which Rodolfo and Mimi introduce themselves to one another, their ensuing love duet, and the waltz song of Mimi's friend Musetta are familiar to every operagoer; but perhaps the most affecting portion of *La Bohème* (curiously, Puccini himself thought it the weakest) is Act III, which seems to capture perfectly in music both the bleakness of a wintry day on the outskirts of Paris and the fading of youthful dreams of love.

Like Manon Lescaut before her, and Tosca and Butterfly after, Mimi is a romantic young woman of beauty and charm but weak moral fiber. This was a feminine type that appealed strongly to Puccini; in fact, almost all his operas have such heroines. He once showed Giuseppe Adami, a librettist who later became his biographer, a lithograph of a Venetian scene in which a nude young girl gazes longingly from behind the bars of a grated window at a husky gondolier. "That," he said, "is the kind of libretto that I want for my next opera."

Puccini followed *Bohème* with *Tosca* (1900), a work in the most obvious *verismo* style, with plenty of onstage brutality. Its three main characters are Floria Tosca, an opera singer; Mario Cavaradossi, a painter who is a political revolutionist; and Baron Scarpia, a police official who lusts after Tosca. The plot is sheer melodrama: Scarpia arrests and tortures Cavaradossi but promises to free him in exchange for the privilege of sleeping with Tosca. After lamenting her plight in the aria "Vissi d'arte" (I have lived for art), Tosca consents, but when the lecherous Baron reaches for her, she stabs him to death. Puccini's music underlines every twist of this lurid story, which ends with all three of the main characters dying by violence; the spontaneity of *La Bohème* seems to give way to a cold calculation of the effect a particular melodic or harmonic turn will create. With its lush roles for soprano, tenor, and baritone, *Tosca* affords boundless opportunities for unrestrained vocal display, but its overall effect is not without a touch of the tawdry.

Madama Butterfly (1904) regains the freshness of *Bohème*; in fact, the geisha girl who is seduced and abandoned by an American naval officer is probably the most universally appealing of all Puccini's heroines, and her duet with Lieutenant B. F. (for Benjamin Franklin) Pinkerton is the most incandescent and rapturous of all Puccini's love music. *Butterfly* comes close to being a one-character opera, since Pinkerton is little more than a stock figure, who disappears completely during the second act and returns only fleetingly during the third, and the other personages are relatively minor. The first performance of *Madama Butterfly* was a failure, but Puccini made some revisions and the work

In a colorful and spectacular scene from the Metropolitan Opera's production of Puccini's Turandot, *the Princess Turandot (Birgit Nilsson) hears a suitor's answer to three riddles that will bring him either her hand in marriage or his execution.*

quickly triumphed as completely as *Bohème* and *Tosca*, with Butterfly's aria "Un bel dì vedremo" (Some day he'll come) being sung in cafés and cabarets as well as in opera houses.

Puccini, as Verdi had noted at the outset of his career, kept his ear attuned to the latest musical trends; he knew his Wagner and his Debussy, and it is possible to trace influences of both in his music. In *Butterfly* he employed occasional Japanese themes and even a snatch of "The Star-Spangled Banner"—the latter in the same scene in which Pinkerton, inviting the United States Consul Sharpless to have a drink, asks him whether he prefers "milk punch, or whiskey." Fortunately the Consul upholds the honor of America by responding, "Whiskey."

By the time of *Butterfly*, Puccini was forty-five years old, rich, famous, and sought after everywhere. He built himself a sumptuous villa at Torre del Lago, and in dress and demeanor he resembled a successful businessman as much as a composer—actually, he combined the two callings very nicely. While he was still in his twenties he began a love affair with Elvira Gemignani, the wife of a former school friend, which, though frequently interrupted by amatory side excursions on his part, continued throughout his life. Puccini and Elvira were formally married in 1904, after the death of Gemignani, but even marriage did

Puccini (photograph above) had a fondness for exotic locales and detail in his work. In 1910, at the request of the Metropolitan Opera Company, he created La fanciulla del West, *an opera based on a play by the American theatrical producer David Belasco and set in California during the Gold Rush. With Toscanini conducting the Metropolitan Orchestra, Enrico Caruso singing the lead role of Dick Johnson, and both Puccini and Belasco in the audience,* La fanciulla del West's *opening night was an especially glamorous occasion. The photograph at left shows the opera's concluding moments as Puccini's heroine Minnie (Emmy Destinn) pleads with a posse to spare Johnson.*

not terminate his encounters with other women. In 1908 the household was rent by a scandal in which Elvira—apparently unjustly—accused a young housemaid of having relations with her husband. The terrified girl committed suicide by swallowing poison, and her family brought suit for defamation of character against Elvira. Eventually the case was settled out of court, but only after considerable anguish and notoriety.

Puccini had visited New York in 1907 to view the first performance at the Metropolitan Opera of *Madama Butterfly*. The Metropolitan asked for the honor of premiering his next opera, and in 1910 he complied by giving it *La fanciulla del West* ("The Girl of the Golden West"), based on a play by David Belasco. But although Puccini expressed the hope that he had reflected in his story of sheriffs and desperadoes in California, "the spirit of the American people and particularly the vigorous nature of the West," the opera did not achieve the lasting success of his previous works. Similarly, *La Rondine* ("The Swallow," 1917), an operettalike work in the Viennese manner, has never been more than an occasional novelty. However, in *Il Trittico* ("The Triptych," 1918), a set of three one-act operas, Puccini reaffirmed his mastery, *Il Tabarro* ("The Cloak") being a taut, *verismo* drama whose setting is a barge in the River Seine; *Suor Angelica* ("Sister Angelica") a mystical-sentimental work that ends barely before it starts to cloy; and *Gianni Schicchi* a lusty farce about a Renaissance rogue who impersonates a corpse to swindle his way into a sizable fortune.

Puccini's last opera, *Turandot* (1926), was left unfinished at his death, and Franco Alfano supplied the final scene. A richly scored opera with a large cast and chorus, it deals with a Chinese princess who sentences to death any suitor unable to solve three riddles. In character, Turandot is hardly the most sympathetic of Puccini's heroines, but she gets to sing some of his most spectacularly difficult music. The score of the opera, with its unusual harmonies and characters not easy to categorize, indicates that Puccini in his sixties was still experimenting and looking for new directions.

But he was never to explore them further. In 1924 a throat ailment from which he had suffered for years was finally diagnosed as cancer, and he traveled by train, coughing blood all the way, to a clinic in Brussels that specialized in the then-new radium therapy. Various treatments were tried; finally, radium needles were inserted directly into the tumor while he was fed liquids through his nose. At first he seemed to improve a bit, but four days later he suffered a fatal heart attack, the needles still in his throat. The entire operatic world mourned; Arturo Toscanini conducted a funeral concert at Milan; and Puccini was buried at his villa in Torre del Lago.

Puccini is the last Italian composer—indeed the last composer of *any* nationality—to have added a whole body of work to the standard international operatic repertory. Of lesser stature than Verdi both as a man and as a musician, he nevertheless continued a great tradition and left it intact for whoever may yet come on the scene to receive it. He is not an unworthy descendant of the Florentine *Camerata*, but it would be saddening to think that he is the last of that noble line.

9

A Particular Accent

OPERETTA WAS ONCE DEFINED by Camille Saint-Saëns, himself the composer of twelve operas, five piano concertos, three symphonies, and innumerable other works, as "a daughter of the *opéra comique*, a daughter who went to the bad. Not that daughters who go to the bad are always lacking in charm. . . ."

Almost from the beginnings of opera, especially opera in France, the lighter forms had coexisted amiably with the more serious. But in the mid-nineteenth century light opera, or operetta, began to emerge as an entity with its own musical values and theatrical style. Jacques Offenbach, the first of the great operetta composers, and presumably the inspiration of Saint-Saëns' definition, created a type of witty and tuneful musical work that raised light opera to a high art.

Like so many important musical personages in France, Offenbach was not French. The German-born son of a Jewish cantor, he began his musical career in Cologne and settled at the age of fourteen in Paris, where he became a cellist, first in the Opéra-Comique orchestra, and then a traveling virtuoso. He married a Spanish Catholic, adopting her religion. In 1855 he opened his own theater, a tiny establishment he called Les Bouffes-Parisiens, where he began to produce the giddy works that created a whole new theatrical genre—*Orphée aux enfers* ("Orpheus in the Underworld," 1858), *La Belle Hélène* ("The Beautiful Helen," 1864), *La Vie Parisienne* ("Parisian Life," 1866), *La Perichole* (1868), and some two dozen others.

Offenbach's operettas have survived because of their swift and dazzling scores, which are, perhaps, the most vivacious since Rossini's. They popularized the cancan and made it a symbol of sexual frivolity. But they are also superb satiric works, transporting Greek mythology into the cynical world of the Emperor Napoleon III, and ridiculing the politics and morality of their day. Thus the story of Orpheus's journey to Hades in search of Eurydice, traditionally a celebration of connubial fidelity, is turned into a saga of husbands and wives busily deceiving one another, with Eurydice carrying on an affair with the god Pluto, disguised as a shepherd, and Orpheus, a violinist by profession, interested only in playing his latest concerto. "C'est le comble de l'art, Il dure une heure un quart," he tells her—"It's the climax of art, it lasts an hour and a quarter." The violin tune begins and soon blends into a duet for the quarreling couple. At the end Orpheus is reluctantly forced to go to Pluto's realm in search of Eurydice by the prodding of a female character called Public Opinion, but Eurydice ultimately decides to remain there while everyone joins in a joyous cancan.

The fame which accrued to Offenbach as a composer of operettas would have satisfied most men, but like the clown who wanted to play Hamlet he longed to write one serious opera that would assure his immortality. In his mid-fifties he began work on *The Tales of Hoffmann*, based on the works of E.T.A. Hoffmann, a German author of weird and romantic stories. *The Tales of Hoffmann* is a masterly blend of the grotesque and the beautiful, a worthy challenge to imaginative singers and stage directors alike. In its pages Offenbach more than achieved his ambition to show that he could write something beyond musical farce, but he died four months before the work had its triumphal premiere at the Opéra-Comique in February, 1881.

Offenbach's success in operetta had a stimulating effect upon composers elsewhere. In Vienna Johann Strauss the Younger, known as the "Waltz King," created a vogue for sentimental operettas written largely in three-quarter time with *Die Fledermaus* ("The Bat"), in 1874. *Fledermaus* epitomizes the Viennese spirit in music and is performed everywhere; when Rudolf Bing took over direction of the Met-

ropolitan Opera in 1950, he staged it there and proved that it could still enchant a sophisticated twentieth-century audience. Johann Strauss followed *Fledermaus* with a succession of similar works including *Der Zigeunerbaron* ("The Gypsy Baron," 1885) and *Eine Nacht in Venedig* ("A Night in Venice," 1883). After his death in 1899 the Viennese tradition was carried on by such operettas as Franz Léhar's *Die lustige Witwe* ("The Merry Widow," 1905) and Oskar Straus's *Der tapfere Soldat* ("The Chocolate Soldier," 1908), the latter based on George Bernard Shaw's play *Arms and the Man*.

Considerably closer to the Offenbach spirit of irreverence were the English operettas of W. S. Gilbert and Sir Arthur Sullivan. Their accomplishment was all the more remarkable in that English opera of any kind had been inert since the death of Henry Purcell in 1695. About the only nineteenth-century works of any consequence were *The Bohemian Girl* (1843) and *Maritana* (1845), and the respective composers of these, Michael Balfe and William Vincent Wallace, were both Irish. Gilbert and Sullivan did more than produce a sequence of enchanting works; they proved that Englishmen were still able to compose operas.

Their collaboration began modestly in 1875 with a short work, *Trial by Jury*, and went on to turn out such masterpieces as *H.M.S. Pinafore* (1878), *The Pirates of Penzance* (1880), *Iolanthe* (1882), *The Mikado* (1885), *The Yeomen of the Guard* (1888), and all the other Savoy operas—so called for the London theater in which they were produced by Richard D'Oyly Carte. Despite differences in personal temperament, they were as ideal a librettist-composer team as has ever existed, with Gilbert's poetic and satiric gifts finding a perfect match in Sullivan's genius for delectable melody and musical parody. Their operettas show little sign of aging, even though many of the Victorian foibles that were the subject of their gibes have long since disappeared. In fact, Sullivan's music, without blunting Gilbert's satire, has always made it seem thoroughly amiable and agreeable. Crusty old King Gama might be speaking for the entire Gilbert and Sullivan canon when he says in *Princess Ida*:

> Whene'er I spoke
> Sarcastic joke
> > Replete with malice spiteful,
> This people mild
> Politely smiled,
> > And voted me delightful!

For all their popularity in the English-speaking world, the Gilbert and Sullivan operettas have never made any great inroads elsewhere. Like many other operas, serious as well as light, they seem to have a distinctively national character both in their texts and in their music. As long ago as the seventeenth century, that sturdy Englishman Samuel Pepys—who once said he could resist everything except women and music—had noticed a tendency of every people to produce a musical style and sound that reflected their own heritage and traditions. "I am convinced more and more," he wrote in his diary for April 7, 1667,

"that, as every nation has a particular accent and tone in discourse, so as the tone of one not to agree with or please the other, no more can the fashion of singing to words, for that the better the words are set, the more they take in of the ordinary tone of the country whose language the song speaks, so that a song well composed by an Englishman must be better to an Englishman than it can be to a stranger, or than if set by a stranger in foreign words."

In opera, the late nineteenth century was the time for the "particular accent" of each country to show itself, with a great upsurge of nationalism sweeping through countries that previously had made little contribution to the operatic mainstream.

Foremost among these was tsarist Russia, which had listened to imported Italian and French opera for years without producing any of its own until the arrival on the scene of Mikhail Glinka. The son of a well-to-do family, Glinka underwent an extensive musical education, including studies in Italy and Germany. He had a youthful admiration for Bellini but soon concluded that it made no sense for him, a Russian, to imitate Italian styles. "I, a dweller in the North, felt quite differently from the children of the sunny South," he later wrote. "With us, things either make no impression at all, or they sink deep into the soul"—a shrewd and succinct description of Russian music in general.

In 1836 Glinka's opera *A Life for the Tsar* was produced at St. Petersburg; a patriotic epic telling how a simple peasant, Ivan Susanin, saves the life of the founder of the Romanov dynasty by leading astray an army of Polish invaders, it made use of Russian folk songs and choral melodies. Many listeners were delighted with it, but one aristocrat dismissed the score as "coachmen's music." *A Life for the Tsar*, though seldom heard outside Russia, has continued to be a fixture under the Soviets; when it was revived in 1939 it was given under the title *Ivan Susanin*, with the music unchanged but with all references to the tsar deleted from the libretto. Glinka's second opera, *Russlan and Ludmilla* (1842), was even more Russian in its musical coloration, and is widely known through its lively overture.

Glinka's nationalistic approach was carried on by a group known as "The Five," made up of Mily Balakirev, Alexander Borodin, César Cui, Modeste Mussorgsky, and Nikolai Rimsky-Korsakov. Among their works are Borodin's *Prince Igor*, Rimsky-Korsakov's *Le Coq d'or* ("The Golden Cockerel"), and the supreme achievement of Russian opera, Mussorgsky's *Boris Godunov*.

Mussorgsky was a strange figure who gave up a military career because he felt he had a mission to compose music. A strongly built, bearded man, he led a tempestuous life and drank himself to death at the age of forty-two. In *Boris Godunov*, he put on the stage a half-mad Russian tsar who actually reigned from 1598 to 1605—a monarch who comes to his throne by violence and is tormented by conscience. The title role is one of the great bass parts in the operatic literature, calling for a performer of vocal power, regal bearing, and dramatic intensity —qualities combined most memorably, perhaps, in the singer Feodor Chaliapin. Although Boris is the dominant figure in the opera, the true hero is the Russian people, embodied both in massive choruses and in

Russian national opera began with Mikhail Glinka's A Life for the Tsar. *A 1906 edition of the score (left) had a cover by abstract artist Wassily Kandinsky. Rimsky-Korsakov's operas tended toward exotic and Oriental subjects. His* Golden Cockerel *was embellished with a nude scene in Gian Carlo Menotti's 1974 staging in Trieste (right). The soprano shedding her tunic is Gabriella Ravazzi in the role of the Queen of Shemakha. The costume sketches below were created for Prokofiev's* The Flaming Angel.

the piteous wails of a village simpleton. *Boris Godunov* has been performed in French, Italian, and English, yet somehow it almost always manages to "sound Russian." It is usually presented in a version prepared by Rimsky-Korsakov; however, many critics believe that Rimsky's added touches soften the impact of Mussorgsky's rough-hewn, powerful score.

Probably the Russian operas most frequently performed after *Boris* are Peter Ilyich Tchaikovsky's *Eugene Onegin* (1879) and *Pique Dame* (or *The Queen of Spades*, 1890), both imbued with warm lyricism but somewhat lacking in dramatic strength. Neither work is particularly nationalistic in outlook; it is Tchaikovsky's symphonies, rather than his operas, that "sink deep into the soul."

Russian opera has continued to flourish into the twentieth century with at least two composers, Sergei Prokofiev and Dmitri Shostakovich, whose works are performed outside of their homeland. Both spent a good deal of their careers contending with artistic criticism leveled against them by the Soviet regime. Shostakovich, who was born in 1906 and quickly emerged as one of the Soviet Union's brightest young musical talents, suffered the indignity of seeing his opera *Lady Macbeth of Mtzensk* withdrawn by official order in 1936. In revised form and with a new title, *Katerina Izmailova*, it has been performed successfully in recent years both in the Soviet Union and in the West.

Prokofiev spent the first part of his career traveling through the West; his early opera *The Love for Three Oranges* was premiered in 1921 in Chicago. A lively, sardonic updating of an old *commedia dell' arte* play, it is equally well known to symphonic and operatic audiences alike through its famous March and Scherzo. Prokofiev's *The Flaming Angel* was also composed in the West. He wrote several operas following his return to the Soviet Union in 1933; by far the most ambitious and grandiose is *War and Peace* (1955), a four-and-a-half-hour-long setting of Tolstoy's novel of the Napoleonic invasion.

Prokofiev worked on *War and Peace* on and off for twelve years, starting it while Soviet Russia was under attack by Nazi Germany, so that its patriotic fervor had a contemporary urgency. *War and Peace* has only recently begun to be performed in the Western world; in September, 1973, it was chosen to open the spectacular new Sydney Opera House in Australia, and in May, 1974, it was given its United States stage premiere by Sarah Caldwell's Opera Company of Boston. A somewhat uneven and sprawling work, in many of its scenes it approaches the power and grandeur of Tolstoy's great novel.

Czech opera has entered the international repertory through *The Bartered Bride* (1866) by the Bohemian composer Bedrich Smetana. A vivacious and tender comedy with a colorful village background, it has been performed in many languages. Antonin Dvorák's *Rusalka* (1901), about a lovely nymph who dwells in a lake, abounds in lyricism, but its drama, like its heroine, seems a bit watery at times. Leos Janácek, a native of Moravia, wrote highly original operas with a distinctive musical profile. Several, including the folk-flavored *Jenufa* (1903) and the starkly dramatic *Makropoulos Affair* (1924), have attained repeated performances outside their own country.

The best-known Hungarian national opera is Zoltán Kodály's *Háry János* (1926), although most listeners know it only through two orchestral suites extracted from it. Béla Bartók's *Bluebeard's Castle* (1918) is a one-act, two-character opera that is remarkable for its musical intensity.

The "father of Spanish music," Felipe Pedrell, wrote ten operas,

Czech composer Leos Janácek's first opera, Jenufa *(photograph at left, below), was a lyrical setting of a village tragedy. Later he developed a more terse and jagged style, as in* The Makropoulos Affair *(left, above, performed by the New York City Opera with Maralin Niska and Harry Theyard). Francis Poulenc's story of the martyrdom of the Carmelite nuns during the French Revolution,* Les Dialogues des Carmélites *(below) is a deeply moving drama with a message of contemporary importance about the limits of religious freedom.*

few of which are known outside of Spain. His pupil Enrique Granados, who died in 1916 when the *Sussex* was torpedoed by a German U-boat, put together an opera entitled *Goyescas* with music he drew from his own piano pieces. Manuel de Falla's *La vida breve* ("Life is Short," 1913) is a brief tragic opera in the *verismo* vein, though with a strongly Spanish flavor. Its theme comes from a refrain sung by a young gypsy girl: "¡Vivan los que rien! ¡Mueran los que lloran!" (Long live those who laugh! Death to those who weep!). Probably the most frequently performed Spanish musical stage works on both sides of the Atlantic are the *zarzuelas*—light, popular operettas of which the best known are *La Revoltosa* ("The Revolutionary Girl," 1897) by Ruperto Chapí y Lorente and *La verbena de la paloma* ("The Festival of Our Lady of the Dove," 1894) by Tomás Bretón y Hernándéz.

French and Italian opera during the twentieth century have produced a number of notable achievements. Maurice Ravel's piquant and lyrical *L'Heure espagnole* ("The Spanish Hour," 1911) and *L'Enfant et les sortilèges* ("The Child and the Sorceries," 1925) are both delightful works, and the latter has even been the subject of an imaginative television version. Francis Poulenc composed what were probably the two most successful French operas of the post-World War II era, both with a nationalistic tinge. *Les Mamelies de Tirésias* ("The Breasts of Tiresias," 1947) is a madcap satire that concludes with an appeal to the French to reverse their falling birthrate—"Cher Public, faites des enfants" (Dear audience, make children). *Les Dialogues des Carmélites* ("The Dialogues of the Carmelites," 1957), in contrast, is a serious,

even a somber work dealing with religious persecution during the French Revolution but obviously reflecting Europe's travails under the German occupation of the 1940s. In a stunning climactic effect the voices of a chorus of Carmelite nuns one by one fall abruptly silent as the guillotine blade repeatedly descends. With its declamatory dignity and lucid scoring *Les Dialogues des Carmélites* stands in a French tradition going back to Gluck.

Italian composers in the twentieth century have had to work in the shadow of the achievements of Verdi and Puccini. Some have responded by trying to find an individual voice within the general style of their predecessors, but others have broken away completely and adopted more "advanced" procedures. Among the former, Italo Montemezzi is remembered for his *L'amore dei tre rè* ("The Love of Three Kings," 1913), and the half-German Ermanno Wolf-Ferrari for his *Il segreto di Susanna* ("The Secret of Suzanne," 1909) and *I gioielli della Madonna* ("The Jewels of the Madonna," 1911).

Less conservative in style are the operas of Ildebrando Pizzetti, typified in his *Assassinio nella cattedrale* (1958), based on T. S. Eliot's play *Murder in the Cathedral*. And in Luigi Dallapiccola's *Il Prigionero* ("The Prisoner," 1950) and Luigi Nono's *Intolleranza* ("Intolerance," 1961), traditional Italian lyricism gives way increasingly to more radical approaches.

In Germany the establishment of the Weimar Republic after World War I provided an artistic impetus as well as a friendly atmosphere for new and experimental works. It was in Berlin that Berg's *Wozzeck* was first performed in 1925, five years before it reached his native Vienna. The German capital also saw the premiere of the jazzy *Jonny spielt auf*

Combining musical drama and political commentary into biting entertainment, the works of Kurt Weill and his librettist Bertolt Brecht have earned a place in the opera house as well as the theater. Striking stage effects distinguished a 1970 production of Weill's The Rise and Fall of the City of Mahagonny (right) in Spoleto. Carrying forth the legacy of his countrymen Verdi and Puccini, Italo Montemezzi composed L'amore dei tre rè, seen above in a 1953 production at La Scala, marking the fortieth anniversary of the opera's premiere in Milan.

("Johnny Strikes Up," 1927) by another Viennese, Ernst Krenek. Paul Hindemith's operas were given there, climaxing in his *Mathis der Maler* ("Matthias the Painter," 1938), composed just before he fled Hitler's Third Reich.

Among the most original and still-pertinent musical stage works of the period are the satirical commentaries of Kurt Weill and Bertolt Brecht. Using a cabaret rather than an operatic idiom they savagely mocked the social and political practices of their day in such works as *The Rise and Fall of the City of Mahagonny* (1930) and *Die Dreigroschenoper* ("The Threepenny Opera"), which, as already noted, continues to be an American favorite in Marc Blitzstein's English-language adaptation.

Several German composers, including Carl Orff, Werner Egk, and Boris Blacher, have written notable operas in the post-World War II era, as has the Austrian Gottfried von Einem. Many have joined their Italian confreres in adopting avant-garde techniques, among them Hans Werner Henze, whose *Der junge Lord* ("The Young Lord," 1965) has for its hero a trained ape.

Of all European countries, it is the least likely one, Britain, that has produced some of the most substantial and apparently durable twentieth-century operas. Few attempts to compose serious opera had been made in England following the death of Purcell. Dr. Samuel Johnson spoke for all Britons when he described opera as "an exotic and irrational entertainment."

But the growth of English operetta in the Victorian era soon led to efforts to compose more substantial works; in fact, Sir Arthur Sullivan himself made a supreme attempt in his grandiose *Ivanhoe* (1891), which enjoyed an initial run of 160 performances but later fell into a disuse even more profound than that accorded to the Sir Walter Scott novel on which it is based.

Among the first British opera composers of the twentieth century was a woman, Dame Ethyl Smyth. Neither her sex nor her nationality commended themselves to British producers, however, and her major work, *The Wreckers* (1906), received its premiere in Leipzig. The operas of Frederick Delius were also premiered in Germany before Sir Thomas Beecham successfully took up the composer's cause in England. Both Delius' *Koanga* (1904), a work about a slave revolt in America, and his *Village Romeo and Juliet* (1907), a poetic, pastoral opera with a Swiss background, have gained a limited but loyal public. Ralph Vaughan Williams made good use of the British folksong style in *Hugh the Drover* (1924), which became a favorite at Sadler's Wells, a popular North London theater whose opera-in-English performances attracted eager audiences in the 1930s. In more recent years notable English operas include Sir William Walton's *Troilus and Cressida* (1954) and Michael Tippett's *Midsummer Marriage* (1955).

Incontestably the great British operatic master of the twentieth cen-

Britain's leading contemporary composer, Benjamin Britten, has written many successful operas based on literary themes. His first international triumph was Peter Grimes, *set to a poem by George Crabbe. The Canadian tenor Jon Vickers appears at right in the title role. A more recent work, with many dance sequences, is* Death in Venice, *which premiered at Covent Garden in 1973 (below).*

tury is Benjamin Britten. Born in 1913, he has written a dozen operas based on sources ranging from Japanese Noh plays to Thomas Mann's *Death in Venice*. Britten has spent much of his life in Suffolk, on the North Sea, where he established the Aldeburgh Music Festival in conjunction with his long-time friend and interpreter of his roles, tenor Peter Pears. The sea atmosphere pervades Britten's first opera *Peter Grimes* (1945), which is based on George Crabbe's "The Borough," an eighteenth-century narrative poem about a lonely, ill-starred sea captain. Crabbe described Peter Grimes in these terms:

> And though he felt forsaken, grieved at heart
> To think he lived from all mankind apart.

Britten's opera depicts a man destroyed by fate and by his own failings, but it tells his story compassionately and against a dramatically realistic background of life in an English fishing village. *Peter Grimes* is conservative in its approach, with storm music, church music, and a wild celebration in a village inn. But its psychological probing of its characters, its powerful use of symphonic interludes, and the freshness of its choruses all mark it as the work of an original contemporary mind. *Peter Grimes* has been performed all over the world in a variety of languages and seems as likely as any work of the mid-twentieth century to remain in the repertory.

Other operas by Britten have included *A Midsummer Night's Dream* (1960), with an ample orchestral score and many passages of vocal beauty, and three works scored for chamber orchestra—*The Rape of Lucretia* (1946), an oratoriolike composition; *Albert Herring* (1947), a delectable comedy about a not-too-bright young lad who, to his discomfiture, is chosen King of the May; and *The Turn of the Screw* (1954), which skillfully underlines the mysterious horror of Henry James's story. Britten has also composed children's works, such as the delightful, pageant-filled *Noye's Fludde* (1958), and a television opera, the rather austere *Owen Wingrave* (1971).

As a practical man of the theater, a resourceful musician, and a creative spirit attuned to his time, Benjamin Britten has produced a remarkable set of musical achievements. He has also demonstrated—if anyone had any doubts—that opera as an art form continues to have a future.

10

Opera in the New World

To the many definitions of opera already quoted in this book let us add one more, given by the American writer Ambrose Bierce in his *Devil's Dictionary* of 1911: "*Opera, n*: A play representing life in another world, whose inhabitants have no speech but song, no motions but gestures, and no positions but attitudes."

Bierce's view is undoubtedly reflective of a practical, industrious people, such as Americans are traditionally reputed to be. Certainly in the colonial and revolutionary eras there was little time for such niceties as the type of artistic entertainment flourishing at the time in Europe. Yet curiously, a few scattered specimens of musical stage entertainment managed to turn up in the early years of America, like scraggly growths in an inhospitable soil.

The first such presentation to be recorded was that of *Flora*, or *Hob in the Well*, by John Hippisley, an English ballad opera given in a courthouse in Charleston, South Carolina, in 1735. Some years later a troupe of actors and singers known as the London Company was organized in Williamsburg, Virginia, subsequently traveling north to Philadelphia and New York. Although it chiefly performed plays, its repertory also included John Gay's *Beggar's Opera* and two other ballad operas, *The Honest Yorkshireman* and *The Virgin Unmask'd*. It evidently possessed the ability to stir an audience, one way or another, for after a performance in New York in May, 1762, its director, David Douglass, inserted an advertisement in the press offering a reward "to whoever can discover the person who was so very rude as to throw Eggs from the Gallery upon the Stage last Monday, by which the Cloaths of some Ladies and Gentlemen were spoiled and the performance in some measure interrupted."

The first native-born American composer is generally thought to be Francis Hopkinson, the only musician to sign the Declaration of Independence. Hopkinson's *The Temple of Minerva* (1781), an "oratorical entertainment" resembling opera in style, won the approval of most of his contemporaries, including George Washington. It also provoked the creation of an indecent parody, by a disgruntled Philadelphian, entitled *The Temple of Cloacina*. Ballad operas by early American composers include James Hewitt's *Tammany*, or *The Indian Chief*, sponsored in 1794 by the budding Tammany Society of New York—then more a social than a political organization—and J. N. Barker's *The Indian Princess*, based on the story of Pocahontas and performed in Philadelphia in

1808. French-style light operas were given in New Orleans, but elsewhere the British model was preferred. Italian opera did not arrive until 1810, when Paisiello's *Barber of Seville* was given in New Orleans. Rossini's version of the *Barber* was performed in New York in 1819, only three years after its premiere in Rome. Both of these works were sung in English translation.

In 1825 European opera truly established itself on America's shores, conveyed by a remarkable family headed by Manuel García. A Spanish Jew with an adventurous and unconventional spirit, García, after a successful career as a tenor in Europe, impulsively decided to invade the New World. Then fifty years old, he brought with him a company of professional singers, including his son Manuel, Jr., then twenty, and his daughter Maria, seventeen. Manuel, Jr., a baritone, subsequently became a great vocal pedagogue, while Maria, a contralto, married a French merchant in New York, and taking his name, Malibran, developed into one of the most celebrated prima donnas of all time.

This distinguished troupe spent over a year in New York performing operas by Rossini and others, including two by García himself. They were welcomed to the city with especial warmth by Lorenzo da Ponte, Mozart's old librettist, who had emigrated from Europe and was by then teaching Italian at Columbia College. Da Ponte induced the newcomers to add to their repertory "his" *Don Giovanni*. García's visit, as da Ponte says in his *Memoirs*, planted "the first root of the great tree of Italian music in New York."

However, it was a tree that bore fruit slowly. The first grand opera composed in the United States was William Henry Fry's *Leonora* (1845), cast in the mold of Bellini and Donizetti. Even more significant, perhaps, was George F. Bristow's *Rip Van Winkle* (1855), for this was the first American opera based on a native theme. It ran for four weeks at Niblo's Garden in New York City, and its success encouraged Bristow to begin an opera entitled *Columbus*, which he never finished. Bristow, who was a violinist with the New York Philharmonic Society, ended his career as supervisor of music in the New York City public schools.

Few American operas of the late nineteenth and early twentieth centuries met with more than scant or fleeting success, although operatic annals are studded with attempts: Walter Damrosch's *The Scarlet Letter* (1896), American in impulse but Germanic in execution; Frederick S. Converse's *The Pipe of Desire* (1906), the first American work given at the Metropolitan Opera House (1910); Deems Taylor's *The King's Henchman* (1927) and *Peter Ibbetson* (1931); Howard Hanson's *Merry Mount* (1934); and a number of others. Most of these works displayed little in the way of a specifically American impulse; when such a strain did appear it developed from the musical contributions and influences of black Americans—even though the composers utilizing it were not necessarily black themselves. One Negro composer who did complete an opera was Scott Joplin, the "King of Ragtime," whose long-neglected *Treemonisha* (1911), about a black girl who becomes a leader of her people, achieved revival in the 1970s. Afro-American rhythms and songs gave dramatic realism to Louis Gruenberg's *Emperor Jones* (1933), based on Eugene O'Neill's play about a Pull-

Virgil Thomson's opera Four Saints in Three Acts, *set to a libretto by Gertrude Stein, received a "one-time-only" performance in Hartford, Connecticut, to mark the opening of a theater at the Wadsworth Athenaeum (photograph above). However, the interest that greeted this production induced Thomson and his director, John Houseman, to bring the opera to Broadway, where it enjoyed a run of six weeks.*

man porter who becomes ruler of a West Indies island only to go mad in the jungle.

As performers, Negroes played a significant part in the success of Virgil Thomson's *Four Saints in Three Acts* (1934), still one of the most remarkable of all American operas. Thomson's music is a setting of an enigmatic text by Gertrude Stein that includes the famous line, "Pigeons on the grass alas." Of black singers Thomson wrote: "I had chosen them purely for beauty of voice, clarity of enunciation, and fine carriage. Their surprise gift to the production was their understanding of the work."

Thomson's second opera, *The Mother of Us All* (1947), also with a libretto by Stein, centers around the life and times of Susan B. Anthony, the nineteenth-century feminist. Few operas have conveyed American feeling with as much wit, charm, and grace. Thomson's own description of his music is as apt as any:

> The music of *The Mother of Us All* is an evocation of nineteenth-century America, with its gospel hymns and cocky marches, its sentimental ballads, waltzes, darn-fool ditties and intoned sermons. . . . It is a souvenir of all those sounds and kinds of tunes that were once the music of rural America and that still are the basic idiom of our country because they are the oldest vernacular still remembered here and used.

135

The most universally accepted of all American operas is George Gershwin's *Porgy and Bess* (1935), compounded of three elements: black folk idiom, Broadway musical techniques, and the musical resourcefulness and individuality of its composer. Gershwin's career was almost meteoric in its brilliance and brevity. He wrote his first popular hit song "Swanee" at nineteen, composed "Rhapsody in Blue" at twenty-five, completed eight musical shows including *Oh Kay!*, *Strike Up the Band*, and *Of Thee I Sing* between the ages of twenty-eight and thirty-two, and produced *Porgy and Bess* at thirty-six. He died of a brain tumor, July 11, 1937, at thirty-eight.

Porgy and Bess has for its background Negro life in Charleston. Gershwin actually spent some time on the South Carolina coast, absorbing the sounds and sights of the region. Right from its haunting opening lullaby "Summertime," it is an original and nonderivative work, with little use of actual folk tunes. Gershwin intended it as a thoroughgoing opera, and so it is, with highly developed musical ensembles, meticulous orchestration, and a vivid sense of characterization. If

George Gershwin, shown in the photograph at left completing the score of Porgy and Bess, *infused elements of American popular songs and jazz into the sphere of opera in this final major accomplishment. The original Broadway production of* Porgy and Bess *in 1935 and a revival in 1942 showcased the talent of such black singer-actors as Anne Brown (Bess), Todd Duncan (Porgy), and Warren Coleman (Crown) seen at right.*

Overleaf: A rollicking brass band brings out the residents of Catfish Row in their Sunday finery as they prepare for a picnic on Kittiwick Island at the end of Act II of the 1935 production of Porgy and Bess.

the people of Catfish Row at times utilize a language very close to popular song, it is not because a special effect is desired, but because such language is the natural way for them to express themselves in an operatic situation.

When *Porgy and Bess* was performed in New York with an all-black cast headed by Todd Duncan and Anne Brown, the reception was far from enthusiastic. In fact, it was reviewed more favorably by the drama critics than by the music critics. Among the latter, Olin Downes in the *Times* complained that its style shifted between opera and "operetta or sheer Broadway entertainment," and Virgil Thomson characterized it as "crooked folklore and halfway opera," though six years later he reversed himself and called it "a beautiful piece of music and a deeply moving play for the lyric theater." The original production, given in a Broadway theater, ran 124 performances and lost $70,000. Only after Gershwin's death did *Porgy and Bess* really find its audiences, and then, thanks to American touring companies, it found them all over the world.

A great surge in American operatic creativity began immediately after World War II and shows no sign of abating. A lengthy list might be set forth of works premiered in recent years. The New York City Opera, in particular, has made a specialty of introducing new operas, and a number of them, including Douglas Moore's *Ballad of Baby Doe* (1956), Carlisle Floyd's *Susannah* (1955), and Robert Ward's *The Crucible* (1961), seem to have entered its permanent repertory.

At the Metropolitan Opera, Samuel Barber's *Vanessa* (1958) was successful enough for the company to commission a new work from the composer for the inaugural of its new home at Lincoln Center in 1966. However, Barber's *Antony and Cleopatra*, smothered in an overly elaborate production, did not rise to the occasion despite the presence of Leontyne Price in the role of the Egyptian queen.

The Metropolitan Opera also gave the American premiere of Igor Stravinsky's *The Rake's Progress* in 1953, two years after its first per-

formance in Venice. In his later years Stravinsky was an American composer at least in nationality. His previous operas, *Le Rossignol* ("The Nightingale," 1914), *Mavra* (1922), *Renard* (1922), and the oratoriolike *Oedipus Rex* (1927), were all composed in France, but *The Rake's Progress* was written in California to an English text by the poet W. H. Auden. Couched in a neo-Mozartean style, it remains a connoisseur's opera, though it is revived with some frequency. However, it was his ballet scores, far more than his operas, that marked Stravinsky as the dominant composer of the mid-twentieth century.

The composer who has most successfully navigated the operatic mainstream into the contemporary world is Gian Carlo Menotti, Italian by birth and citizenship but American in residence and in approach to stagecraft. Through 1974 Menotti, who was born in 1911, had composed more than a dozen operas. His status as a composer is paradoxical: many critics find him overly imitative of Puccini and the *verismo* school, yet no modern opera composer has won nearly so much popular acceptance or had so many different operas performed in so many different houses.

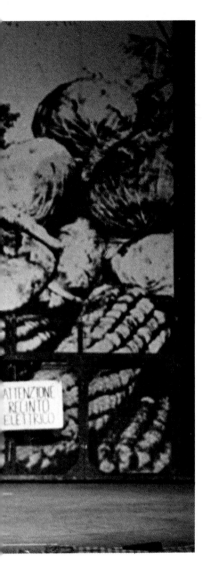

Menotti has written operas for radio (*The Old Maid and the Thief*, 1939) and for television (*Amahl and the Night Visitors*, 1951). Indeed, as *Amahl* has become a regular Christmas feature, its repeated holiday telecasts may well mean that more people have viewed it than any other opera ever written—a sobering thought. Among Menotti's most powerful tragic operas are *The Medium* (1946), *The Saint of Bleecker Street* (1954), and especially *The Consul* (1950), which expresses the searing agony of modern political refugees. Menotti's comedic gift is displayed in *Amelia Goes to the Ball* (1937), *The Telephone* (1947), and *Help! Help! The Globolinks* (1968)—a delightful and tender work about a busload of schoolchildren confronted by invaders from outer space who know no language except electronic music.

Menotti writes his own librettos and often directs his own productions. Sometimes he emphasizes the drama rather than the music in his operas, but his are works of genuine passion and abundant melody, and are none the worse for being the products of a craftsman who is a shrewd judge of theatrical effect.

In some ways the most striking American contribution to the lyric stage has occurred not in the opera house but in the Broadway theater. Its origins go back to the romantic operetta style represented in the works of Victor Herbert, Rudolf Friml, and Sigmund Romberg, all European-born, but it was in Jerome Kern's *Show Boat* (1927) that it first displayed its individuality and distinctively American flavor. Subsequently musical comedy was raised to a fine art by such songwriters as Irving Berlin, Vincent Youmans, Cole Porter, and a dozen others.

The Broadway musical also began to take on a greater social pertinence and substance, as in Gershwin's *Of Thee I Sing* (1931), a political satire, and Harold Rome's *Pins and Needles*, a revue produced in 1937 by the International Ladies' Garment Workers' Union. Marc Blitzstein's *The Cradle Will Rock* (1937) was a frankly proletarian drama with music. Blitzstein later composed *Regina* (1949), an operatic version of

Gian Carlo Menotti's Festival of Two Worlds in Spoleto, Italy, has earned a worldwide reputation for its adventurous and imaginative presentations of opera, dance, and concert music. The 1972 season featured Igor Stravinsky's rarely produced opera Renard, *performed by the experimental theatrical troupe La Mama (above), as well as a revival of Menotti's dramatic opera* The Consul *(right).*

Lillian Hellman's play *The Little Foxes*, and, of course, made the supremely successful American adaptation of Kurt Weill's *The Three-penny Opera*. He was working on what he hoped would be his masterpiece, a score for the Metropolitan Opera based on the Sacco-Vanzetti Case of the 1920s, when he was attacked and fatally beaten by thugs while vacationing on Martinique in 1964.

Kurt Weill, who had fled Nazi Germany with his wife, the singer Lotte Lenya, made a remarkably deft stylistic adjustment from Berlin to Broadway, as demonstrated in such shows as *Lady in the Dark* (1941), *One Touch of Venus* (1943), and *Lost in the Stars* (1949). Even his relatively unsuccessful *Knickerbocker Holiday* (1938) was made memorable by the wistfully beautiful "September Song." Weill's folk-opera *Down in the Valley*, first given at Indiana University in 1948, achieved performances throughout the United States, and his *Street Scene* (1947), with lyrics by Langston Hughes, entered the repertory of the New York City Opera after an initial failure on Broadway.

Probably the most distinguished career in recent years among Broadway composers has been that of Richard Rodgers. For eighteen years he collaborated with lyricist Lorenz Hart to produce such brilliant shows as *On Your Toes* (1936), *The Boys from Syracuse* (1938), and *Pal Joey* (1940). When Hart died in 1943 Rodgers began an association with Oscar Hammerstein II that resulted in works of still

greater musical depth. Their *Oklahoma!* (1943) created a new standard in American show music, blending a cogent story, fresh and inventive melodies, tasteful dances, and a strong sense of characterization. It had a quality of candor and conviction that seemed to banish forever the traditional operetta tales about dashing hussars and pretty peasant girls.

The Rodgers-Hammerstein collaboration was equally successful in *Carousel* (1945) and *The King and I* (1951), and achieved perhaps its finest work in *South Pacific* (1949), a moving and credible depiction of a World War II romance between a young United States Navy nurse and a middle-aged French planter. Metropolitan Opera bass Ezio Pinza was enlisted to play the role of the planter, Emile de Becque, a significant sign that the distance between opera and Broadway was perhaps much less than had been previously supposed.

This new type of show, with musical and dramatic elements closely integrated, has continued to flourish in the American theater. Some of its outstanding exemplars are Frank Loesser's *Guys and Dolls* (1950) and *The Most Happy Fella* (1956), Alan Jay Lerner and Frederick Loewe's *My Fair Lady* (1956), Leonard Bernstein's *West Side Story* (1957), Sheldon Harnick and Jerry Bock's *Fiddler on the Roof* (1964), and Mitch Leigh's *Man of La Mancha* (1965). It is a list that seems certain to grow as the gap between popular musical theater and opera continues to narrow in the years ahead.

The "Broadway musical" has added a new category to the list of satellite theatrical forms that surround opera. In Rodgers and Hammerstein's South Pacific *the celebrated opera basso Ezio Pinza played alongside one of the American theater's most famous musical personalities, Mary Martin (left, above). Reflecting the diversity of subject matter portrayed in musicals is Lerner and Loewe's elegantly costumed comedy* My Fair Lady *(left, below) and the brilliant, colorful story of New York City ghetto life created by Bernstein and Sondheim in* West Side Story *(below).*

Epilogue:

The Lively Corpse

HECTOR BERLIOZ ONCE CHIDED his fellow composer Felix Mendelssohn for being "a little too fond of the dead." In like manner, opera itself has been accused of being too firmly rooted in the past, of living on ancient glories rather than future prospects. Admittedly there is a measure of truth in the charge, for ordinary subscription audiences will flock to Verdi or Puccini, especially when a celebrated soprano is in the leading role, but shy away from contemporary or experimental works.

Yet it also is possible to exaggerate both the extent of this conservatism and its effect upon the repertory offered even in the world's more traditional houses. The most productive era of opera is generally accounted to be the 101 years between 1786, when Mozart's *Marriage of Figaro* was written, and 1887, the year of Verdi's *Otello*. Yet of the twenty-five operas on the 1974–1975 schedule of the Metropolitan Opera—no bastion of modernity—thirteen were composed *after* 1887. And four of these, Britten's *Death in Venice* (1973), Berg's *Wozzeck* (1925), Bartók's *Bluebeard's Castle* (1918), and Janácek's *Jenufa* (1903), are decidedly modern products. If opera in the twentieth century is dead, then it is, like Puccini's Gianni Schicchi, an extremely lively corpse.

Composers in recent years have been exploring new techniques and expanding opera's dimensions. Atonalism, serialism, electronic, synthesizer, and computer music all have had or are having their day. Karl-Birgir Blomdahl's spaceship opera, *Aniara*, produced in Stockholm in 1959, made use of taped electronic sounds along with conventional music. *Faust Counter Faust* (1971) was an avant-garde concoction by the Center Opera of Minneapolis in which an original score was mixed in with tape recordings of previous Faust operas and various other electronic interjections. At least two rock operas have been performed successfully, *Tommy* (1969) and *Jesus Christ Superstar* (1971), though both were essentially pop-culture phenomena with more commercial than aesthetic significance. Some theatrical works, like Leonard Bernstein's *Mass*, commissioned for the opening of the John F. Kennedy Center for the Performing Arts in Washington, D.C., in 1971, adroitly blend operatic elements into a multimedia mixture in which dance, drama, and electronic elements all play their part.

With all its innovations, opera seems more likely than many other musical forms to maintain a strong link of continuity with the past. Essentially a vocal art, it is distinguished by the human quality brought

In keeping with trends in theater, modern dance, ballet, and concert music, adventuresome opera companies have been experimenting with new and unusual technical approaches. One spectacular attempt was the Minneapolis Center Opera Company's production of Faust Counter Faust *(scene at left), an opera within an opera pitting the story of a modern-day Faust against the image created by Berlioz and Gounod.*

to it by the singers without whom it cannot function. However its format changes, whatever experimentation it undergoes, its four cornerstones remain soprano, alto, tenor, bass. It is no accident that the most popular and frequently performed operatic composers of the day are Benjamin Britten and Gian Carlo Menotti, both of whom prefer to work within the tradition even as they seek to create operas of and for their own times.

Whatever the opera of the future may sound like, it is almost certain to *look* far different from the opera of the past. Modern production techniques, including the use of film projections, cinematic effects, stroboscopic lighting, superimposed images and the like, have brought a new flexibility and excitement to the musical stage. And with them, opera seems to be regaining the position it held in the seventeenth century as the most scenically innovative of all forms of theater.

Perhaps even more important is technology's contribution to the development of new audiences for opera. Radio, television, and movies have brought opera to thousands who might never have known it otherwise. The impact of recordings can hardly be overstated. The record industry, which started by making wax pressings of single arias sung by Caruso and other luminaries of the 1900–1920 Golden Age, and played on hand-wound Victrolas, assumed enormous proportions in the era of long-playing stereophonic records and tapes that began after World War II. Today some three hundred different operas are available in complete recorded form, and many others in excerpts, covering the

entire operatic experience from the *Camerata* to *Carmen Jones*.

This broad range of interest and understanding is one of the most heartening aspects of modern operatic life. No other era has had as much knowledge of or appreciation for the achievements of past gener ations, or done more to restore them to life. Monteverdi and Mozart, Bellini and Berlioz, early Verdi and late Prokofiev—all have been res cued from obscurity, neglect, or misunderstanding. The revival has taken place not only on recordings, but in actual stage performances from Boston to Berlin. Some of the most adventurous work in the United States has been done by the hundreds of opera workshops scattered throughout the country, many of which are connected with a university or conservatory.

As it enters the last quarter of the twentieth century, opera shows every sign of remaining a viable and vital art form. In fact, its most critical current problem is monetary rather than musical. Opera still is, as John Evelyn wrote, a "magnificent and expensive" diversion, and its financial crisis has been made more acute than ever because box-office receipts are increasingly unable to keep up with escalating production and labor costs. The old aristocracy that once maintained houses and companies for its own pride and pleasure has long since vanished; having gone public, opera now looks for support from the modern world's main repositories of available cash—government, foundations, and business corporations. In Europe, virtually all opera houses are state supported. In the United States, government response is more grudging,

The first space opera, Aniara *(scene at left), with an electronic music score by the Swedish composer Karl-Birgir Blomdahl, depicts the gradual mental and emotional deterioration of refugees fleeing a doomed planet Earth only to become trapped in a malfunctioning spaceship. Leonard Bernstein's* Mass *(below) is a multimedia concert work employing traditional musical forms to illustrate biblical themes.*

and years of financial struggle lie ahead.

But the story of opera for four centuries has been a triumph of art over economics, and there is no reason to despair of the outcome at this late date. In 1634, Pietro de' Bardi, son of Giovanni de' Bardi, patron of the Florentine *Camerata*, sat down to recall the emotions with which he, as a young man, had heard the first opera ever written, Peri's *Dafne*.

I was left speechless with amazement. . . . It was sung to the accompaniment of a consort of instruments, an arrangement followed thereafter in all the other comedies. Caccini and Peri were under great

Contrary to the usual progression of most musical works from stage to recording studio, the rock opera Jesus Christ Superstar *(above) first appeared as a commercially successful long-playing record album and only later was turned into a theatrical presentation.*

obligation . . . to Signor Jacopo Corsi, who, becoming ardent and discontent with all but the superlative in this art, directed these composers with excellent ideas and marvelous doctrines, as befitted so noble an enterprise. . . . Nor was there any want of men to imitate them, and in Florence, the first home of this sort of music, and in other cities of Italy, especially Rome, these gave and are still giving a marvelous account of themselves on the dramatic stage.

And so they still are, for in the world of opera the Golden Age is always the present.

BACKSTAGE
AT THE OPERA

Under the leadership of the Italian-born impresario Giulio Gatti-Casazza, the Metropolitan Opera joined the ranks of the foremost opera companies in the world. Shortly after his retirement from the Met in 1935, Gatti-Casazza began writing his memoirs, in which he recalled some of the more unusual incidents that occurred during his tenure.

In general, I did not have much to complain about with regard to artists—men and women. I must confess that, in their relations with me, they have always been reasonable, and save for rare exceptions, well disciplined and agreeable. This has been due to the fact, in part, that I have always treated them with the greatest possible justice and courtesy, but without too much intimacy. My door has always been open to them at any moment, and I have always maintained contact with them. Naturally, there are artists who require much patience and not too much praise. And one must try to have as great a number of doubles or replacements as possible. The artist for whom there is no substitute is likely to be more difficult than the one whose place can be taken by someone else.

For the rest, prima donnas and tenors I have found in every walk of life: in the personnel of the university, in the army, the navy, journalism, politics, etc. To tell the truth, vanity, hypersensitivity and rivalry are not the exclusive inheritance of the lyric artist.

Some artists are extremely naïve, so much so as to baffle by their excuses the most exigent drillmasters. I remember the marvellous excuse one of them offered Toscanini. It was the tenor De Marchi. The occasion was a performance of "Huguenots," when he sang a false note during a performance unsatisfactory in several respects, which roused the ire of Toscanini. De Marchi was standing in the wings, reviling himself, when he heard the voice of Toscanini, who had just come on the stage, after conducting. Toscanini was scolding vigorously the men in charge of the lighting, who had kept the scene too dark. De Marchi went up to Toscanini and said:

"Bravo, Maestro! This darkness is a real outrage. It caused me to sing a bad note. Those electricians are beasts. The blame is all theirs!"

Sometimes the verdicts of the press complicate matters. This even applied to Caruso at the height of his career.

One day I was sitting in my office at the Metropolitan preparing a program for the following season, when Mr. Otto Kahn came to me and said:

"Why don't you give 'Rigoletto'?"

"It is not easy," I said.

"Why? What's the trouble? You have plenty of tenors. You have Caruso."

"Caruso?" I replied. "His voice is now too heavy for 'Rigoletto.' "

But he insisted so much that I said, "All right, we will give 'Rigoletto' with Caruso."

I went to Caruso and said to him, "Next season we must do a revival of 'Rigoletto.' "

In 1974 Theoni V. Aldredge designed the costumes for the New York City Opera's new production of Die Fledermaus. *Her original sketches are shown above and on the following pages.*

"Oh, for the love of God," he cried, "let me alone! 'Rigoletto' is no longer for me."

But I insisted, explaining to him that they had asked for this opera with him in the cast.

"All right," he said, "if you must have it, then I shall sing it."

The next season we presented the revival. It is impossible to make clear now how bad a performance we gave. Every one, the artists, the orchestra, we were all agreed that it had been pretty bad. I was enraged with myself.

"Why did I give this role to Caruso?" I said to myself. "What was the use of the revival? It was not necessary. Tomorrow the critics will slay the poor fellow, who is so thoroughly conscientious."

And Caruso left the theatre that evening, followed by his usual entourage, which was always at his side. He had his collar up, and his head buried inside his coat. Every one was in vile humor, and no one spoke a word.

I went to my hotel, saying, "What stupidity to give this performance!" The next morning I did not even have the courage to go into the press room . . . where I usually glanced at the reviews. I was so sure of the accounts that I preferred not to see or ask anything, and I went directly to my own office. I sat there working, when I heard, from the end of the hall, the voice of Caruso. He was singing loudly and joyously the aria "La donna è mobile." He reached up to my door and knocked, still singing. I called out to him.

"Eh, Gatti," he cried out as soon as he walked in, "we had a success last night. Have you read the papers?"

"No," I said. "I have not read the papers, but I have no doubt of what they say."

"Well, look," Caruso cried out, and thrust several clippings on my desk. "A marvel! Every paper has a splendid account! Nothing but praise!"

I asked myself whether I was not mad. The artists had agreed with me in pronouncing the performance bad. It occurred to me, then, that what had happened was that "Rigoletto" had not been performed for a number of years and the magic of the opera had caused the writers to forget the bad performance.

Then Caruso said, "I think I can sing a good 'Rigoletto.' Last night I was tired. But now I am completely sure of myself."

The year after this revival we gave "Rigoletto" again, and this time we had a really good performance. The next day the critics wrote in terms of strong disfavor.

Caruso came to me early and said, "Tell me, Gatti, didn't I sing better than last year?"

"Yes, yes," I said.

"Have you read the papers?" he asked.

"I have seen them," I replied, "and it proves that a man like you does not need to read them. You are above all that sort of thing. The young artists are worried about what the papers say, what the critics say, but you shouldn't be. The press does its work. You should do yours, without worrying about them."

Giulio Gatti-Casazza
Memories of the Opera, 1941

Among the general public and opera aficionados alike the career of Enrico Caruso stands as one of the ultimate achievements in the art of singing. Blessed as he was with extraordinary natural ability, Caruso remained mindful of the need for careful husbanding of these gifts. And, in the latter part of his career, Caruso recorded some of his techniques in a practical guidebook entitled How to Sing.

Of the thousands of people who visit the opera during the season, few outside of a small proportion of the initiated realise how much the performance of a singer whom they see and hear on stage is dependent on previous rehearsal, constant practice, and watchfulness over the physical conditions that preserve that most precious of our assets, the voice.

Nor does the same great public know of what the singer often suffers in the way of nervousness or stage fright before appearing in front of the footlights, nor that his life, outwardly so fêted and brillant, is in private more or less of a retired, ascetic one, and that his social pleasures are strictly limited....

I am perhaps more favored than many in the fact that my voice was always "there," and that, with proper cultivation, of course, I have not had to overstrain it in the attempt to reach vocal heights which have come to some only after severe and long-continued effort. But, on the other hand, the finer the natural voice, the more sedulous the care required to preserve it in its pristine freshness and bloom. This is the singer's ever-present problem—in my case, however, mostly a matter of commonsense living.

... I wish to say here a word in regard to the practical significance of ... nervousness. Artists who do not experience it are those who lack real genius. There are really two kinds of fear—that arising from a realisation of the importance of what is to be done, the other from a lack of confidence in one's power. If a singer has no conscience in his performance he never is nervous, but full of assurance.

It is best to remain absolutely quiet and see no one on the day of the performance, so as not to be enervated by the effort of talking much, to say nothing of tiring the vocal cords. One prima donna of my acquaintance occupies herself in trimming hats on the days when she sings. ... It is just as well not to "pass through" the role that is to be sung on the day of appearing, but in the morning a few technical exercises to keep the voice in tune, as it were, are to be recommended. The great Italian singers of other days followed this rule, and it still holds good.

If the singer gives much of himself, as well as his voice, to the public, he should still hold his breathing supply in, so to speak, as he would guard the capital from which comes his income. Failure should thus be impossible if there is always a reserve to draw on. So the more one sings with good breath control the more beautiful the voice becomes.

We of the opera are often inclined to be superstitious. One woman, a distinguished and most intelligent artist, crosses herself repeatedly before taking her "cue," and a prima donna who is a favorite on two continents, and who is always escorted to the theatre by her mother, invariably goes through the very solemn ceremony of kissing her mother good-bye and receiving her blessing before going on to sing.

Another famous singer wears a small bracelet that was given to her [when an infant] by Gounod. She has grown somewhat stout of late years, and the hoop of gold has been reinforced so often that there is hardly any of the great composer's original gift left. Still, she feels that it is a charm which has made her success, and whether she sings the part of a lowly peasant or a princess the bracelet is always visible.

. . . These little traits, trivial in themselves, are of vital importance in that they create a sense of security in the soul of the artist, who goes on his way, if not rejoicing, at least convinced that the fates are not against him.

I would say to all young people who are ambitious to enter on a career of opera: Remember, it is a thoroughly hard-worked profession, after all; that even with a voice of requisite size and proper cultivation there is still a repertory of roles to acquire, taking long months and years of study and requiring a considerable feat of memory to retain . . . even after they are learned. Then there is the art of acting to be studied. . . . Then, as opera is sung nowadays, the knowledge of the diction of at least three languages—French, German and Italian—if not essential, is at least most helpful.

ENRICO CARUSO
How to Sing, 1913

The premiere performance of the Virgil Thomson-Gertrude Stein opera Four Saints in Three Acts *represented important firsts for many people involved in the production. It was the inaugural venture for a new theater built at the Wadsworth Athenaeum in Hartford, Connecticut, by its director A.E. (Chick) Austin; it was Thomson's first opera; and, finally, it was John Houseman's directorial debut. Naturally with so much at stake, the final few days of rehearsal became quite hectic, as Houseman describes in his autobiography,* Run-through.

On the afternoon of Wednesday, February 1, 1934, Virgil and I were driven up to Hartford, to be followed by Freddy [Frederick Ashton] and the company two days later. It was near zero when we arrived and it grew colder from day to day. Each evening thousands of starlings, chirping piteously, sought refuge under the eaves of the Wadsworth Athenaeum. But inside all was light and beauty and warmth. Unlike most new buildings, the Avery Memorial wing was complete and ready for its inauguration. . . .

Austin was there to welcome us and proudly took us on a grand tour of the Museum, ending with his new theatre in the basement. Then he drove us to his house for dinner, the last serious meal I was to have in a week. Over brandy, under the seventeenth-century Venetian panels, which were his latest acquisition, he informed us with a boyish smile that the Friends and Enemies [of Modern Music, sponsors of the performance] were in a financial bind. The ticket sale was going swimmingly: we were already sold out for three of our five performances. Unfortunately most of the tickets had been ordered by out-of-towners and would not be paid for until the people arrived. I pointed out that the cast and technicians expected to be paid before the weekend. Chick said he would try to think of something. Then he drove me back to the theatre where Feder and his men were at work spotting lines and hanging equipment on the empty stage. They were a curious crew: his close friend and counsellor, Teddy Thomas (born Tomashevsky of the illustrious Yiddish theatre dynasty), and a silent apprentice whose name I never knew—not even when he sliced off the tip of his little finger while cutting gelatins at five in the morning and we had to drive him to the hospital to have it sewn back on while Feder kept abusing him for getting blood on the equipment. Chief of the local helpers was a gargoyle of a man, bald as an egg, with a huge beak of a nose, a former acrobat and escape artist, whom Chick used as an assistant and victim in his magic shows. Since he was also something of a human fly, it was he who was sent up the high ladders to do all the impossible jobs. He never complained, but during one of our interminable night shifts we were startled by a loud, continuous, hollow banging overhead. It was the escape artist, high up on a twenty-foot ladder, bashing his head against the back wall of the theatre to keep himself awake.

I have said that the new wing was complete: this was not strictly true. Since the theatre lacked rigging, ropes, pipe, cable and many of the necessities of a professional stage, several cars and a truck were in constant motion between New York and Hartford that week bringing urgently needed equipment, over two hundred costumes, our so fragile props and the huge mass of our cellophane firmament, which arrived with Kate Lawson on Thursday morning and took all of that day and most of the following night to install. Owing to the lowness of the proscenium and grid it was impossible to achieve the feeling of sky and space suggested in Florine's models. Kate solved this, in part, by sewing hundreds of tapes into the mesh and then using these to create an infinite number of cellophane loops, which gave the impression of a grand opera drape ready to soar into the flies at any moment.

The company [which was all black] arrived with Freddy by bus at noon on Friday. They were greeted by the Negro Chamber of Commerce and billeted in black households all over town. That afternoon we began transferring our rehearsal movements to the stage. We worked until midnight, then sent the company home till noon of the

next day. As the singers left, the technicians moved in and began their nightly task of lighting the show.

Abe Feder was the first of the prima donnas in the American lighting field. *Four Saints* was his big chance, and he was determined to make the most of it at no matter what human cost. Lighting in those days, before electronic switchboards and reasonably reliable intercommunication systems existed, was an agonizing process of trial and error, of exasperated howling back and forth between the front and back of the house. And Florine Stettheimer's decor, with its dazzling, diamond-bright background was, in Feder's words, "a creeping bitch"—especially the first act, which she wanted inundated with pure white light. In vain Feder attempted to explain (to Florine, to Virgil, to me, to anyone who would listen) that there was no such thing as white light in the spectrum—that it was obtained by the expert mixing of primary colors projected through various shades of red, blue and yellow gelatin in the two hundred or more projectors with which he had covered the ceiling and sides of Chick's theatre. Florine repeated that she wanted clear white light—as in her model. Feder refused to believe her. For three successive nights he had the escape artist and his crew clambering up and down ladders, changing gelatins, which he then blended with infinite care and skill at diverse intensities. And each morning, when he proudly exhibited his night's work to Florine, she would say quietly that what she wanted was clear white light. Reluctant and unconvinced, he finally gave it to her at dress rehearsal, and she was grateful. He had a more rewarding time with the light blues and greens of the second act picnic and deeper cobalt of the Spanish sky darkening for the appearance of the Holy Ghost and achieving a livid splendor during the procession in the third.

On Sunday afternoon, with Kate Lawson alternately scolding and cajoling, we held a dress parade—act by act. . . . This was followed by a run-through in costume with props. . . . When it was over, I invited the company to meet me in the main court in front of the baroque marble nude. Against this impressive background, at one-thirty in the morning, I told them of the Friends and Enemies' financial straits. They looked at me and said nothing. I said we would be most grateful if they could wait until opening night for their money. Though most of them must have been close to penniless, not one of them demanded payment.

The next morning Alex Smallens and his orchestra of twenty arrived from New York and held their first musical reading in the pit, which could barely hold them. This resulted in one of our worst crises, the only time in thirty-seven years I have seen Virgil Thomson seriously shaken. To save money, he and Maurice [Grosser] had prepared the orchestral score together on the Mediterranean island of Porquerolles the previous summer: Virgil composing in pencil at the rate of ten pages a day and Maurice keeping up with him, going over the notes in ink. Proofreading by eye (no piano being available) proved unreliable: hundreds of errors survived in the score and were copied into the orchestral parts. Smallens was furious as hours and hundreds of dollars in musicians' overtime were spent while Virgil, white and tight-lipped, corrected his errors. But by the next evening we were ready to hold our first full dress rehearsal with orchestra. It ran far into the night with only one major blowup—the classic conflict of conductor and director over performers so placed on the stage that they had difficulty in following the beat. Smallens was a bully and a shouter. His yelling drove Freddy Ashton up the aisle in tears, stopping long enough to shout "I have worked with Sir Thomas Beecham! A genius! And he never spoke to me as you have!" before leaving the theatre. Since it was fifteen below zero outside, he returned almost immediately and the rehearsal continued. When it was over, members of the Saints' chorus on the upper tier of their pyramidal bleachers on either side of the stage complained that their off-stage ears had been blistered by seven hours of continuous exposure to Feder's massed overhead projectors.

On February seventh and eighth the New Haven Railroad added extra parlor cars to its afternoon train for the New York fashionables, the press and members of the international art world coming to Hartford to honor the new wing's opening and to see the Picasso show and the opera. It was known that Mrs. Harrison Williams, America's perennial best-dressed woman of the year, had ordered a special dress for the occasion: a cocktail dress on the train, it loosened to full-length for the reception and the theatre. I remember that evening vaguely as through a bright, heavy haze: the terrible cold outside as the cars began to arrive and the starlings screaming their heads off and the galleries overhead filled with people in evening dress with champagne glasses in their hands moving among the strong colors of the Picasso canvases.

Backstage everyone except me seemed surprisingly confident and relaxed. Fifteen minutes before curtain time I went out to get a breath of air. The birds were still screeching, and as I stood in the street for a moment, pierced by the icy wind, I became aware of an astonishing thing: silently, as in some German film of the early twenties, there appeared out of the darkness a huge smooth object unlike anything I had ever seen. Black and shiny and shaped like a gigantic raindrop, it came to a stop before the Museum; and from a sliding panel in its side stepped two beautiful ladies, one blonde and one dark, in shimmering evening dresses accompanied by a small, wiry, balding man in a dinner jacket, who, I discovered later, was Buckminster Fuller, creator of the Dymaxion car (of which this was the first specimen) escorting Dorothy Hale and Clare Boothe. Leaving their vehicle at the curb, they entered the building and disappeared into the crowd that was beginning to flow down from the galleries into the theatre.

When I got back downstairs the Saints were assembling on the stage, ascending their pyramids and checking their costumes and props. At 8:47 Chick Austin appeared to tell us that everyone was seated and we could begin. We embraced each other. Then the Saints took their opening positions and waited for the sharp drum roll that announced the start of the opera.

Since I spent the entire time of the performance rushing around backstage, checking entrances, light cues, props and effects, I do not have the faintest recollection of how the opera looked or sounded that night. Virgil was pleased and so, apparently—each in his own way— were our distinguished audience and critics.

JOHN HOUSEMAN
Run-through, 1972

No matter how well established an artist may be, each debut of a new work is an ordeal that affects him and those close to him. On September 11, 1951, Igor Stravinsky's The Rake's Progress *premiered at the Teatro la Fenice in Venice. In the audience was the composer's wife, Vera, whose observations on the evening's events and the preparations for it provide an intimate look at this opening night.*

Venice, September 11, 1951. A night of stifling heat and a sirocco that blows like a bellows. The alleys near the theater have been roped off to keep the Fourth Estate at bay during the arrival procession, though the Higher Estates come not as pedestrians but are deposited by gondolas and motor launches directly at the theater door from a strongly redolent canal. Our own (pedestrian) party includes Nadia Boulanger (who carries Igor's valises), Wystan Auden and Chester Kallman (both nervous in spite of liquid fortifications—a moat of martinis, in fact), Stephen Spender (shy, deferential), and Louis MacNeice (handsome, arrogantly silent, but perhaps pickled).

A familiar unfamiliar face veers toward me as I enter the foyer, but no sooner have I identified it as Maxim Gorky's adopted son, Zinovy Peshkov (last seen in the Caucasus during the Revolution), than others crowding around me crowd General Peshkov out. The list of old friends who have come to criticize and otherwise "assist" at the performance is too copious to be continued.

La Fenice, the most beautiful theater in the world, has never glittered as it does tonight in honor of the debut, and as an extra garnishing, bouquets of roses, like debutantes' corsages, have been pinned to each loge. Unfortunately, the beauty of these stalls on the inside is even less than "skin deep." The plush seems to have had chicken—or rather, moth—pox, and it and everything else is badly in need of deodorants. Another discomfort is that the seats are like European railroad compartments. The occupants on the side nearer the stage (i.e., the men) face in the wrong direction as if their ears were encased in their legs and abdomens, like grasshoppers.

The audience glitters, too; everyone, that is, except a New York newspaperman who has no doubt already prepared a jobbery on the event consistent with his apparel and life-long devotion to the commonplace. (*Note:* Air travel was not yet the rule at that time and therefore neither were blue denims and Beethoven sweaters.)

In Italy nothing respectable begins on time. During tonight's long delay my thoughts drift back through the weeks of preparation, to the first conferences with stage directors and music coaches, which took place in Naples. I spent the mornings in the Naples aquarium then, drawing an old *joli laide* crustacean, a "liquid prisoner pent in walls of glass" (Shakespeare). But I also think, during the wait, about echoes in the opera of Igor's so-called private life—of how, for example, the card game stemmed from his own fondness for cards; to me, Shadow's harpsichord arpeggio is an imitation of Igor's way of shuffling cards, as the *staccato* of that instrument recalls the way he snaps playing cards on a table. Perhaps Auden had actually observed Igor playing solitaire and heard him utter Russian *gros mots* when the wrong card appeared, which may have given him the idea for "the Deuce!" I think, too, of how the *Epilogue*, and the idea of pointing to the audience—"you and you"—was inspired by Walter Huston in *The Devil and Daniel Webster*, a film Igor admired.

At 21:35, a prompt thirty-five minutes late, Igor enters the pit and bows to the audience which, though ultra *mondaine*, applauds him with (it seems to me) a core of genuine appreciation. He then turns quickly to the orchestra so that we can see only his extraordinary occipital bumps and small, vital beat. The singers are Robert Rounseville, who has only recently emerged, or not quite fully emerged, from a film career and manner, but who is aptly cast as Tom Rakewell; Elizabeth Schwarzkopf, who is a cool and perfect Anne; Hugues Cuénod, a subtle, mysterious, and believable Sellem; and Jennie Tourel, who as the diva, Baba, could swagger through her grand exit on an elephant without risking a snigger from the audience. At first-act intermission we drink *caffè espresso* in the Campo San Fantin, mercifully rescued from impertinent judgments by the unforgettable effect on everyone of Frl. Schwarzkopf's high C.

Igor claims no more for the music than that it is conventional, but what beautiful *inventions* are in it, too. I would mention, for a preliminary list, the chord progressions at the end of the first half of the Cavatina, the modulation to "O wilful powers" (following Anne's "how evil in the purple prose they seem"), the transformation of the Ballad Tune in the final two scenes, and the double appoggiaturas, those wonderfully style-embalmed representations of Tom's graveyard fear which reappear during his madness. But it seems to me that Igor has saved the finest moments of all for the final scene. These are the music of "Venus, mount thy throne," the duet "In a foolish dream," and—the most touching music Igor ever wrote—Tom's "Where art thou, Venus?"

The *prima assoluta* is tentative in many ways, and it shows more "might" as the preterite of "may" than power; at every change of tempo the opera could "fall apart" (as the Americans say). Nevertheless, it conveys much of the opera's "inner resonance" (as the British say), and all of us except the unglittering New Yorker are deeply moved. The post-mortem party does not break up until . . . dawn.

VERA STRAVINSKY
Themes and Episodes, 1966

Although today it clearly ranks as one of the major opera companies in the world, in its early years the New York City Opera depended upon generous amounts of energy and inventiveness to compensate for the small budgets and cramped performing quarters provided by the City Center. But as the distinguished director Margaret Webster recalls in her autobiography Don't Put Your Daughter on the Stage, *in spite of these handicaps the City Opera produced an outstanding repertoire of classic and modern operas.*

Once upon a time the Met had a poor relation who lived in a hideous old building up on West 55th Street. It was a Masonic Temple which the city had taken over for nonpayment of taxes, and it housed indigent opera, indigent ballet and fragments of penniless drama. Now the New York City Opera Company confronts its rival from an equally stately palace across the Plaza at Lincoln Center. Fountains splash for both alike; distinguished feet cross the patio toward both imposing portals; rival *Traviata*'s resound from west and south; and the New York City Opera very often wins on points. I don't know whether they like each other any better. In my day the Met was lofty and disparaging about the City Opera, and the poor relation was spiteful, envious and resentful about that old rich-bitch downtown. I should be surprised if propinquity has bred affection.

I have said that the old Met ran on zeal. So did the City Center; even more zeal and far, far less money. There were no VIP nights, no white ties and tiaras, but a large "popular-price" audience. Opera was sung almost always in English by mostly American singers. New American operas were produced here often; very rarely at the Met. Of the four I directed, two should certainly have been done by the Met (William Walton's *Troilus and Cressida* and Strauss's *Schweigsame Frau*); one never could have been (Vittorio Giannini's *Taming of the Shrew*); and one *was*—good old Verdi again, with *Macbetto*.

Bing's reason for not doing new operas was that his audience would only support a very limited number of performances, too few to make so much as a dent in the production costs. When he put a tentative toe into the waters of novelty, even so distinguished a novelty as Stravinsky's *The Rake's Progress*, the best he could get from it was seven performances spread over two seasons. The New York City Company gave only five of *Troilus and Cressida*, also spread over two seasons; but they somehow managed to make *Faust* or "Cav and Pag" subsidize a lot more experimental work than the Met ever got out of *Carmen* and *Aida*.

At first the City Opera paid no rent, though it always paid taxes; from 1954 it paid 1½ percent of the gross as rent; but it got no subsidy, ran on a tiny budget, and had to raise funds from opera lovers just like the Met. The President of the City Council, Newbold Morris in my day, was a member of its Board and Morton Baum its ardent moving spirit. The vague aura of public service which clung to it only meant that everyone was desperately underpaid. It was always in a chronic state of deficit—as it is still, on a far grander scale, despite some public subsidy. It played regular seasons at the City Center, sharing the building with George Balanchine's New York City Ballet Company and sporadic infusions of musical comedy or plays. With the aid of short tours it managed to keep together a company which, while not "permanent," was reasonably steady.

I had reason to know "the Mecca Temple," to give it its old name, all too well. I had done battle with its problems twice for Maurice Evans and once (*Richard III*) for José Ferrer during the drama seasons. The auditorium lacked charm to a spectacular degree and was very difficult either to sing or speak in. The stage had reasonable depth but no side space whatever. The electrical equipment had been salvaged from Noah and Sons; but it was less complicated to handle and far more imaginatively used than the Met monsters. The rehearsal space was even more limited, the chorus every bit as hardworked, the pressures were just as lethal—but somehow it was a good deal more fun; perhaps it was because nobody expected so much, and they were always being agreeably surprised.

The first opera I did there, in 1955, was William Walton's *Troilus and Cressida*. The original production had only recently taken place, at Covent Garden. I had not seen it, there were no recordings and no one to play me the score. The libretto was a fine piece of work in its own right. I knew the author, Christopher Hassall, and through him met Walton in London and got permission from the BBC to hear the recording they had taken from a Covent Garden broadcast. Lots of chorus again, and extras and costumes and complicated scenery, but glorious music and all in English and all new to everybody. . . . The singers were all American, the bass a Chinese American, the baritone a Negro. Josef Rosenstock conducted and Phyllis Curtin sang Cressida.

Not least, the composer and author had written the opera with contemporary theatre minds. Hassall was an actor and a playwright as well as a poet; Walton loved words as much as he did notes; and above all, no one had been able to coach the singers in prefabricated, second-hand, "traditional" interpretations. They had learned the score, of course, and were musically prepared, but Dr. Rosenstock and I "got at them," if I may so phrase it, together. I had always thought this was the way things should be. All four of the operas I did at the City Center were entirely new to the singers. At the same time there was a continuity of personnel and musical staff which gave cohesion to the company, and though there were no great singing "names," the cast stayed put. This, however, did involve dangers. When Troilus got a throat infection a few days before we opened, there was nobody else on the American continent who had ever sung the role or even studied it. Mercifully, he recovered in time. The Chorus were as full of effort and good will as they had been at the Met, and there were the usual small, fat tenor and gaunt, elderly bass, always in the wrong places at the wrong time.

There came one really terrible day when I found out that the designer had allocated to the Chorus in the last act a wide assortment of clothing which bore no relation whatever either to who was supposed to be what or to the various vocal divisions. Cooks' sons, Dukes' sons and sons of Earls for whom the City Center couldn't afford belts, jostled each other impartially, mixing first tenors with second basses "irregardless" and hopelessly shattering my careful plans. The only thing I had absolutely counted on was the only thing there wasn't, viz: an army.

I realized I would have to restage the entire scene overnight, unless Rosenstock would allow me to mix the voices. He was sympathetic, but adamant. The costumes, limited by budget, had been fitted and could not be changed. Working almost all night I managed to get everybody sorted out in time for the day's rehearsal, at the expense of a couple of extra pairs of tights and a slight lack of solidarity among the second tenors. I also discovered that the Chorus had never had a chance to read the libretto and tended to think it was Shakespeare's. They were simultaneously rehearsing *Carmen, Bohème, Golden Slippers* (a new production), *The Merry Wives of Windsor, The Love of Three Oranges* and *Cenerentola*. I marveled. The executive staff worked even harder. They all seemed to have acquired a peculiar yellowish-grey pallor and didn't always have time to get together with a razor.

The opera season opened while *Troilus* was still in rehearsal and every singer was needed to work on some other opera. It was hard to do a sextet with two principals, one understudy and the pianist. Walton arrived, which frightened everybody very much but quite unnecessarily. It was odd to have a real, live composer around; odder still to hear him refer to the tenor's most tenorish aria as "that beastly little tune." He seemed pleased and was helpful except for one rather strange orchestra rehearsal when he himself conducted in the Pit and Rosenstock duplicated from a small podium behind him.

The opening night went well, except for one episode.... Much of the plot centered around a crimson scarf given by Troilus to Cressida (Act I), by her to Diomed (Act II) and fought over by the two men (Act III). After Troilus's death it was absolutely essential for her to have it in her hands for her final aria, to hide the sword with which she kills herself. Despite Awful Warnings from me to Troilus, Cressida and the two soldiers who had to drag the body of Troilus offstage... the scarf got dragged off with him. No end to opera. A swift, silent mass evacuation of the auditorium by me, Julius Rudel and sundry others, a frantic dash backstage; somehow we managed to push it back, under a curtain; somehow Cressida saw it, retrieved it, sang about it, killed herself with élan. I aged several years.

The reviews were fine and the libretto praised as it deserved. But oh, I thought, all this blood, sweat and tears for something which will be seen exactly five times! If it is wearing and dispiriting to direct opera, surely only lunatics with a strong bent toward self-immolation can devote years of their time and talents to writing it.

MARGARET WEBSTER
Don't Put Your Daughter on the Stage, 1972

During his twenty-three years as general manager of the Metropolitan Opera, Sir Rudolf Bing established a reputation as a skillful master of his company. In a volume of memoirs published in 1972, Bing gives those on the outside a glimpse of the many competing needs and desires he had to balance in order to produce a season at the Met.

Planning the schedule is the opera manager's expertise. There is an almost endless chain of considerations before firm decisions can be made. The first step is to look at the two preceding seasons and decide which operas you wish to repeat and which you don't, considering primarily the success of the productions and how often a particular work has been done in the past. Then you look at what hasn't been done and deserves to be done, either as a revival or as a new production. In my twenty-two years at the Metropolitan I had an average of about four new productions a season, involving something like eighty operas— *Aida, Carmen, Cav* and *Pag, Faust, Fidelio, Otello, Traviata,* and *Tristan* were each given two new productions in my time.

You must ask how many different productions you need, which is partly a function of the works chosen. If you have *Pelléas et Mélisande* or *Wozzeck* on the list, you know that you cannot schedule twelve or fifteen performances of it, because the public will not come. Every *Pelléas* or *Wozzeck* must be balanced by a *Traviata* or a *Bohème*. You must ask, have I got a cast? Special problems arise: for years I felt the Metropolitan could not do *Falstaff,* because I could not imagine either a *Falstaff* with Leonard Warren or . . .without him. Once an artist forced me to give an opera by refusing to accept an engagement unless that work were scheduled—Renata Tebaldi simply had to sing the glamorous actress Adriana Lecouvreur in New York. (Then she took sick and canceled, and we had to do the wretched opera *without* Tebaldi.) Once an opening night had to be changed late in the planning process, when Joan Sutherland decided she was not yet ready to attempt *Norma.* More commonly, the problem is simply the availability of a necessary star: there is very little chance of doing *Carmen* successfully at the Metropolitan unless you have under contract at least one, and preferably two, internationally known Carmens.

The need for "covers" complicates planning at all stages. In Frankfurt, if someone is ill, the manager can put in a call to Hamburg or Cologne or Munich or Zurich at two in the afternoon, and borrow a mezzo-soprano for the night. I could call Hartford, Connecticut, until I was blue in the face without finding a possible Carmen. And an opera like *Carmen* is easy, because there are only a few difficult roles to cast. Consider *Die Walküre,* with its eight Valkyries in addition to the principal singers; to cast *Die Walküre,* the Metropolitan should have sixteen of them. The Three Ladies needed for *The Magic Flute* become six ladies at the Metropolitan. In my early years, most singers came by the week, and were permitted to take outside engagements only with the consent of the management; they could cover performances they were not scheduled to sing. But now nearly all even slightly important singers are engaged on a per-performance basis. You have someone who sings Wednesday whom you would like to have as a cover for a role on Saturday; but he takes an engagement in Philadelphia on Friday, and that's that.

Important artists hate to cover, and do so only when there is a husband or a lover or a baby in New York to make the sacrifice of pride seem worthwhile. Among my most unpleasant duties during my last years at the Metropolitan were the annual negotiations with Lucine Amara, who was invaluable for this purpose: a well-trained artist with an accurate, flexible voice, she could be counted on to manage at least acceptably most of the soprano roles in the Italian repertory—but somehow she had never acquired the projection of a star. In return for her courtesy in covering, she was entitled to whatever courtesies I could offer and when a role suited to her low-profile temperament came up in a new production—Ellen, the schoolteacher, in *Peter Grimes*—I felt obliged to assign it to her, even though Georg Solti, who was to conduct, had a rival candidate for the role and left our roster when Miss Amara was chosen.

Quite apart from such moral obligations, you must ask yourself *practically*, to whom do I owe a new production? In the normal course of events, most artists couldn't care less about new productions: they would just as soon not rehearse. But starring in a new production has become a status symbol, and all the artists fight for the roles. Indeed, they even fight to have the first night in a revived older production, because the critics come to the first nights. Fortunately, we have two plums on the tree, because the broadcast rates almost as highly as the premiere in the status it confers.

Once the new productions are determined, you must put together the team of conductor, director, and designer who can bring about the result. Bringing together director and designer is one of a general manager's hardest jobs for these two must work on terms of complete conceptual harmony. . . .

Having chosen repertory, you must decide where on the year's program to place each opera. The first problem is opening night. Certain operas, in general the most popular, lend themselves to opening nights, and others do not. *Pelléas* is impossible—it's . . . an opera where people go off to Sherry's in the intermission and don't come back for the next act. Ordinarily *Don Carlo* would not be a good opening-night opera, either, but we got away with it, twice.

Placement of opera must be governed by the availability of singers. Corelli comes for perhaps three months, and will not sing more than six times a month. (Planning seasons in the 1960s, I always talked first to Corelli, and always signed him last. He would say yes, then no, then I don't think so; he would come in and talk out his troubles, and I would say, "Well, Franco. . . .") Miss Nilsson comes for less than two months; certain Wagner operas have been all but unthinkable without her, though the new management will have to start thinking. Miss Price, having accepted a silly theory about the dangers of overexposure, may be available as little as three or four times a season. Miss Sutherland will sing only if her husband conducts. The sequence in which roles appear is important in determining whether an artist can undertake two parts: a soprano needs more time to go from *Aida* to *Traviata* (lightening the voice) than to go from *Traviata* to *Aida*.

You must worry constantly about the subscribers. People have to get a mixture—a certain number of Italian works, a certain number of German works, a French opera, a Mozart if there is one, a modern if they're unlucky. Each subscription series justly demands its share of the electrifying artists and of the new productions. Obviously, rehearsal schedules must be meshed with performances. You find you cannot do *Tristan* on the night you had planned because that day you need a stage rehearsal of *Turandot*, and Miss Nilsson can't do both. Indeed, technically, the stage itself can't do both. Some days . . . the stage is unavailable to performers, because the designer needs it for lighting rehearsals. At the new house in Lincoln Center the machinery is so complicated that whole days must be reserved for its maintenance. Now that we make all our own sets, and nearly all our own costumes, there are other scheduling needs, for the shops must never be without work: designers must deliver their designs according to a prearranged schedule that may have relatively little to do with when the opera is to be put onstage.

Then there are the union contracts, which become more burdensome with each renewal. What were once "weekly artists" who sang comprimario roles as needed are now "plan artists" who can be asked to sing twice and cover three times or sing once and cover four times, according to complicated formulas. You write in Velis for a role, and the watchdogs come and say, "That takes him over his number for the week, it will cost X dollars penalty," and you take Velis out and put in someone not as good.

Under the 1969 contracts, the chorus cannot be asked to sing more than five performances a week without the imposition of heavy overtime penalties. Making the final plans for 1971–72, back in 1970, we had everything lined up just so—Nilsson's dates and Corelli's dates, Böhm's dates, Colin Davis's dates, the new productions, the rehearsals, the covers, the plan artists, the balance among the different subscription series—and suddenly somebody looked at the list and said: "Oh, my God, there's no chorus-free opera that week." And somebody else—I think it was I—said, "Oh, forget it; that's just tough," Someday . . . all these things will be done by computer; I have no desire to see it. . . .

Yet despite all this complexity, I believe we created at the Metropolitan Opera an atmosphere in which people worked effectively and cheerfully. Our plans almost always held up. In twenty-two years, the Metropolitan missed only three-and-a-half performances—one in the power blackout, two in the aftermath of the assassination of President Kennedy, and one half when Leonard Warren died onstage in the middle of a performance. Conductors and directors both almost always received as many rehearsals as they said they needed (as early as 1953, I was able to promise Monteux no fewer than eight orchestra rehearsals for *Pelléas et Mélisande*); and the fact is, despite much apparently authoritative statement to the contrary, that the average Metropolitan Opera performance has more rehearsal hours behind it than the average performance at any other opera house in the world. Moreover, everyone in the house knows long in advance exactly what will be expected of him—not only the performance schedule but the full rehearsal schedule is fixed many months ahead.

SIR RUDOLF BING
5,000 Nights at the Opera, 1972

Since Sarah Caldwell founded the Opera Company of Boston in 1958, that city has been treated to operatic performances that reach consistently high levels of excellence and excitement. The combination of talent and attention to detail that makes Miss Caldwell one of the world's leading opera directors was succinctly captured in a New Yorker *magazine profile by Winthrop Sargeant.*

In her appearance and manner, Miss Caldwell reminds one of a gentle locomotive. She stands about five feet five and weighs in the neighborhood of two hundred pounds, and carries herself with remarkable agility for such a large woman. Her energy is boundless. She has been known to rehearse her cast half the night and then roll herself up in a piece of carpet and go to sleep in the aisle of the theatre. Her habits of dress are correspondingly offhand. She wears an old print dress summer and winter, covered in cold weather by an overcoat that looks like a bathrobe. In winter, she wears boots indoors and out; in summer, sneakers. Her gray-streaked hair is parted slightly to one side and then functionally combed back, and during rehearsals she wears horn-rimmed glasses, through which she peers at scores, the stage, and the orchestra. Her voice is a deep contralto (it has even been described as a baritone), and when she is conducting a full stage rehearsal she often makes a megaphone of her hands and roars at the people onstage. Despite all this, Miss Caldwell is a very feminine woman. Her manner at more intimate rehearsals is invariably gentle, humorous, and infinitely patient. She addresses the singers who are working with her as "ladies and gentlemen." She often takes suggestions from them, and makes her own suggestions in the form of questions ("Shouldn't we all look up at this point?") or as tentative proposals ("I think it would be better if you stood over there"). She practically never loses her temper, and when she does the only evidence of it is a slightly reddened patch in the middle of each cheek. Most of the time, with her bulky figure dressed any which way, with her spectacles askew and her hair hanging straight around her face, she could be taken for the theatre's janitress rather than its director. Only when she has finished rehearsing does she get her hair set, in anticipation of a curtain call . . . , and this, she claims, is to please her mother, with whom she shares a Boston apartment.

Actually, it is inaccurate to describe Miss Caldwell as an operatic stage director. Sarah Caldwell *is* the Opera Company of Boston. She herself conducts most of its performances. She sits in on all the meetings of the company's board of directors and helps raise money to cover its budget. She decides which prominent singers to hire, and what operas to produce. She is . . . Boston's all-purpose operatic impresario. . . . In short, she can do everything connected with the production of an opera except sing it, and when she functions merely as a stage director she is using only a fraction of her talents.

These talents approach genius, and consequently, as the old saying has it, consist of infinite pains. She begins by learning the score of the opera in question at the piano . . . . Then she immerses herself in a study of everything that has ever been written about the opera—the circumstances in which it was composed, the style of the period, the composer's notes and correspondence concerning it, any variations in tradition as to its performance . . . the general history of the period of composition, such variations in the manuscript as have turned up from time to time, and so on. By the time she has finished all this, she has become an encyclopedia on the subject. Her next step is to work with her designers, usually Herbert Senn and Helen Pond. This involves much more than merely turning out a stage set or two. She often takes Mr. Senn and Miss Pond to Europe to examine the background of the opera and to hear different performances of it. . . . Once these preliminary decisions have been made, Miss Caldwell begins holding a series of conferences—with her board of directors about expenses, with her designers about the geography of the stage, with her electricians about the lighting, with her prop man about where props are to be placed, and so on. Then she is ready for sessions with her performers, who come to Boston eager and willing to spend all the time on rehearsals that she may require. At first, these sessions consist merely of discussions—not about musical matters but about characterization, the general tone of the opera, and how each character fits into the whole. Then comes the coaching of each singer in his role—a process in which a pianist helps by playing the orchestral score while the singer sings his part. "After that, the flurry of concentration begins," Miss Caldwell says. "Up to this time, it has been a pleasant and leisurely experience, but now everything is in dead earnest." The process that follows differs markedly from that used by most other stage directors. She takes her dramatic cues not from the libretto but from the music. After each singer has been rehearsed separately, all the members of the cast are brought together and rehearsed as a unit. Unlike most of her colleagues, Miss Caldwell never starts by blocking a scene. "I don't like to do that," she said recently. "It leads to concentration on mechanical problems and kills spontaneity. From the very beginning, I focus on character and on musical matters. The text provides clues, of course. In the legitimate theatre, you can time things easily. Not so in opera. In opera, the inflection of the words and music suggests what one does." On another occasion, she said, "I'm no Svengali. I never try to force a

preconceived notion of a role on any artist. I work with what the artist already has, and try to arrive at the character as reflected through his or her own personality, letting the artist achieve the best that he can at that moment of his career." Thus, Sarah Caldwell productions of the same opera . . . with different casts would be altogether dissimilar, because of differences in the artists' personalities. "One person must be responsible for the style of a production, but the most interesting part of this profession is collaboration," Miss Caldwell continued. "Every chorister must feel responsible for a separate characterization. A chorister is an important artist. The idea is to stimulate each person onstage to his best efforts. Opera represents an extraordinary level of achievement, and opera singers, despite rumors to the contrary, are highly intelligent people. An opera singer *has* to be intelligent. Otherwise, considering the competition, he would never get anywhere. The idea that I mold artists like clay is nonsense. I simply sit down with the singer and help him save time. Of course, chamber music represents a high order of achievement, too. But chamber music involves the best efforts of only a few players, who rehearse together. An opera singer has to create a whole dramatic life. He has to sing, dance, and do many other things. It's no wonder operatic artists are occasionally nervous."

The spectacle of Miss Caldwell during a rehearsal is an interesting one. She is a master of the English language and always makes remarkably articulate comments. She employs an assistant, who wanders around the stage area taking notes and seeing to it that orders are carried out precisely. ("All assistants expect to be stage directors themselves someday," she remarked to a reporter during one of these rehearsals, and when things are in full swing she sometimes allows her assistant to take over.) Almost invariably, there will be a number of children looking on from crannies of the auditorium. Some are children of the Opera Company trustees, some belong to members of the cast, and others have simply wandered in off the street. Miss Caldwell refers to them as "the knothole gang," and from time to time she employs a few of them as supernumeraries. A Boston critic once complained, "Is it absolutely necessary for Miss Caldwell to use children in every performance?" The knothole gang was as outraged at this slight as any prima donna would have been. "Did you see what that sour s.o.b. on the *Herald* wrote?" one of them exclaimed to her the following day. Miss Caldwell is also lavish in her use of animals. She feels they add flavor to a production, and at one time or another she has used ponies, dogs, cats, bears, horses, monkeys—and even Peruvian llamas. During her production of Arnold Schoenberg's "Moses and Aaron," which she presented for the first time in America, she was a bit too lavish with animal life. There is an orgy scene in "Moses and Aaron," and she thought that some animals would add a pagan flavor to it. "I had engaged some sheep and goats and a calf from a theatrical-animal supply house, but I hadn't thought about where they were to be kept," she said. "The only possible place was under a ramp in front of the stage. But during the final rehearsals the animals bleated and bawled to such an extent that

the music could hardly be heard." Osborne McConathy, a former horn
player with the Boston Symphony, who at that time conducted many
of Miss Caldwell's productions, was presiding in the pit as patiently as
he could, but eventually he could take no more. "It's either me or the
animals," he told Miss Caldwell. Miss Caldwell gave in, and though
the production may have been a bit less colorful, it was at least audible
on opening night.

WINTHROP SARGEANT
The New Yorker, December 24, 1973

*Frustrated in his attempts to gain more substantial roles, the American
tenor James McCracken and his wife, soprano Sandra Warfield, left
contracts at the Metropolitan Opera Company in 1957 in order to
study and work in Europe. However, even in the capital of Italian
opera, Milan, McCracken faced important obstacles to his advancement.*

We were in Italy because we thought it the only place where we could
get a real start singing Italian opera. It seemed to me that all you had to
be was an Italian tenor and Mr. Bing would engage you very quickly at
the Met. We weren't Italian, but if we could make good in Italy, this
Italian aura would rub off on us, and Mr. Bing would call us back. We
had been at the Met and we were going back there. . . .   ,

Milan was and is the headquarters of Italian opera. Many of the
aspiring singers we met said they would much rather have lived in
Rome, but Milan was the place to be, and there must have been a mil-
lion aspiring singers there, studying with all the best teachers, waiting
in the outer offices of all the important agents, hoping for a chance to
audition. Theoretically a singer could audition in Milan for impresarios
from opera houses anywhere in Italy, or for that matter anywhere in
the world—even Moscow. The impresarios would come to an agent
and ask him to set up an audition. The agent controlled who sang at
each audition.

I began to make the rounds of the agents: Anseloni, Finzi, Moresco,
Vaccari, Del Signore. On our first tour two summers before, still under
contract to the Metropolitan Opera, these people had all been eager to
hear me. But now they were remarkably difficult to get in to see.

I didn't speak Italian well enough to do any business on the phone.
The only thing was to sit in their outer offices waiting till they would
see me. Also there was always the chance that someone I knew would
come in, some conductor or impresario. Not only could I get a line
from him on what was going on, he might even be holding auditions
there in the agent's office—and once the agent saw that I knew the
man, he couldn't very well refuse me the chance to sing for him.

It didn't take long to realize that Signor Liduino was the great Italian agent. He was like an octopus; he sat over everything in Italy.
There wasn't anything happening in the musical world that Liduino
didn't have his tentacles on, or his say-so—yes or no. So there was only

one thing to do: to see if I couldn't get into the graces of Liduino. I went to Liduino's office and sat there. Some days I sat there for five or six hours and no one so much as nodded to me; other days something might happen.

In those days I was dyeing my hair black. I hoped it would make me look more Italian. The Italians couldn't pronounce my name, so the black hair didn't help very much. I refused to change my name to something Italian, but I did have calling cards printed up on which I changed James to Giacomo . . . and added a vowel to my last name, so it wouldn't start with four straight consonants. This gave the Italians at least a chance to pronounce it. The calling cards read:

GIACOMO MAC CRACKEN

TENORE

Once in a great while, after waiting in the outer office, I would actually get in to see the great man, Signor Liduino. He would promise to get me something soon and tell me that I had to have patience. To this day, I don't understand why he didn't just tell me that there was no use waiting around there and to go on back to wherever I came from. Once in a while he would throw me a crumb and allow me to audition for someone there, in his suite of offices, usually someone from a town so small I didn't even know where it was. . . .

As spring drew near and I still hadn't sung anywhere, even a single performance, I noticed in the paper where several conductors whom I had worked with or had contact with in the past were coming to Milan to give concerts. I remember, and get a kind of sick feeling in my stomach even now, how I forced myself to approach them and ask, "Do you remember? I'm James McCracken. I sang the Majordomo in *Rosenkavalier* with you at the Metropolitan Opera." I would ask how long they were going to be in Milan and would they possibly have time to hear me sing. Rudolph Kempe heard me the next morning after such an occasion and was very encouraging. I cornered Thomas Schippers after his rehearsal and asked him to have a Campari with me at Biffi's. I had sung the student in *Tales of Hoffman* with him at the Met, one of my better parts: a half a dozen good phrases. I convinced him over that drink that he'd really never heard me and should listen to me again. Several days later I auditioned for him and Gian-Carlo Menotti. They gave me plenty of time, talked to me afterwards and encouraged me to keep trying. This did a lot more for my morale than waiting in the office of Liduino. After the concert by Leonard Bernstein, I went backstage to ask him if he remembered me. I had done a small part in the *Mamelles de Tirésias* at Brandeis University with him in 1953. But when I saw how exhausted he was—he really looked dead on his feet —I didn't have the nerve to ask him for his time. So I remember I told him how much I enjoyed his conducting and the concert and I left. I went home disappointed in myself that I didn't have more guts; but now, ten years later, knowing how I feel after some performances of *Otello*, I'm sure that I did the right thing. . . .

[Herbert] Von Karajan was coming to Milan for a concert. I heard he was having auditions on the stage of La Scala and decided to try to crash the party. However, I had no appointment, and the auditions had been arranged for Liduino's singers. Herr Mattoni, Von Karajan's secretary, said that if there happened to be time at the end of the audition, the Maestro might hear me. He put me in a little room off the stage with the other singers, all of them nervously clearing their throats and humming. We could hear whoever was singing onstage. We heard one tenor blow all his high notes. The room emptied out until only I was left, at which point Mattoni announced that the auditions were over and that I should then go home. I pushed Herr Mattoni aside, walked out on the stage, put the music in front of the befuddled accompanist, and started to sing. It was the *Turandot* aria "*Nessun dorma.*" I always had something short so that I could get through one whole aria before people stopped me. Von Karajan listened, and asked me to sing something else. I did. He then told me to come back the next day and sing the *Meistersinger* aria.

I did that too.

He is a very small man. He had gray in his hair, looked about forty-five, and was built like a sprinter. He was the emperor of opera in Austria.

He said, "That's it." He spoke to Mattoni in German, and went out.

Von Karajan is as efficient as a robot. He knows how much time it takes to change his shirt on the way to his car. He exuded efficiency even when standing there listening to me. . . .

When he was gone, Mattoni said, "Herr von Karajan said that if you will learn Bacchus in *Ariadne auf Naxos*, he will give you one performance in Vienna next season."

I went home elated. There were tears in my eyes, I was so hysterical. I told Sandra, "The most famous conductor in Europe has hired me for Vienna." We bought the records and the score that very day—they cost more than twenty dollars, a fortune to us—and I started in to study the part immediately. It was a terrific part.

JAMES MCCRACKEN AND SANDRA WARFIELD
A Star in the Family, 1971

In the past several years Beverly Sills has emerged as one of the reigning operatic performers of this era. Beyond her superb abilities as a singer and actress, Miss Sills possesses the aplomb of a seasoned trouper as she proved in the spring of 1974 when she stepped on stage at the New York State Theater to perform—without benefit of rehearsal—in a production of La Traviata.

Champagne glass in hand, Beverly Sills was beaming as she spun gracefully through the crowd on stage in the first act of "La Traviata." She was doing what theater people call bits of business—flirting here, laughing there, sharing a toast with someone on the side.

She was singing, too, of course—exquisitely. But theater people have another term for what she was doing most of all: Miss Sills was winging it.

An hour before the opera began, she had set foot on the New York City Opera's "Traviata" set for the very first time. At the last moment in the best tradition of the "show must go on" spirit, she had agreed to pinch hit in a crisis and sing the role of Violetta in Verdi's opera, without a rehearsal, in a production she had never even seen before. Had she not done so, there would have been no opera at the New York State Theater Wednesday night.

When it was all over, the audience was in a riotous state of ecstasy. They had arrived expecting a production of "Medea." And now they were whistling, cheering, screaming, stamping their feet and throwing confetti at Miss Sills.

"It may be a terrible admission," said Julius Rudel, the company's director and maestro, "but sometimes the spontaneity itself can do wonders. A performance in those circumstances can be . . . galvanizing."

No one would have disagreed that evening, least of all the stage hands, extras and members of the chorus who worked frantically for a smooth production and, in moments at ease, stood transfixed in the wings, gaping as Miss Sills improvised with exuberance.

For the audience, the story-book evening began when Mr. Rudel emerged on stage at 8 P.M., announced the cancellation of "Medea" because of the illness of its star, Maralin Niska, and told how the only soprano available for the night was Miss Sills.

She had sung the part some 275 times, but never before with Mr. Rudel at the podium, and never before in this production, which makes a great many directorial demands on the singers. But, said Mr. Rudel, "wonderful trouper and member of the company as she is, Miss Sills has agreed to do it."

At the same time, Miss Sills had requested that newspapers not review her performance.

Only moments before, Miss Sills, in a radiant white organza and silk taffeta gown, was sitting at a pink circular divan at center stage, toying with her gardenia and concentrating on Mr. Rudel's last-minute instructions.

Having sung two "Anna Bolenas" the week before, and scheduled to do "I Puritani" the night following, she and the conductor had decided to dispense with rehearsals as too taxing.

"I don't mind if you linger a bit on 'Addio,'" Mr. Rudel was saying.

"Fine," she replied, and then grinning mischievously, added: "In case you forget, I'll be the rather tall girl in the red hair standing somewhere in the middle of things."

The curtain rose, and suddenly Miss Sills, as Violetta, was giddy from champagne at her party for her friends. Not one of the two dozen chorus members, partygoers all, had the slightest idea of where she was going to move, but move she did.

At the end of the rollicking drinking song, the chorus members darted away, only to stand in the wings and watch Miss Sills launch into "Sempre Libera." One singer clutched her fists and whispered: "Sing it, baby!"

Just before Act II, Miss Sills was being told where to move, and at which point, by Patrick Bakman, the twenty-nine-year-old stage director. She was looking very dubious.

"Now," said Mr. Bakman, "here is where Annina comes in with the tea table."

"What do I do with it?" Miss Sills asked impatiently.

"You pour tea with it."

Miss Sills looked even more dubious. "I'm not going to be able to do all of this," she said firmly. "I'll pick up the writing paper, I'll take the locket, I'll even close the windows. But I can't do everything."

The act played without mishap, and Miss Sills rushed out to the wings at the end, grinning broadly. "Some day you'll have to tell me where that tea can be served," she said to Mr. Bakman. "Where! Where! The only time I could see for it was at 'Di due figlia.' What a time to serve him tea!"

Mr. Rudel, meanwhile, was worrying about the orchestra's second percussionist, who had been lent for the evening to the Metropolitan Opera, but who was now needed for "La Traviata." As a result, the percussionist had to race back and forth across Lincoln Center to catch his cues in each opera house. "If you hear a cymbal crash," Mr. Rudel said, chuckling, "you'll know he made it."

All during the evening, Miss Sills continued to startle her colleagues, not least of all her co-star, John Stewart, who played Alfredo. In the third act's most dramatic moment, for instance, Mr. Stewart flung his gambling winnings at her, and Miss Sills stood stunned at stage right.

Behind the scenes, everyone was wondering whether Miss Sills was going to remember to move to center stage. She did, collapsing violently to the floor, but only after pausing as if paralyzed by emotion. "That surprised me," Mr. Stewart said later. "But, boy, did it work well."

Shortly before 11 P.M., Beverly Sills completed the opera, her first "Traviata" in New York in more than twelve years. "Now," she said offstage between curtain calls, "let's see what happens tomorrow night."

In her dressing room, Mr. Rudel congratulated her again, and then came a surprise. Frank Corsaro, who originally staged the evening's production back in 1966 had been in the audience, and now he rushed up to Miss Sills.

"Beverly," he said, "you were superb! I've never seen the death scene played better—never."

"What a nice thing to say," said Miss Sills. "I had visions of your coming backstage shouting, 'Where is that woman!' "

Everybody laughed uproariously, and Miss Sills said to Mr. Corsaro at last: "Frank, where the hell does she serve that tea?"

STEVEN R. WEISMAN
The New York Times, March 22, 1974

After seven years in retirement Maria Callas returned to the opera world—but in a classroom, not on the stage. Engaged to instruct a master's class in voice at New York City's Juilliard School of Music, Callas tried to keep herself in the background. But, as Los Angeles Times *free-lance writer Robert Jacobson notes in a diary he kept during the six-week course, the Callas aura soon dominated the proceedings.*

With horn-rimmed glasses perched on her nose, long auburn hair streaming down her back and wearing simple pants and blouse with chains of jewelry around her neck, Callas was the schoolteacher to the quick—often angered by those who came to worship rather than learn. She had chosen her pianist carefully: Young Eugene Kohn was with her every step of the way.

Those who know Callas only from her performances or recordings might not have expected the sincerity of purpose which emanated from her. Her familiar virtues, and the basic ones of all—great singing and interpreting—were stressed. Square attack, correct application of *rubato* and *portamento*, the use of the voice for dramatic purpose, fidelity to the composer, attention to the words, the noble presentation of the body and arms to shape a phrase. . . .

Feb. 7: Exactly at 5:30 Callas makes an auspicious entrance in a long print outfit, raising her left hand to discourage applause (at this she is not effective, nor is she throughout the sessions). Since Juilliard is preparing a new production of *La Bohème*, today is devoted to that opera. Kyung Woo Park is first, singing through "Si, mi chiamano Mimi." There is applause and Callas shakes her head, "We're all wonderful, but no applause, eh!"

She asks the young soprano for less movement and to bring her sound more forward. "Mimi is not Vestale. Make it simple, not too heavy." She tries to show her how to put a smile into her singing, how to color and caress the phrases. Phrase by phrase, she helps her build the aria and clean up the sound. With "Son andate," she works on giving it passion and opening up the voice. "Always vibrate the sound."

At the death scene she stresses the legato phrasing on "morbida." She tells a young bass, "you have a beautiful face and wonderful body —give it to the public." She suggests he treat the "Coat Aria" like poetry. "You're making it too dark. Give it pathos." To tenor Mario Fusco she asks, "How long do you hold that note?" "As long as they'll let me," he replies in the tenor fashion.

Feb. 10: Barrie Smith, a young blond soprano who started in the fall as a mezzo, works on "Madre, pietosa" from *La Forza del Destino*. Callas suggests: "You're a little nervous." The other confesses, "I'm scared to death!" The main problem is bridging the lower and middle voice, giving support to sustain and project the notes. The eager student is absorbed by Callas and seems to draw inspiration. The object here is to mix the voice. Callas is sympathetic to the difficulties of the aria—its range, the pronunciation, the rhythmic changes. "You have a lot of work to do" is her final challenge.

Sheila Nadler, a mezzo formerly with the San Francisco Opera, launches into Rosina's "Una voce poco fà" from *Barbiere*. The soprano's criticism is that there are too many pauses, the rhythm doesn't keep going. She also insists on the double C at the end, to which the mezzo responds with her playful half smile.

Feb. 14: Callas congratulates her students on their work in *Bohème*. Miss Smith begins with "L'altra notte" from *Mefistofele*. "Your dynamics are not right," Callas begins. The beginning must be more solid, more tragic, more dramatic in impact; she needs an expression of pain and terror. The low chest tones, she explains, are a problem to everyone. "The new style is to have high notes and no chest tones. But this is not so. Listen to records and you'll hear that even the lightest soprano with top, top tones also has chest tones."

Bridging notes needs more focus too. "Keep the chiaroscuro in your dynamics, in your light and dark sounds." She urges a focusing of the voice. "And you have to have those chest notes," Callas reiterates. "They're the basis of the repertoire, including Verdi." Singing, she tells all her people, "is the most difficult job in the world. That's why we must take it seriously." She explains that the two bridges in the voice—the lower one and the approach to the top—are a common problem.

Willard White sings "Il lacerato spirito" from *Simon Boccanegra*. She asks him for better diction, more authority and a warmer sound. When Callas sings the bass aria, there is immense nobility to her Verdi style. She works for true tones and a pianissimo within the focus of the voice, within its basic substance. "Richen the sound and let loose," she finally tells him.

A Korean soprano unsuccessfully attempts a big aria from Verdi's *La Battaglia di Legnano*. "It's a difficult aria," Callas assures everyone. "I was supposed to record it and haven't so we both have difficulties with it." In the andante, Callas reminds her of the trill. "Do I have to sing it?" she asks. "Well, he wrote it!" Callas responds.

Another Oriental soprano sings from *La Sonnambula*. "Sing it with more force," she is told. "Give it dramatic emphasis and shading and more life, but always *on* the note." The girl begins to force, has pitch problems and tightens up. Also, she has no idea of style or meaning.

Miss Park sings the first act *Forza* aria with a covered tone, flatting consistently. It's a large, healthy voice, but is much too thick and throaty—and she tends to slur notes. Callas herself sounds like a car engine running without gas today; but everyone is under the weather and she concedes that a general throat malaise is the demon....

March 9: In the act one duet from *Butterfly*, a Korean soprano and Fusco are both admonished for their lack of passion. Callas says to him, "I'd rather have a phrase louder and supported than have it fall out. Sustain more. And more warmth—you're Neapolitan! There's no excuse!"

A light tenor works on "Pourquoi me reveiller" from *Werther*. "Why did you breathe there," she stops him. "Because I ran out of breath," he returns. She works on the difference between a portamento and sliding at the end.

Miss Smith is back with Leonora's first-act aria in *Forza*, bringing with her the problems of support and sustaining of phrases. She finds the aria tiring. "I warned you it was difficult, but you insisted and now you're going to sing it," Callas shakes her head. "I would have preferred 'Pace, pace.' " Finally Miss Smith throws up her hands. "There are three or four notes in my voice I can't sing today." "Likewise," replies Callas. . . .

March 16: For the final session, Callas's desk is filled with presents, flowers and a shiny apple. She explains, "There has been a program behind this justice, even though some have thought it unjust." Miss Terzian begins on "Nacqui all'affanno" from Rossini's *Cenerentola*. Callas remarks she is singing it too heavily. "Remember, this is a girl with a change of position. There has to be niceness, kindness, and beauty in your attitude. Don't push it so." She stresses legato, rather than choppy vocalizing in the scales—and the necessity of the trill. "If an instrumentalist couldn't trill or have an *attaccatura* or embellish, he couldn't pass his first examination here," she warns. "We singers must have all this technical equipment."

Miss Terzian works hard on better breathing and Callas gets the fiorature lighter. Mr. Carlson and Miss Hendricks work on act two of *Lucia*. When the girl takes some optional high notes, Callas intervenes: "I know you have nice high notes, but . . . this is an unhappy duetto. Fireworks are wrong!" To the baritone she also insists, "As it's written . . . and it's not written to sing a cadenza there." Callas makes them look to the dramatic meaning of this music and finding it in pronouncing and legato. "How about the high notes at the end?" the baritone asks. "Sure, of course, save them for that," she concedes. "When you are older, you'll hate yourself if you've wasted them."

In deciding about the cut at the end of the duet, she remarks, "Some conductors like to 'open' our hearts out." As for colleagues, she states, "Good ones hold a note the same—bad ones do not. Just don't make it sound like 'Here comes the high note.' " Callas stresses that the voice for Lucia is the same for *Norma*, *Pirata*, and *Puritani*—none are light, but later traditions changed that.

Miss Smith and Fusco end with White in the *Forza* final Trio. "Are you warming up now?" Callas asks the girl. "Yes, now that I've gone to heaven!" she laughs.

Finally, Callas turns to students and observers: "Please try and remember that all this effort I've given you, and put it into other scores. It's not an easy career. Sing properly and apply whatever knowledge I've given you. It doesn't stop here. You are the young generation, and the only thanks I want is diction, feeling and expression. I'm not good with words," she shrugs and walks off, to tumultuous applause.

ROBERT JACOBSON
Los Angeles Times, April 30, 1972

A Chronology of Opera

Appearance of the liturgical drama; *The Play of Daniel* is performed at Beauvais	1100-1200
Development of the pastorale	c.1200 Incas begin to build empire in Peru; Aztecs enter the valley of Mexico
Adam de la Halle composes *Le Jeu de Robin et de Marion*	1283 Reign of Edward I in England; his "Model Parliament" represents all classes of society
Madrigals become popular; *sacre rappresentazioni* are performed for the public in Italy	1300 Wenceslas II of Bohemia becomes king of Poland
Vocal and instrumental *intermedi* begin to be used in the intervals of spoken dramas	1450 Nicholas V forms the Vatican Library
Vincenzo Galilei sets forth the principles of the Florentine *Camerata* in his "Dialogue About Ancient and Modern Music"; the *Camerata* renounces polyphony and favors the recitative	1581 Sir Philip Sidney discusses the nature and status of poetry in his *Defence of Poesie*
Orazio Vecchi combines farce with music in the premiere of his madrigal comedy *L'Amfiparnaso*	1594 Shakespeare writes the *Taming of the Shrew*
Jacopo Peri's musical fable *Dafne*, often considered as the first opera, is performed at the palace of Jacopo Corsi; opera becomes the preferred entertainment of the aristocracy	1597 Shakespeare completes *Merchant of Venice*, *Richard II*, and *Romeo and Juliet*
Peri composes *Euridice*, the earliest opera for which a score has been preserved	1600 British East India Company is established; Shakespeare writes *Henry V* and *Much Ado about Nothing*
Claudio Monteverdi explores the potential of the new musical style in *Orfeo*	1607 Francis Beaumont writes his burlesque drama *The Knight of the Burning Pestle*; Ben Jonson publishes *Volpone*
Singer-composer Francesca Caccini's *The Liberation of Ruggiero* is the first opera to be composed by a woman	1625 Francis Bacon publishes his *Essays*; Charles I ascends the throne of England
Heinrich Schütz's version of *Dafne* represents the first indigenous German opera	1627 Huguenots revolt; English occupy Nova Scotia
Vergilio Mazzocchi and Marco Marazzoli create the first real comic opera, *Chi soffre, speri*; the San Cassiano Theater, the first public opera house, is built in Venice	1637 Descartes writes *Discours de la Méthode*; Corneille's *Le Cid* is performed in Paris
Monteverdi develops vivid characters and stirring music in *The Return of Ulysses to His Country*; one year later he completes *The Coronation of Poppea* for its Venice premiere	1641 Massacre of Protestants in Ulster; outbreak of Irish rebellion
Cardinal Mazarin introduces Italian opera to the French court of King Louis XIV	1643 Louis XIV succeeds to the throne of France
Castrato singers begin to dominate Italian opera	1650 Frontier between English and Dutch colonies in North America defined
British composer William D'Avenant develops the "masque" in his *Siege of Rhodes*	1656 Diego Velázquez paints *The Maids of Honor*, considered his finest work
Jean-Baptiste Lully establishes L'Academie Royale de Musique in Paris; he develops the opera-ballet and the two-part overture	1672 Admission charged for the first time at a number of London concerts
The Hamburg State Opera opens under the direction of Reinhard Keiser	1678 John Bunyan publishes the first part of his allegorical *Pilgrim's Progress*
Alessandro Scarlatti founds the Neapolitan School of opera, which establishes the *da capo*, or three-part, aria; its adherents abandon mythological themes in favor of historical material	1685 Louis XIV revokes the Edict of Nantes; Protestants flee abroad
Henry Purcell writes the first English operatic masterpiece, *Dido and Aeneas*, performed by the young ladies at Josias Priest's fashionable finishing school in Chelsea	1689 Racine writes *Esther*, ending a twelve-year separation from the theater; two years later his major work, *Athalie* is produced
George Frideric Handel travels to Italy, where he composes *Rodrigo* and *Agrippina* in the traditional *opera seria* form	1706

Handel's *Rinaldo* creates a sensation at the Haymarket Theatre in London	1711	Joseph Addison and Richard Steele begin publishing *The Spectator* in England
The L'Opéra-Comique is established in Paris	1715	The Age of Reason begins
Handel composes *Giulio Cesare* and begins work on *Rodelinda*, his two most popular operas	1723	Voltaire writes his epic poem on King Henry IV, the *Henriad*
John Gay's ballad opera, *The Beggar's Opera*, features popular airs and a satiric text that pokes fun at English politics and social mores	1728	English poet Alexander Pope attacks literary hacks in his satirical *Dunciad*
Giovanni Battista Pergolesi establishes *opera buffa* as a viable form in the first important comic opera, *La serva padrona*	1733	English inventor John Kay patents the flying shuttle for weaving
Opening of London's Royal Opera House, Covent Garden, situated in the heart of the city's produce market	1734	J. S. Bach composes his *Christmas Oratorio*
John Hippisley's *Flora* is the first opera performed in America	1735	William Hogarth publishes a series of engravings called *The Rake's Progress*
The Burgtheater opens in Vienna to perform important court productions	1742	Henry Fielding's second parody of the epistolary novel, after *Shamela*, evolves into a wholly original work, *Joseph Andrews*
Jean Jacques Rousseau composes *Le Devin du village*; In Paris, adherents of traditional Italian opera lash out against French-opera lovers in La Guerre des Bouffons	1752	Benjamin Franklin invents the lightning rod; Gregorian calendar is adopted by Great Britain; Scottish philosopher David Hume writes *Political Discourses*
Christoph Willibald von Gluck collaborates with librettist Ranieri de' Calzabigi in *Orfeo ed Euridice*, marking revolutionary changes and reform in *opera seria*	1761	Performance of *L'amore delle tre melarance* by Carlo Gozzi, who seeks to preserve the influence of *commedia dell' arte* in Italy
Gluck's *Alceste* is premiered at the Burgtheater; Wolfgang Amadeus Mozart's *Apollo et Hyacinthus*, written at the age of eleven, is performed by Salzburg University students	1767	Eccentric Irish clergyman Laurence Sterne completes his nine-volume comic masterpiece, *Tristram Shandy*
Mozart composes *Bastien et Bastienne* for an outdoor performance at the Vienna home of Dr. Anton Mesmer	1768	The Petit Trianon, completed at Versailles, marks the Classic revival in architecture
La Scala, Italy's leading opera house, and one of the world's most renowned, is built in Milan	1776	American Declaration of Independence is signed in Philadelphia
Mozart composes *Idomeneo*, his first mature opera, tailoring it to the talents of his singers	1780	Benedict Arnold's treason is exposed
Mozart composes the Turkish-flavored *Abduction from the Seraglio*, the first of his operas produced in Vienna	1782	Rama I founds the Chakin dynasty in Thailand
	1785	*The Times* of London is founded by John Walter
Mozart collaborates with Lorenzo da Ponte on *The Marriage of Figaro*; he completes *Don Giovanni* the following year	1786	Massachusetts insurrectionists attack U.S. arsenals in Shays' Rebellion
Emperor Joseph II establishes a company in Vienna to present the German brand of comic opera known as *singspiel*	1788	The United States Constitution is ratified
	1789	Parisians storm the Bastille; Declaration of the Rights of Man proclaimed
Mozart completes *Così fan tutte*, the last of his Italian comic operas	1790	Thomas Saint invents the first sewing machine
Mozart's *Magic Flute* is the first true opera to be written in German	1791	Thomas Paine publishes the *Rights of Man*
Beethoven's only opera, *Fidelio*, is modeled on the popular French "rescue opera"	1805	British admiral Horatio Nelson destroys the Franco-Spanish fleet in the Battle of Trafalgar
J. N. Barker's *The Indian Princess*, based on the story of Pocahontas, is performed in New Orleans	1808	Beethoven completes his Fifth Symphony, perhaps the most popular piece of serious music ever written
	1812	United States and Britain go to war
Giuseppi Verdi is born at Le Roncole, and Richard Wagner in Leipzig; they embody the antitheses of operatic style—vocal versus orchestral	1813	
Rossini completes his musical farce *The Barber of Seville;* a year later he completes his lighthearted *Cenerentola* and *La gazza ladra*	1816	Johann Maelzel invents the metronome
Karl Maria von Weber features Teutonic fairy tale and the supernatural in *Der Freischütz*	1821	Mexico wins independence from Spain; Greece rises against Turkey

Opera and Music	Year	World Events
Rossini marries soprano Isabella Colbran and settles in Paris, leaving Italian opera in the hands of Donizetti and Bellini	1823	Construction of the British Museum begins; Monroe Doctrine closes America to further colonization or interference in its affairs by European powers
European opera is established in America with the arrival of Manuel García's singing troupe; García's daughter, Maria Malibran, is to become a celebrated prima donna	1825	Robert Owen establishes a communal experiment at New Harmony, Indiana; Erie Canal is opened
Daniel Francois Esprit Auber's political opera *La Muette de Portici* helps ignite an uprising that leads to Belgium's independence; a year later Rossini adopts Auber's style in *William Tell*	1828	Andrew Jackson is elected as first Democratic President; he introduces the spoils system on a national level
Giacomo Meyerbeer, collaborating with Eugène Scribe, creates the grotesque *Robert le Diable*, his first grand opera; Bellini establishes the *bel canto* style in *Norma*, *La Sonnambula*, and, four years later, *I Puritani*	1831	Nat Turner leads major slave revolt in Virginia; William Lloyd Garrison founds *The Liberator*, an antislavery journal
Gaetano Donizetti introduces the "mad scene" in *Lucia di Lammermoor*	1835	In Africa, the "Great Trek" establishes the republics of Transvaal, Natal, and Orange Free State
Meyerbeer composes *Les Huguenots*, an operatic spectacular based on the French religious wars of the sixteenth century; Mikhail Glinka contributes Russian national accents to opera with *A Life for the Tsar*	1836	Charles Dickens's *Pickwick Papers* marks debut of the most popular novelist of all time
Verdi composes his first opera, *Oberto*, in the style of Bellini	1838	Beginning of regular steamship communication between England and America
Verdi recounts the story of Nebuchadnezzar in *Nabucco*; the Dresden Opera produces Wagner's *Rienzi* and *The Flying Dutchman* and offers him the post of musical director	1842	Dickens's maiden tour of the United States; Honoré de Balzac issues the first of seventy-odd volumes on life in nineteenth-century France, works known collectively as *La Comédie humaine*
William Henry Fry's *Leonora* is the first grand opera to be composed in the United States; Wagner completes *Tannhäuser*	1845	Emily Brontë writes *Wuthering Heights*
Verdi emphasizes musical characterization in *Rigoletto*; two years later he completes *La Traviata* and *Il Trovatore*	1851	The Crystal Palace is erected in Hyde Park to house the Great Exhibition
Verdi composes *Les vêpres siciliennes* for the Paris Opéra; George F. Bristow's *Rip Van Winkle* is the first American opera to be based on a native theme	1855	Aluminum is produced on a commercial scale; Walt Whitman publishes *Leaves of Grass*
Jacques Offenbach raises operetta to a high art and popularizes the cancan in *Orphée aux enfers*; Hector Berlioz completes his five-hour-long panorama *Les Troyens*	1858	Abraham Lincoln and Stephen Douglas debate the slavery issue in the United States
Charles Gounod consummates the era of French grand opera with *Faust*; Roman officials censor Verdi's *Masked Ball* for depicting the assassination of a king onstage	1859	Gustav Kirchhoff and Robert Bunson discover a method of spectrum analysis of light; Ferdinand de Lesseps begins construction of the Suez Canal; Charles Darwin publishes *Origin of Species*
	1861	American Civil War breaks out
The Five—Russian composers Mili Balakirev, César Cui, Alexander Borodin, Nicolai Rimsky-Korsakov, and Modeste Mussorgsky—dedicate themselves to Russian national music	1862	Victor Hugo completes his last major novel, *Les Misérables*; Ivan Turgenev, the most cosmopolitan of Russian writers, completes *Fathers and Sons*
Wagner composes *Tristan und Isolde* and sets forth the concept of *Gesamtkunstwerke*, the "total work of art"	1865	Assassination of Abraham Lincoln; Joseph Lister introduces method of surgical asepsis
Czech opera enters the international repertory with Bedrich Smetana's *The Bartered Bride*	1866	Alfred Nobel invents dynamite; Feodor Dostoevsky writes *Crime and Punishment*
Wagner's *Die Meistersinger* celebrates the struggle between the old and the innovative in art	1868	First transcontinental railroad is completed in the United States
Verdi blends tragedy and ceremonial panoply in *Aïda*, the final great opera of his middle period	1871	German Empire is proclaimed; Heinrich Schliemann identifies and excavates the site of ancient Troy; trade unions legalized in England
Mussorgsky's powerful *Boris Godunov* captures the spirit of the Russian people; Johann Strauss the Younger establishes the waltz form in his opera *Die Fledermaus*	1874	Henry Morton Stanley begins Congo River explorations; Whiskey Ring is exposed in the U.S.; Factory Act in England institutes a 56½-hour working week
W.S. Gilbert and Sir Arthur Sullivan produce their first joint venture, *Trial by Jury*; Bizet's *Carmen* scandalizes audiences at the Opéra-Comique	1875	Irish nationalist leader Charles Stewart Parnell is elected to Parliament and begins movement for Irish independence
Wagner completes *The Ring*, a titanic cycle of four musical dramas, performed at the opening of his new theater in Bayreuth	1876	Alexander Graham Bell invents the telephone; Peter Ilich Tchaikovsky composes *Swan Lake*

Gilbert and Sullivan's *H.M.S. Pinafore* pokes fun at Victorian England; two years later the D'Oyly Carte Opera Company performs *The Pirates of Penzance* in New York	1878	Congress of Berlin convenes; Germany introduces factory inspection; Bland-Allison Act reintroduces silver standard in America
Offenbach composes his one serious opera, *The Tales of Hoffmann*	1881	Italian choreographer Luigi Manzotti stages *Excelsior*, a ballet extravaganza
New York's Metropolitan Opera House opens with Gounod's *Faust*	1883	The Fabian Society is founded in England
Jules Massenet combines religion and eroticism in one of his most characteristic works, *Manon*	1884	Elie Metchnikoff introduces the theory of phagocytosis, showing the antibacterial function of white blood cells
Otello embodies the dramatic and musical cohesiveness of Verdi's new style	1887	Emile Berliner invents the gramophone and a method for duplicating disc records
Pietro Mascagni wins the Sonzogno competition for one-act operas with his fiercely melodramatic *Cavalleria rusticana*	1890	William James writes *The Principles of Psychology*; Henrik Ibsen completes his feminist drama *Hedda Gabler*; Oscar Wilde finishes *Dorian Gray*
Ruggiero Leoncavallo completes the *verismo* classic, *I Pagliacci*	1892	The first diesel engine is constructed
Puccini becomes world famous with the production of *La Bohème*	1896	First electric submarine is built in France; production of Anton Chekhov's *The Seagull*
Ruperto Chapí y Lorente's *La Revoltosa* typifies the *zarzuela* in Spain	1897	Edmond Rostand writes *Cyrano de Bergerac*; discovery of gold in Klondike
Puccini completes the brutally realistic *Tosca*; Gustave Charpentier composes *Louise*, about a young working girl who longs for the liberation of women	1900	Founding of the Labour Party in Great Britain; Boxer Rebellion is crushed in China; Picasso makes his first trip to Paris
Claude Debussy introduces impressionism in *Pelléas et Mélisande*	1902	George Méliè's film *A Trip to the Moon* makes use of special effects and trick photography
Moravian composer Leos Janácek completes his folk-flavored *Jenufa*; a year later Puccini completes *Madama Butterfly*	1903	Orville and Wilbur Wright fly their first airplane at Kitty Hawk, N.C.; in London, Social Democrats split into Mensheviks and Bolsheviks, forming nascent Communist party
Richard Strauss's *Salome* shocks its audience at the Dresden Opera	1905	Einstein begins to formulate his special and general theories of relativity
Puccini composes *The Girl of the Golden West*	1910	Union of South Africa is formed
Richard Strauss and Hugo von Hofmannsthal collaborate on their romantic comedy *Der Rosenkavalier*; Ravel composes the piquant *L'heure espagnole*	1911	Sun Yat-sen leads Chinese Revolution, forcing Manchu emperor to abdicate; painters Wassily Kandinsky and Franz Marc found Der Blaue Reiter
Spanish composer Enrique Granados creates *Goyescas* with music drawn from his own piano compositions	1916	Allied and German forces suffer enormous casualties at Verdun and the Somme
Béla Bartók's *Bluebeard's Castle* is written for only two characters	1918	Republic proclaimed in Germany; Communist revolt in Hungary is organized by Béla Kun
	1919	Treaty of Versailles ends World War I
Sergei Prokofiev composes his *Love for Three Oranges* for the Chicago Opera	1921	Austrian philosopher Ludwig Wittgenstein publishes the *Tractatus Logico-philosophicus*
Ralph Vaughan Williams uses British folksong style in Sadler's Wells favorite, *Hugh the Drover*	1924	Nikolai Lenin dies; Joseph Stalin becomes ultimate dictator in Russia
Alban Berg adopts atonal composition and *sprechstimme*, or speech-song, in his phantasmagoric opera *Wozzeck*	1925	Death of Sun Yat-sen, the father of the Republic of China
Puccini's last opera, *Turandot*, has its premiere at La Scala; Zoltán Kodály's *Háry János* represents Hungarian national opera	1926	Richard Byrd and Floyd Bennett become the first men to fly over the North Pole; Union of Soviet Socialist Republics is established
The Broadway musical establishes its link with opera in Jerome Kern's lyric *Show Boat*	1927	Charles Lindbergh makes first solo, nonstop transatlantic flight in *The Spirit of St. Louis*
Kurt Weill and Bertolt Brecht satirize social and political practices in Germany with *The Threepenny Opera*, updating Gay's *The Beggar's Opera*	1928	Sir Alexander Fleming discovers penicillin; Stalin initiates Five Year Plan for rapid industrialization and farm collectivization
	1929	Stock market crash on Wall Street leads to worldwide economic depression
The Metropolitan broadcasts Engelbert Humperdinck's *Hänsel und Gretel* as the first of its weekly Saturday matinee radio programs	1931	Mao Tse-tung is elected chairman of the Soviet Republic of China; Germany and Japan abandon gold standard; Japan invades Manchuria
Louis Gruenberg's *Emperor Jones* features Afro-American songs and rhythms	1933	Adolf Hitler becomes chancellor of Germany; André Malraux writes *La Condition Humaine*
Virgil Thomson uses an all-black cast in his *Four Saints in Three Acts*, which has its premiere in Hartford, Connecticut	1934	Arnold J. Toynbee begins his ten-volume work, *A Study of History*

George Gershwin combines black folk idiom and Broadway musical techniques in *Porgy and Bess*	1935	Culmination of the legendary "long march" of the Red Army in China led by Mao Tse-tung
Richard Rodgers and Lorenz Hart produce *On Your Toes*; within four years they complete *The Boys from Syracuse* and *Pal Joey*; Shostakovich's *Lady Macbeth of Mtzensk* is censored in Moscow	1936	Rome-Berlin-Tokyo Axis formed; Spanish Civil War begins; three years later Franco's forces emerge victorious
Gian Carlo Menotti composes *The Old Maid and the Thief* for radio	1939	German invasion of Poland marks the beginning of World War II
A tabloid version of *I Pagliacci* marks the beginning of televised opera in the U.S.	1941	Japanese attack Pearl Harbor; the United States enters the war
Rodgers and Oscar Hammerstein II create new standards for American show music with *Oklahoma!*; New York City Opera is organized to provide good opera at popular prices	1943	German defeat at Stalingrad marks turning point in the war on the eastern front; Italy surrenders unconditionally to Allies and declares war on Germany
Benjamin Britten bases his first opera, *Peter Grimes*, on George Crabbe's poem about an ill-fated sea captain; Rodgers and Hammerstein win new fame with *Carousel*	1945	Allies defeat German forces; the first atomic bombs are used against Japan to end World War II in the Pacific; United Nations is organized; first television sets reach the public market
Thomson's second opera, *The Mother of Us All*, centers around the life of Susan B. Anthony; Francis Poulenc's satire *Les Mamelles de Tirésias* advocates an increase in the French birthrate	1947	India attains independence from Great Britain; dominion of Pakistan is created
Long-playing records make feasible complete opera recordings for the mass market	1948	Creation of the state of Israel
The NBC Television Opera Theater is formed, meeting a growing public demand to view performances at home	1949	Mao Tse-tung establishes Chinese People's Republic in Peking; NATO organized for collective self-protection of Western Powers
Luigi Dallapiccola extols human liberty and dignity in *Il Prigionero*; Frank Loesser completes his musical comedy *Guys and Dolls*	1950	President Truman sends American forces to Korea
Menotti's television opera *Amahl and the Night Visitor* becomes a popular Christmas feature; Igor Stravinsky's *The Rake's Progress* has its premiere in Venice	1951	Twenty-second Amendment to the Constitution is ratified, limiting president to two terms in office
Britten bases his gripping *Turn of the Screw* on Henry James's novel; Menotti composes the Pulitzer-Prize-winning *Saint of Bleecker Street*	1954	Launching of the U.S.S. *Nautilus*, the first American nuclear-powered submarine
Michael Tippett composes *Midsummer Marriage*; Carlisle Flood's *Susannah* is a study of persecution; Prokofiev completes *War and Peace*	1955	U.S. civil-rights leader Martin Luther King leads bus boycott in Montgomery, Alabama; Tennessee Williams writes *Cat on a Hot Tin Roof*
Douglas Moore hails America's past in *The Ballad of Baby Doe*; Alan Jay Lerner and Frederick Loewe produce *My Fair Lady*	1956	Suez Canal crisis; Russia crushes anti-Communist uprising in Hungary
Leonard Bernstein completes *West Side Story*	1957	*Sputnik I*, the first artificial satellite, is launched by the Soviet Union
Britten composes *Noye's Fludde*, a children's opera based on the story of Noah; Samuel Barber composes his first opera, *Vanessa*	1958	National Aeronautics and Space Administration (NASA) is created to study the problems of space travel
Karl-Birgir Blomdahl combines electronic and conventional music in his spaceship opera *Aniara*	1959	Charles de Gaulle is inaugurated as president of the new Fifth Republic in France
Robert Ward's *The Crucible* has as its theme the late-seventeenth-century Salem witch trials	1961	Soviet astronaut Yuri Gagarin becomes the first man in space; Berlin Wall is built
Jerry Bock's *Fiddler on the Roof* is an immediate Broadway success	1964	Civil Rights Act is passed by the U.S. Congress; World Trade Center is proposed in New York
Hans Werner Henze's satire *The Young Lord* has as its hero a trained ape; Mitch Leigh completes *Man of La Mancha*	1965	United States begins bombing Viet Nam; India and Pakistan fight over Kashmir; Mao Tse-tung launches "cultural revolution" in China
The new Metropolitan Opera opens at Lincoln Center with Barber's *Antony and Cleopatra*	1966	Indira Gandhi becomes prime minister of India
A busload of curious schoolchildren confronts visitors from outer space in Menotti's *Help! Help! The Globolinks!*	1968	Russian troops invade Czechoslovakia to stifle liberal regime of Alexander Dubcek; assassination of Martin Luther King and Robert Kennedy
	1969	American astronauts are first to walk on the moon
Rudolf Bing retires after twenty-two years as manager of the Metropolitan Opera; Bernstein composes a multimedia *Mass* for the opening of the J. F. Kennedy Center for the Performing Arts	1971	Chilean poet Pablo Neruda wins the Nobel Prize for Literature
The Metropolitan Opera presents the American premiere of Britten's *Death in Venice*	1974	President Nixon, facing impeachment over Watergate scandal, resigns

Selected Bibliography

Anderson, Emily, ed. *The Letters of Mozart and His Family.* 3 vols. London: Macmillan, 1938. (Second edition: 2 vols. St. Martin's Press, Inc. 1966.)

Broder, Nathan, ed. *The Great Operas of Mozart.* New York: Norton, 1964.

Chase, Gilbert. *America's Music: From the Pilgrims to the Present.* New York: McGraw-Hill, 1955. (Revised edition: McGraw-Hill, 1966.)

Cooper, Martin. *Opéra Comique.* New York: Chanticleer Press, 1949.

Crosten, William L. *French Grand Opera: An Art and a Business.* New York: King's Crown Press, 1948. (Reprint: DaCapo Press, 1972.)

Dent, Edward J. *Foundations of English Opera.* Cambridge: The University Press, 1928. (Second edition: DaCapo Press, 1967.)

———. *Mozart's Operas: A Critical Study.* Second edition. London: Oxford University Press, 1947.

———. *Opera.* New York: Penguin Books, 1945.

Grout, Donald Jay. *A Short History of Opera.* Second edition. New York: Columbia University Press, 1965.

Harewood, Earl of, ed. *Kobbe's Complete Opera Book.* Revised edition. New York: Putnam, 1972.

Marek, George R. *Puccini.* London: Cassel, 1952.

Martin, George. *The Opera Companion: A Guide for the Casual Operagoer.* New York: Dodd, Mead & Company, 1961. (Reprint: Apollo Editions, 1971.)

Morgenstern, Sam, ed. *Composers on Music.* New York: Pantheon Books, 1956.

Newman, Ernest. *Wagner as Man and Artist.* New York: Vintage Books, 1960. (Reprint: Peter Smith, 1963.)

Pleasants, Henry. *The Great Singers.* New York: Simon and Schuster, 1966.

Raynor, Henry. *A Social History of Music.* New York: Schocken, 1972.

Rolland, Romain. *Some Musicians of Former Days.* Translated by Mary Blaiklock. New York: Henry Holt, 1915.

Smith, Patrick J. *The Tenth Muse: A Historical Study of the Opera Libretto.* New York: Alfred A. Knopf, Inc., 1970.

Strunk, Oliver, ed. *Source Readings in Music History.* New York: Norton, 1950.

Toye, Francis. *Italian Opera.* London: Parrish, 1952.

Werfel, Franz and Stefan, Paul, eds. *Verdi: The Man in His Letters.* New York: L. B. Fischer, 1942. (Reprint: Vienna House, 1973.)

Picture Credits

The Editors would like to thank the following individuals and organizations for their invaluable assistance:

Metropolitan Opera Guild—Robert A. Tuggle and Stephanie Bodene
The Granger Collection, New York—William and Erica Glover

The following abbreviations are used:

(BB)—Photograph © by Beth Bergman
(FD)—Frank Dunand, Metropolitan Opera Guild
(FF)—Fred Fehl
CR, M—Civica Raccotta di Stampe Bertarelli, Milan
MS, M—Museo Teatrale alla Scala, Milan
NL, F—National Library, Florence
(M)—Mondadori Archives

HALFTITLE: Symbol designed by Jay J. Smith Studio FRONTISPIECE: (BB)

CHAPTER 1 **6** NL,F (Scala) **8–9** MS,M (Marzari) **9** Museo Correr, Venice (Mercurio) **10** CR,M (Dani) **11** CR,M (SEF) **12–13** All: NL,F (Scala) **14** NL,F (Pineider) **15** Top: NL,F (Pineider); bottom: (Arborio Mella) **16** NL, F (Pineider) **17** Salzbürger Festspiele **18** Top: The Granger Collection, New York; bottom: CR, M (Dani) **19** (BB)

CHAPTER 2 **20** Theatermuseum, Munich (Blauel) **22** Janos Scholz Collection, New York (CEAM) **23** CR,M (Panicucci) **24** Museo Civico, Turin (Scala) **25** Both: MS,M (Marzari) **26** MS,M (Marzari) **27** (Zoe Dominic) **28** National Portrait Gallery, London **29** (Zoe Dominic) **30–31** Tate Gallery, London (Marchiori) **32–33** Theatermuseum, Munich (Blauel) **33** New York City Opera Company

CHAPTER 3 **34** Museo Civico, Turin (Rampazzi) **36–37** Bibliothèque Nationale, Paris **38–39** Theatermuseum, Munich (Blauel) **40** Top: The Granger Collection, New York; bottom: (Piccagliani) **41** MS,M (Dani) **42** National Library, Paris (CEAM) **43** Top: both, Bibliothèque de l'Opéra, Paris (Lalance) **43** Bottom, MS,M (Dani) **44** MS,M (Dani) **44** Bibliothèque de l'Opéra, Paris (Pucciarelli) **45** Bibliothèque de l'Opéra (CEAM)

CHAPTER 4 **46** Staatsgalerie, Stuttgart **48–49** Austrian National Tourist Office **49** Top, CR,M (Arborio Mella) **50** (Archives De Cesare) **51** (Toepffer) **52** Bottom: (BB) **52–53** CR,M (Archives De Cesare) **54–55** (FD) **56** Salzbürger Festspiele **57** Theatermuseum, Munich (Blauel) **58–59** (BB)

CHAPTER 5 **60** CR,M (Dani) **62** Top: MS,M (Dani); bottom: CR,M (Archives De Cesare) **63** (Lotti) **64** Top: (FD); bottom: CR,M (Archieves De Cesare) **65** MS,M (Marzari) **66** (FD) **67** Top: Bibliothèque de l'Opera, Paris (Pucciarelli); bottom: MS,M (Dani) **68** CR,M (Dani) **69** (Piccagliani) **70–71** Bibliothèque de l'Opéra, Paris (Lalance) **72–73** (Zoe Dominic) **74** The Granger Collection, New York **75** Top: CR,M (Dani); bottom: *Opera News* from The Granger Collection, New York

CHAPTER 6 **76** MS,M (Marzari) **78** Top: (M); bottom: MS,M (M) **79** CR,M (C.A. Pin) **80** CR,M (Dani) **81** Top: (Louis Melançon); bottom: CR,M (Dani) **82** (Vernon Smith, *Opera News*) **83** Top: MS,M (Begotti); bottom: CR,M (Dani) **84–85** (Mori) **86** Top: Musée des Arts Décoratifs, Paris (Kimmel); **86–87** bottom: CR,M (Dani) **88** Palace of Prefecture, Milan (SEF) **89** Left: (M); right: (Marchiori)

CHAPTER 7 **90** Württenbergisches Landesmuseum, Stuttgart **92** (BB) **93** CR,M (Dani) **94–95** (FD) **96** CR,M (Dani) **97** Top: MS,M (Dani); bottom: Bibliothèque de l'Opéra (Bert) **98–99** Top: CR,M (Dani); bottom: (Piccagliani) **100** CR,M (Archives De Cesare) **101** (Archives De Cesare) **102** (Enar Merkel Rydberg) **103** (Lionello Fabbri)

CHAPTER 8 **104** (FD) **106** CR,M (Dani) **107** CR,M (Dani) **108** (Lionello Fabbri) **108–109** (Piccagliani) **110** Top: CR,M (Dani); bottom: CR,M (Dani) **111** (Louis Melançon, Metropolitan Opera Guild) **112** MS,M (CEAM) **113** CR,M (Brogi) **114–115** (FD) **116** Culver Pictures **117** The Granger Collection, New York

CHAPTER 9 **118** Magnum (E. Lessing) **120** Top: CR,M; bottom: (FD) **121** Bibliothèque de Musée des Arts Décoratifs, Paris (Lalance) **122–123** D'Oyly Carte Opera Company (John Watt, Associated Press) **124** Top: (M) **124–125** MS,M (Dani) **125** (Ansa) **126** Top: (Associated Press); bottom: (Piccagliani) **127** (Agence Bernand) **128** (Piccagliani) **129** (Lionello Fabbri) **130–131** (Sydacation International) **131** Covent Garden Opera Company

CHAPTER 10 **132** Musée Carnavalet, Paris (SEF) **134–135** New York Public Library **136** The Granger Collection, New York **137** Culver Pictures **138–139** (Vandamm Studio) **140** (FF) **140–141** (FF) **142** (Lionello Fabbri) **143** (Lionello Fabbri) **144** Top: Culver Pictures; bottom: (FF) **145** (FF)

EPILOGUE **146** (McKay) **148** Top: Opera House, Stockholm; **148–149** (Fletcher Drake) **150–151** Robert Stigwood Organization, New York **152** (Antonia Mulas)

BACKSTAGE AT THE OPERA **154–179** Costumes from *Die Fledermaus* designed by Theoni V. Aldredge

Index

Abduction from the Seraglio, The (Mozart), 45, 49–50
Acis et Galatée (Lully), 36
Adam, Adolphe-Charles, 67
Adami, Giuseppe, 114
Addison, Joseph, 7
Affligio, Giuseppe, 48
Africaine, L' (Meyerbeer), 71
Agrippina (Handel), 29
Aïda (Verdi), 83, 86, 113
Albert, Eugène d', 100
Albert Herring (Britten), 131
Alceste (Gluck), 40, 41
Alceste (Lully), 36, 37
Alcina (Handel), 16, 32, 33
Aldeburgh Music Festival, 131
Alfano, Franco, 117
Algarotti, Francesco, 37
Amadis de Gaule (Lully), 36
Amahl and the Night Visitors (Menotti), 143
Amelia Goes to the Ball (Menotti), 143
American opera, 133 ff.
Amfiparnaso, L' (Vecchi), 11, 14–15
Amore dei tre rè, L' (Montemezzi), 128
Andrea Chénier (Giordano), 109
Andromeda (Manelli), 22
Aniara (Blomdahl), 147, 149
Anna Bolena (Donizetti), 65
Anthony, Susan B., 135
Antony and Cleopatra (Barber), 141
Apollo et Hyacinthus (Mozart), 48
Arabella (Strauss), 100
Aria, 15, 16
  da capo, 26
Ariadne auf Naxos (Strauss), 100
Arianna (Monteverdi), 18
Ariodante (Handel), 33
Ariosto, Lodovico, 16
Aristi, Attilio, 32
Arsace, L' (Feo), 35
Ascanio in Alba (Mozart), 48
Assassinio nella cattedrale, L' (Pizzetti), 128
Astianatte (Bononcini), 33
Atalanta (Handel), 32
Attila (Verdi), 79
Auber, Daniel Francois Esprit, 67–68
Auden, W. H., 142
Austrian opera, 26–27, 37, 101–3
  light, 120–21

Bach, Johann Sebastian, 27, 29
Balakirev, Mily, 124
Balfe, Michael, 121
Ballad of Baby Doe (Moore), 140, 141
Ballad opera, 33, 43
Ballo à cavallo, 16
Ballo in maschera, Un (Verdi), 82, 83
Barber, Samuel, 141

Barber of Baghdad (Cornelius), 98
Barberini, 21
Barber of Seville (Paisiello), 44, 134
Bardi, Giovanni de', 8, 150
Bardi, Pietro de', 150
Barezzi, Antonio, 77–78
Bargagli, Gerolamo, 10
Barker, J. N, 133
Baroni, Leonora, 35
Bartered Bride, The (Smetana), 126
Bartók, Béla, 126
Basso continuo, 16
Bastien und Bastienne (Mozart), 48
Battaglia di Legnano, La (Verdi), 79
Bayreuth, 91, 92, 98, 109
Béatrice et Bénédict (Berlioz), 75
Beaumarchais, 65
Beecham, Thomas, 130
Beethoven, Ludwig van, 61–62, 67
Beggar's Opera (Gay), 29, 33, 121, 133
Beginning of opera, 8 ff.
Belasco, David, 117
Bel canto, 65
Belle Hélène, La (Offenbach), 119
Bellini, Vincenzo, 65
Bennuci, Francesco, 53
Benvenuto Cellini (Berlioz), 75
Berenice (Handel), 32
Berg, Alban, 101–3, 128
Berlin, 101, 128–29
Berlioz, Hector, 71, 74–75, 147
Bernstein, Leonard, 145, 147, 149
Berton, Henri Montan, 67
Bierce, Ambrose, 133
Bing, Rudolf, 120, 166 ff.
Bizet, Georges, 105–6
Blacher, Boris, 129
Blitzstein, Marc, 33, 129, 143–44
Blomdahl, Karl-Birgir, 147, 149
Blow, John, 28
Bluebeard's Castle (Bartók), 126, 147
Bock, Jerry, 145
Bohème, La (Puccini), 113–14
Bohemia, 53, 56, 126
Bohemian Girl (Balfe), 121
Boieldieu, François-Adrien, 67
Boito, Arrigo, 86, 87, 88
Bolshoi Theater, 153
Bondini, Pasquale, 53
Bononcini, Giovanni, 32–33
Bordoni, Faustina, 33
Boris Godunov (Mussorgsky), 119, 124–25
Borodin, Alexander, 124
"Borough, The" (Crabbe), 131
Boston Opera Company, 169 ff.
Bouffes-Parisiens, Les, 119
Boys from Syracuse, The, 144
Brecht, Bertolt, 33, 128, 129
Bretón y Hernándéz, Tomás, 127
Bristow, George F., 134
British opera, 28 ff.
  light, 121, 124
  in twentieth century, 129–31
Britten, Benjamin, 131, 148
Broadway musicals, 143–45
Broschi, Carlo (Farinelli), 25
Brown, Anne, 136, 140

Browning, Robert, 44
Büchner, Georg, 103
Bühnenfestspiel, 97
Bülow, Cosima von, 93
Buontalenti, Bernardo, 7, 8
Burney, Charles, 21
Busoni, Ferruccio, 100
Buxtehude, Dietrich, 29
Byrom, John, 32

Caballé, Montserrat, 80, 153
Caccini, Francesca, 16, 22
Caccini, Giulio, 8, 15, 16
Caffarelli (Gaetano Majorano), 25
Cain, James M., 63
Caldwell, Sarah, 126, 169 ff.
Callas, Maria, 65, 67, 177–79
Calzabigi, Ranieri de', 40
Camerata fiorentina, 8–9, 15
Capriccio (Strauss), 100
Carmen (Bizet), 105–6, 107
Carmen Jones (Hammerstein II), 106
Carousel, 145
Carte, Richard D'Oyly, 121
Caruso, Enrico, 79, 110, 117, 154–55, 156–57
Castor et Pollux (Rameau), 37
Castrati, 22, 24–25, 33, 35, 100
Catalani, Alfredo, 109
Catena d'Adone (Mazzocchi), 16
Cavalieri, Caterina, 49
Cavalieri, Emilio de', 8, 16
Cavalleria rusticana (Mascagni), 109, 110, 113
Cenerentola (Rossini), 63
Cesti, Marc' Antonio, 26–27
Chagall, Marc, 59
Chaliapin, Feodor, 124
Chapí y Lorente, Ruperto, 127
Charpentier, Gustave, 108
Cherubini, Luigi, 67
Chi soffre, speri (Mazzocchi), 18, 43
Chopin, Frédéric, 65, 71
Cimarosa, Domenico, 44
City Center, 163, 164
Claque, 74
Clemenza di Tito, La (Mozart), 26, 56
Coffee Cantata (Bach), 27
Coffey, Charles, 45
Colbran, Isabella, 65
Colloredo, Hieronymus von, 49
Columbus (Bristow), 134
Comic opera, 25–26, 43–45, 50, 67, 100, 101, 106, 121, 143
Comte Ory, Le (Rossini), 68
Consul, The (Menotti), 143
Converse, Frederick S., 134
Cooke, Henry, 28
Coq d'or, Le (Rimsky-Korsakov), 124, 125
Corelli, Franco, 167, 168
Cornelius, Peter, 98
Corsi, Jacopo, 15, 151
Così fan tutte (Mozart), 50, 56, 57, 59
Covent Garden, 29, 33, 62, 67, 71, 119, 131
Crabbe, George, 131

Cradle Will Rock, The, 143
Cristina of Lorraine, 7, 10
Crociato in Egitto, Il (Meyerbeer), 71
Crucible, The (Ward), 140, 141
Cui, César, 124
Cuzzoni, Francesca, 32, 33
Czar and Carpenter (Lortzing), 98
Czech opera, 126

Da capo, 26
Dafne (Peri), 3, 15, 150
Dafne (Schütz), 27
Dallapiccola, Luigi, 128
Dal Prato, Vincenzo, 49
Dame blanche, La (Boieldieu), 67
Dame aux Camelias, La (Dumas), 81
Damnation de Faust, La (Berlioz), 75
Damrosch, Walter, 134
Danaïdes, Les (Salieri), 74
Da Ponte, Lorenzo, 50, 53, 56, 134
D'Avenant, William, 28
Death in Venice (Britten), 131, 147
Debussy, Claude, 98, 108–9
Delibes, Léo, 106
Delius, Frederick, 130
Dent, Edward J., 49
Devin du village, Le (Rousseau), 45
Dialogues des Carmélites, Les (Poulenc), 127–28
Dido and Aeneas (Purcell), 28, 29, 75
Doktor Faust (Busoni), 100
Don Carlos (Verdi), 82
Don Giovanni (Mozart), 7, 47, 48, 50, 53, 59
Donizetti, Gaetano, 64, 65–67
Don Pasquale (Donizetti), 65, 67
Don't Put Your Daughter on the Stage (Webster), 163–65
Douglass, David, 133
Downes, Olin, 140
Down in the Valley, 144
D'Oyly Carte Opera Company, 121
Draghi, Antonio, 37
Dramma giocoso, 53
Dramma per musica, 15
Dumas, Alexandre, fils, 81
Duni, Egidio, 45
Dvořák, Antonin, 126

Edgar (Puccini), 113
Egk, Werner, 129
Einem, Gottfried von, 129
Elektra (Strauss), 99–100
Eliot, T. S., 128
Elisir d'amore, L' (Donizetti), 65
Emperor Jones (Gruenberg), 134–35
Enfant et les sortilèges, L' (Ravel), 127
Entführung aus dem Serail (Mozart), 45, 49–50
Ernani (Verdi), 79
Eugene Onegin (Tchaikovsky), 125
Euridice, 41, 119
Euridice (Caccini), 15
Euridice (Peri), 14, 22
Euryanthe (Weber), 62
Evelyn, John, 149
Experimental opera, 147 ff.

Falla, Manuel de, 127
Falstaff (Verdi), 87–88
Fanciulla del West, La (Puccini), 117
Farinelli (Carlo Broschi), 25, 33
Farnese, Elizabeth, 25
Faure, Jean-Baptiste, 74
Faust (Gounod), 74, 75, 100
Faust Counter Faust, 147
Favart, Charles Simon, 44–45
Feen, Die (Wagner), 92
Feo, Francesco, 35
Fernand Cortez (Spontini), 67
Fiddler on the Roof, 145
Fidelio (Beethoven), 61–62, 63, 67
Figaro, 50–52, 53, 64, 65
Fille du regiment, La (Donizetti), 65
Finta giardiniera, La (Mozart), 48
Finta semplice, La (Mozart), 48
Fischer, Ludwig, 49
5,000 Nights at the Opera (Bing), 166 ff.
Flaming Angel, The (Prokofiev), 125
Fledermaus, Die (Strauss), 120–21, 154
Flora (Hippisley), 133
Florence, beginning of opera in, 8 ff.
Florence Music Festival, 88
Flotow, Friedrich von, 98
Floyd, Carlisle, 141
Flying Dutchman (Wagner), 92
Foire Saint-German, 44
Folk opera, Russian, 124, 125
Forza del destino, La (Verdi), 82, 83
Four Saints in Three Acts (Thomson), 134, 135, 157 ff.
Franklin, Benjamin, 41–42
Frau ohne Schatten (Strauss), 100
Freischütz, Der (Weber), 62, 63
French opera, 35–37, 41–42
    comic, 43, 44–45, 67, 106
    light, 119–20
    in nineteenth century, 61, 67 ff.
    realism, 105 ff.
    in twentieth century, 127–28
French Revolution, 61, 67
Friml, Rudolf, 143
Fry, William Henry, 134
Fuoco eterno custodito dalle Vestali, Il (Draghi), 37
Furtwängler, Wilhelm, 96
Future of opera, 149–51

Galilei, Vincenzo, 8, 9
Galuppi, Baldassare, 44
García, Manuel, 134
Gatti-Casazza, Giulio, 154–56
Gay, John, 29, 33, 121, 133
Gazza ladra, La (Rossini), 63
Gemignani, Elvira, 116–17
George I, 29, 32
German opera, 26–27, 47 ff.
    comic, 43, 45, 50, 58
    Mozart and, 47 ff.
    in nineteenth century, 61–62
    Strauss and, 99–100
    in twentieth century, 128–29
    Wagner and, 91 ff.
Gershwin, George, 136, 140, 143
Gesamtkunstwerke, 77, 93

Geyer, Ludwig, 92
Gianni Schicchi (Puccini), 117
Gilbert, W. S., 121, 124
Gioconda, La (Ponchielli), 109
Giordano, Umberto, 109
Giorno di regno, Un (Verdi), 78, 87
Giovanna d'Arco (Verdi), 79
Giulio Cesare (Handel), 33
Glinka, Mikhail, 124, 125
Gluck, Christoph Willibald von, 37 ff., 45, 74
Glyndebourne Opera Festival, 59
Goetz, Hermann, 98
Gioielli della Madonna, I (Wolf-Ferrari), 128
Goldoni, Carlo, 44
Gonzaga, Francesco, 18
Gonzaga, Vincenzo, 18
Götterdämmerung (Wagner), 96
Gounod, Charles, 74, 75
Goyescas (Granados), 127
Granados, Enrique, 127
Grand opera, 8, 67 ff.
Greek music, 8–9
Grétry, André, 45
Grisi, Giulia, 65
Gruenberg, Louis, 134
Guadagni, Gaetano, 41
Guerre des Bouffons, La, 37, 41
Guiraud, Ernest, 106
Guys and Dolls, 145

Halévy, Jacques Fromental, 71
Halle, Adam de la, 35, 44
Hammerstein, Oscar, II, 106, 144–45
Handel, George Frideric, 16, 25, 29 ff., 40
Hanneton, Le, 61
Hänsel und Gretel (Humperdinck), 98
Hanson, Howard, 134
Harnick, Sheldon, 145
Hart, Lorenz, 144
Háry János (Kodály), 126
Hasse, Johann, 44
Haydn, Joseph, 44
Haymarket Theater, 40
Heldentenor, 98
Hellman, Lillian, 144
Help! Help! The Globolinks (Menotti), 143
Henry IV, 15
Henze, Hans Werner, 129
Herbert, Victor, 143
Hérold, Ferdinand, 67
Heure espagnole, L' (Ravel), 127
Hewitt, James, 133
Hiller, Johann Adam, 45
Hindemith, Paul, 129
Hippisley, John, 133
Hippolyte et Aricie (Rameau), 37
H.M.S. Pinafore (Gilbert-Sullivan), 121
Hob in the Well (Hippisley), 133
Hoffmann, E.T.A., 120, 121
Hofmannsthal, Hugo von, 100
Hogarth, William, 25, 29
Honest Yorkshireman, The, 133

Hopkinson, Francis, 133
Horne, Marilyn, 68, 105
Houseman, John, 134, 157 ff.
Hugh the Drover (William), 130
Hughes, Langston, 144
Hugo, Victor, 79
Huguenots, Les (Meyerbeer), 71, 100
Humperdinck, Engelbert, 98
Hungarian opera, 126

Idomeneo, rè di Creta (Mozart), 49
Impresario, The (Mozart), 50
Impressionism, 108, 109
Incoronazione di Poppea, L' (Monteverdi), 19, 22
Indes galantes, Les (Rameau), 36–37
Indian Princess, The (Barker), 133
Innovations in opera, 147 ff.
Intermedi, 7, 8, 10
Intolleranza (Nono), 128
Iolanthe (Gilbert–Sullivan), 121
Iphigénie en Tauride (Gluck), 41
Italiana in Algeri, L' (Rossini), 63
Italian opera, 21 ff., 37
  beginning of, 8 ff.
  in nineteenth century, 61, 62 ff.
  realism, 109 ff.
  in twentieth century, 128
  in United States, 134
  Verdi and, 77 ff.
Ivanhoe (Sullivan), 129–30
Ivan Susanin (Glinka), 124
Ivrogne corrige, L' (Gluck), 45

Jacobson, Robert, 177–79
Jagd, Die (Hiller), 45
James, Henry, 131
Janácek, Leos, 126, 127
Jenufa (Janácek), 126, 127, 147
Jesus Christ Superstar, 147, 151
Jeu de Robin et de Marion, Le (Halle), 35
Johnson, Samuel, 129
Jommelli, Nicola, 37
Jongleur de Notre Dame, Le (Massenet), 107
Jonny spielt auf (Krenek), 128–29
Joplin, Scott, 134
Joseph (Méhul), 107
Joseph II, 45, 48, 49, 56
Juive, La (Halévy), 71
Julius Caesar (Handel), 32, 33
Junge Lord, Der (Henze), 129

Kandinsky, Wassily, 125
Karajan, Herbert von, 92, 173–74
Katerina Izmailova (Shostakovich), 125
Keiser, Reinhard, 27
Kelly, Michael, 52–53
Kennedy Center, 147
Kern, Jerome, 143
King and I, The, 145
King's Henchman, The (Taylor), 134
Kirsten, Dorothy, 110
Knickerbocker Holiday, 144
Koanga (Delius), 130
Kodály, Zoltán, 126

Korngold, Erich, 100–101
Krenek, Ernst, 129

Lady Macbeth of Mtzensk (Shostakovich), 125
Lakmé (Delibes), 106
Lalo, Eduard, 106
Landi, Stefano, 16
La Scala, 63, 68, 77, 78, 88, 109, 128
Laussot, Jessie, 93
Lawes, Henry, 28
Léhar, Franz, 121
Leigh, Mitch, 145
Leitmotiv, 96, 98
Leoncavallo, Ruggiero, 110
Leonora (Fry), 134
Leonore Overtures, 61
Leopold I, 26
Leopold II, 56
Lerner, Alan Jay, 145
Levasseur, Auguste, 74
Liberazione di Ruggiero dall' isola d'Alcina (Caccini), 16
Liebesverbot, Das (Wagner), 92
Life for the Tsar, A (Glinka), 124, 125
Light opera, 119 ff.
Lind, Jenny, 65
Lisimaco, 25
Liszt, Franz, 93
Locke, Matthew, 28
Loesser, Frank, 145
Loewe, Frederick, 145
Lohengrin (Wagner), 92, 93
Lombard, I (Verdi), 79
London, 28 ff., 40
London Company, 133
Loreley (Catalani), 109
Lortzing, Gustav Albert, 98
Lost in the Stars, 144
Louis XIV, 35, 37
Louise (Charpentier), 108
Louis Philippe, 74
Love for Three Oranges (Prokofiev), 125
Lucia di Lammermoor (Donizetti), 67
Lucio Silla (Mozart), 48
Ludwig II, 97, 98
Lully, Jean-Baptiste, 35–36, 37
Lulu (Berg), 103
Lustige Witwe, Die (Léhar), 121

Macbeth (Verdi), 86, 87
Madama Butterfly (Puccini), 114–16
Madrigal, 10–11
Madrigal comedies, 11
Maeterlinck, Maurice, 108
Magic Flute, The (Mozart), 57–59
Majorano, Gaetano (Caffarelli), 25
Makropoulos Affair, The (Janácek), 126, 127
Malibran, Maria, 65, 133, 134
Mamelles de Tirésias, Les (Poulenc), 127
Manelli, Francesco, 22
Man of La Mancha, 145
Mann, Thomas, 131
Manon (Massenet), 107

Manon Lescaut (Puccini), 110, 113
Mantua, Duke of, 18
Manzoni, Alessandro, 86
Marazzoli, Marco, 18, 43
Marcello, Benedetto, 37
Margherita of Savoy, 18
Margherita of Spain, 26
Maria Stuarda (Donizetti), 65
Marie-Antoinette, 45, 47
Maritana (Wallace), 121
Marlborough, duke of, 32
Marriage of Figaro (Mozart), 50 ff.
Martha (Flotow), 98
Martin, Mary, 145
Martin y Solar, Vicente, 53
Masaniello (Auber), 67–68
Mascagni, Pietro, 109 ff.
Masked Ball, A (Verdi), 82, 83, 86, 100
Masques, 28
Mass (Bernstein), 147, 149
Massenet, Jules, 107–8
Mathis der Maler (Hindemith), 129
Matrimonio segreto, Il (Cimarosa), 44
Mattheson, Johann, 29
Mavra (Stravinsky), 142
Mayr, Johann Simon, 62–63
Mazarin, Cardinal, 35
Mazzocchi, Domenico, 16
Mazzocchi, Vergilio, 18, 43
McCracken, James, 105, 172–74
Médée (Cherubini), 67
Medici, Fernando de', 7, 10
Medici, Maria de', 15, 16
Medium, The (Menotti), 143
Mefistofele (Boito), 86
Méhul, Etienne, 107
Meistersinger, Die (Wagner), 91, 96–97
Mendelssohn, Felix, 62, 147
Menotti, Gian Carlo, 125, 142–43, 148
Merelli, Bartolomeo, 78
Merry Mount (Hanson), 134
Merry Wives of Windsor (Nicolai), 98
Mesmer, Franz Anton, 48
Metastasio (Pietro Trapassi), 26, 47
Metropolitan Opera, 7, 59, 67, 75, 80, 83, 92, 99, 105, 113, 117, 120–21, 141–42, 147, 154–56
Meyerbeer, Giacomo, 70–71
Midsummer Marriage (Tippett), 130
Midsummer Night's Dream, A (Britten), 131
Mignon (Thomas), 106
Mikado, The (Gilbert-Sullivan), 121
Miller, Arthur, 140
Milton, John, 28
Minneapolis Center Opera, 147
Mireille (Gounod), 75
Mitridate, ré di Ponto (Mozart), 48
Modern-dress opera, first, 81
Moïse en Egypte (Rossini), 68
Mondo della luna, Il (Haydn), 44
Monsigny, Pierre Alexandre, 45
Montemezzi, Italo, 128
Monteverdi, Claudio, 18–19, 22
Moore, Douglas, 140, 141

Moses and Aaron (Schoenberg), 101, 171
Most Happy Fella, The, 145
Mother of Us All, The (Thomson), 135
Mozart, Anna Maria, 48
Mozart, Leopold, 47, 48
Mozart, Nannerl, 47
Mozart, Wolfgang Amadeus, 26, 45, 47 ff.
Muette de Portici, La (Auber), 67–68
Munich, 50, 97
Munich Carnival, 48, 49
Musical drama, 15
   Wagnerian, 91, 93–94
Musicals, Broadway, 143–45
Mussorgsky, Modeste, 119
My Fair Lady, 145
Mysteries of Isis (Mozart), 59

Nabucco (Verdi), 78
Nacht in Venedig, Eine (Strauss), 121
Napoleon I (Bonaparte), 67
Napoleon III, 119
Nationalism, 121, 124
Naturalism, 105, 108
New Orleans Opera, 107
New York City Opera, 163–65
   Donizetti and, 65
   new operas and, 141
Niblo's Garden, 134
Nicolai, Otto, 98
Nietzsche, Friedrich, 97, 105
Nilsson, Birgit, 98, 99, 113, 167, 168
Nono, Luigi, 128
Norma (Bellini), 65
Noyes, Alfred, 77
Noye's Fludde (Britten), 131
Nuove Musiche, Le (Caccini), 16

Oberon (Weber), 62
Oberto, Conte di San Bonifacio (Verdi), 78
Oedipus Rex (Stravinsky), 142
Offenbach, Jacques, 106, 119–20, 121
Of Thee I Sing, 143
Oklahoma!, 145
Old Maid and the Thief, The (Menotti), 143
One-act operas, 109–10
One Touch of Venus, 144
On Your Toes, 144
Opera
   beginning of, 8 ff.
   definition of, 8, 133
   first, 15
   houses, 21, 35, 91
Opera buffa, 7, 25–26, 43–44
   Mozart and, 50 ff.
Opéra comique, 43, 44–45, 67, 106
Opera seria, 25, 26
   in France, 43
   in London, 28, 33
   Mozart and, 48, 49, 56
Operetta, 119 ff.
Oratorio, 16
Orchestra, 16, 36
   Wagner and, 96, 98

Orfeo (Monteverdi), 18
Orfeo (Rossi), 35
Orfeo ed Euridice (Gluck), 40–41
Orff, Carl, 129
Orlando furioso (Ariosto), 16
Orphée aux enfers (Offenbach), 119
Orpheus, 14, 15, 18, 119
Otello (Verdi), 86–87, 88
Owen Wingrave (Britten), 131

Pagliacci, I (Leoncavallo), 110, 113
Paisiello, Giovanni, 44
Palestrinia, Giovanni Pierluigi da, 8
Palestrina (Pfitzner), 100
Pal Joey, 144
Panerai, Rolando, 88
Paris, 35, 41, 92. *See also* French opera.
Paris Opéra, 70, 71, 74, 106
   Verdi and, 81–82, 87
Parsifal (Wagner), 91, 97
Passion According to St. Matthew (Bach), 27
Pasta, Giuditta, 65
Pastorales, 10, 35
Pears, Peter, 131
Péchés de Vieillesse, Les (Rossini), 68
Pêcheurs de perles, Les (Bizet), 105
Pedrell, Felipe, 126–27
Pélissier, Olympe, 68
Pelléas et Mélisande (Debussy), 108, 109
Pellegrina, La (Bargagli), 7, 10
Pepusch, Johann Christoph, 33
Pepys, Samuel, 121
Pergolesi, Giovanni Battista, 25, 37, 43, 44
Peri, Jacopo, 8, 14, 15, 22, 27, 150
Perichole, La (Offenbach), 119
Peter Grimes (Britten), 131
Peter Ibbetson (Taylor), 134
Petite Messe Solennelle, La (Rossini), 68, 70
Pfitzner, Hans, 100
Philidor, François André, 45
Philip V, 25
Phoebus and Pan (Bach), 27
Piccinni, Nicola, 41–42
Pins and Needles, 143
Pinza, Ezio, 59, 145
Pipe of Desire, The (Converse), 134
Pique Dame (Tchaikovsky), 125
Pirates of Penzance (Gilbert–Sullivan), 121
Pizzetti, Ildebrando, 128
Planer, Minna, 93
Play of Daniel, The, 35
Political opera, 68, 129
Pomo d'oro, Il (Cesti), 26–27
Ponchielli, Amilcare, 109
Porgy and Bess (Gershwin), 136, 140
Porpora, Niccolò, 25, 33
Postillon de Longjumeau, Le (Adam), 67
Poulenc, Francis, 127
Price, Leontyne, 141, 167
Priest, Josias, 28
Prigionero, Il (Dallapiccola), 128
Prince Igor (Borodin), 124

Princess Ida (Gilbert–Sullivan), 121
Prokofiev, Sergei, 125–26
Prophète, Le (Meyerbeer), 71
Public opera houses, 21
Puccini, Giacomo, 110, 113 ff.
Puchberg, Michael, 59
Purcell, Henry, 28, 29, 75, 121
Puritani, I (Bellini), 65, 67

Quattro rusteghi, I (Wolf-Ferrari), 44
Queen of Spades (Tchaikovsky), 125
Quinault, Philippe, 35

Raaf, Anton, 49
Rake's Progress (Hogarth), 25
Rake's Progress (Stravinsky), 141, 142, 161–62
Rameau, Jean-Philippe, 36–37, 40
Rape of Lucretia, The (Britten), 131
Rappresentazione di anima e di corpo (Cavalieri), 16
Ravel, Maurice, 127
Realism, 105 ff.
Recitativo (recitative), 9, 15
   French, 36
   secco, 43
Recordings, operatic, 148
Reform movement, 37 ff.
Regina (Blitzstein), 143
Religion, musical plays and, 9–10
Renaissance, 8, 9
Renard (Stravinsky), 143
Requiem Mass (Verdi), 86
Rescue operas, 67
Revoltosa, La (Chapí y Lorente), 127
Reyer, Ernest, 98
Rheingold, Das (Wagner), 92, 96
Richard Coeur de Lion (Grétry), 45
Rienzi (Wagner), 92
Rigoletto (Verdi), 79–80
Rigueurs du cloître, Les (Berton), 67
Rimsky-Korsakov, Nikolai, 119, 124, 125
Rinaldo (Handel), 29
Ring des Nibelungen, Der (Wagner), 92, 93, 96, 98
Rinuccini, Ottavio, 8, 15, 27
Rip Van Winkle (Bristow), 134
Rise and Fall of the City of Mahagonny (Weill), 128, 129
Risorgimento, 79
Ritorno d'Ulisse in patria, Il (Monteverdi), 19, 22
Robert le Diable (Meyerbeer), 70, 71
Roberto Devereux (Donizetti), 65
Robin et Marion (Halle), 44
Rock opera, 147, 151
Rodelinda (Handel), 33
Rodgers, Richard, 144–45
Rodrigo (Handel), 29
Roi d'Ys, Le (Lalo), 107
Roland (Lully), 36
Rolland, Romain, 35
Romanticism, German, 62, 63, 98
Romberg, Sigmund, 143
Rome, 16, 22 ff., 109 ff.
Rome, Harold, 143
Roméo et Juliette (Gounod), 75

Rondine, La (Puccini), 117
Rosenkavalier, Der (Strauss), 100, 101
Rossi, Luigi, 35
Rossignol, Le (Stravinsky), 142
Rossini, Gioacchino, 61, 63–65, 68–70, 80
Rousseau, Jean Jacques, 45, 48
Royal Academy of Music, 32
Run-through (Houseman), 157 ff.
Rusalka (Dvořák), 126
Russian opera, 124–26
Russlan and Ludmilla (Glinka), 124

Sacre rappresentazioni, 9–10
Sadler's Wells, 130
Saggio sopra l'opera in musica (Algarotti), 37
Saint of Bleecker Street (Menotti), 143
Saint-Saëns, Camille, 107, 119
Salieri, Antonio, 70, 74
Salome (Strauss), 99
Samson et Dalila (Saint-Saëns), 107
San Cassiano Theater, 21, 22
Sant' Alessio (Landi), 16
Sargeant, Winthrop, 169 ff.
Savoy Theatre, 121
Scala di seta, La (Rossini), 63
Scarlatti, Alessandro, 26
Scarlet Letter, The (Damrosch), 134
Scenery, Italian, 21, 22, 25
Schauspieldirektor, Der (Mozart), 50
Schikaneder, Emanuel, 57–59
Schoenberg, Arnold, 101, 171
Schubert, Franz, 62
Schumann, Robert, 62
Schütz, Heinrich, 27
Scott, Walter, 67
Scribe, Eugène, 71
Segreto di Susanna, Il (Wolf-Ferrari), 128
Semiramide (Rossini), 65
Serenade (Cain), 63–64
Serse (Handel), 25
Serva padrona, La (Pergolesi), 25, 37, 43, 44
Shaw, George Bernard, 57, 59, 82, 98, 121
Shepherd King, The (Mozart), 48
Shostakovich, Dmitri, 125
Show Boat (Kern), 145
Siège de Corinthe, Le (Rossini), 68
Siege of Rhodes, The, 28
Siegfried (Wagner), 96
Sigurd (Reyer), 98
Sills, Beverly, 32, 65, 68, 140, 174–76
Simon Boccanegra (Verdi), 82
Singers
  Italian, 22 ff., 65
  Mozart and, 49
  Wagner and, 98
Singspiel, 43, 45, 50, 58
Smetana, Bedrich, 126
Smithson, Harriet, 75
Smyth, Dame Ethyl, 130
Socialist opera, first, 108
Sogno di Scipione, Il (Mozart), 48
Solera, Temistocle, 78

Solti, Georg, 96
Sondheim, Stephen, 145
Sonnambula, La (Bellini), 65
Sonzogno, 109, 110, 113
South Pacific, 145
Spaceship opera, 147, 149
Spanish opera, 126–27
Spontini, Gasparo, 67
Sprechtstimme, 103
Standfuss, Johann Christian, 45
Star in the Family, A (McCracken-Warfield), 172–74
Stein, Gertrude, 134, 135, 157
Stephanie, Gottlieb, 49, 50
Straus, Oskar, 121
Strauss, Johann, the Younger, 120–21
Strauss, Richard 99–100
Stravinsky, Igor, 141–42, 143, 161-62
Stravinsky, Vera, 161–62
Street Scene, 144
Strepponi, Giuseppina, 80, 81
Striggio, Alessandro, 18
Sullivan, Arthur, 121, 124, 129
Suor Angelica (Puccini), 117
Susannah (Floyd), 141
Sutherland, Joan, 65, 67, 121, 168

Tales of Hoffmann (Offenbach), 106, 120, 121
Taming of the Shrew (Goetz), 98
Tammany (Hewitt), 133
Tannhäuser (Wagner), 93, 97
Tasso, Torquato, 11
Taylor, Deems, 134
Tchaikovsky, Peter Ilyich, 125
Teatro alla moda, Il (Marcello), 37
Technology, 141–49
Telemann, Georg Philipp, 27
Telephone, The (Menotti), 143
Temple of Cloacina, The, 133
Temple of Minerva, The (Hopkinson), 133
Teufel ist Los, Der (Standfuss), 45
Thaïs (Massenet), 107
Theater auf der Wieden, 57
Theaters, opera, 21, 35, 91
Théâtre des Italiens, 61, 68
Théâtre de l'Opéra-Comique, 44–45, 105, 106–8, 120
Thésée (Lully), 36
Thomas, Ambroise, 106
Thomson, Virgil, 134, 135, 140, 157, 159–60
Threepenny Opera (Weill), 33, 129
Tiefland (d'Albert), 100
Tippett, Michael, 130
Tommy, 147
Tosca (Puccini), 113, 114
Toscanini, Arturo, 63, 117, 154
Tote Stadt, Die (Korngold), 100
Traetta, Tommaso, 37
Trapassi, Pietro, 26
Traviata, La (Verdi), 81
Treemonisha (Joplin), 134
Trial by Jury (Gilbert-Sullivan), 121
Tristan und Isolde (Wagner), 92, 93, 96
Trittico, Il (Puccini), 117

Troilus and Cressida (Walton), 130
Trouser roles, 100
Trovatore, Il (Verdi), 80–81
Troyens, Les (Berlioz), 71, 74, 75
Turnandot (Puccini), 113, 117
Turn of the Screw (Britten), 131

Una cosa rara (Martin), 53

Vanessa (Barber), 141
Vecchi, Orazio, 11, 14
Venice, 18, 21–22, 161
Vêpres sicilennes, Les (Verdi), 80, 81–82
Verbena de la paloma, La (Bréton y Hernándéz), 127
Verdi, Giuseppe, 77 ff., 109
  on Puccini, 113
  on Wagner, 88–89
Verismo, 105, 110, 114, 117, 127
Versailles, 37
Vestale, La (Spontini), 67
Victor Emmanuel II, 79
Vide breve, La (de Falla), 127
Vienna, 26, 37, 40, 44, 45, 48 ff., 101, 120–21
Vienna Opera House, 48
Vie Parisienne, La (Offenbach), 119
Village Romeo and Juliet (Delius), 130
Villi, Le (Puccini), 113
Virgin Unmask'd, The, 133

Wadsworth Athenaeum, 134, 157
Wagner, Richard, 91 ff.
  Verdi and, 88–89
Wagner, Wieland, 92
Walküre, Die (Wagner), 96
Wallace, William Vincent, 121
Wally, La (Catalani), 109
Walton, William, 130, 164
Ward, Robert, 140, 141
Warfield, Sandra, 172–74
War and Peace (Prokofiev), 125–26
Weber, Constanze, 49, 62
Weber, Karl Maria von, 62, 63
Webster, Dorothy, 163–65
Weill, Kurt, 33, 128, 129, 144
Weisman, Steven R., 176
Werther (Massenet), 107
Wesendonk, Mathilde, 93
West Side Story (Bernstein), 145
Williams, Ralph Vaughan, 130
William Tell (Rossini), 68
Wolf-Ferrari, Ermanno, 44, 128
Wozzeck (Berg), 101–3, 128, 147
Wreckers, The (Smyth), 130

Yeomen of the Guard (Gilbert–Sullivan), 121

Zampa (Hérold), 67
Zarzuela, 43, 127
Zauberflöte, Die (Mozart), 57–59
Zazzerino, Il, 15
Zeno, Apostolo, 26
Zigeunerbaron, Der (Strauss), 121
Zuffi, Piero, 41